Fun with the Family™ Missouri

Praise for the Fun with the Family™ series

"Enables parents to turn family travel into an exploration."
—Alexandra Kennedy, Editor, *Family Fun*

"Bound to lead you and your kids to fun-filled days,
those times that help compose the
memories of childhood."
—Dorothy Jordan, *Family Travel Times*

Help Us Keep This Guide Up to Date

Every effort has been made by the authors and editors to make this guide as accurate and useful as possible. However, many changes can occur after a guide is published—establishments close, phone numbers change, hiking trails are rerouted, facilities come under new management, etc.

We would love to hear from you concerning your experiences with this guide and how you feel it could be improved and be kept up to date. While we may not be able to respond to all comments and suggestions, we'll take them to heart, and we'll make certain to share them with the authors. Please send your comments and suggestions to the following address:

The Globe Pequot Press
Reader Response/Editorial Department
P.O. Box 480
Guilford, CT 06437

Or you may e-mail us at: editorial@GlobePequot.com

Thanks for your input, and happy travels!

INSIDERS'GUIDE®

FUN WITH THE FAMILY™ SERIES

fun WITH the Family™

MISSOURI

HUNDREDS OF IDEAS FOR DAY TRIPS WITH THE KIDS

RANDY AND JANE COSBY

FOURTH EDITION

INSIDERS'GUIDE®

GUILFORD, CONNECTICUT
AN IMPRINT OF THE GLOBE PEQUOT PRESS

The prices, rates, and hours listed in this guidebook were confirmed at press time. We recommend, however, that you call establishments to obtain current information before traveling.

To buy books in quantity for corporate use or incentives, call **(800) 962–0973** or e-mail **premiums@GlobePequot.com**.

INSIDERS' GUIDE®

Copyright © 1997, 1999, 2002, 2004 Morris Book Publishing, LLC

Insiders' Guide is a registered trademark of Morris Book Publishing, LLC.
Fun with the Family is a trademark of Morris Book Publishing, LLC.

Text design by Nancy Freeborn and Linda Loiewski
Maps by Rusty Nelson © Morris Book Publishing, LLC
Spot photography throughout © Photodisc

ISSN: 1535-8100
ISBN-13: 978-0-7627-2769-8

Manufactured in the United States of America
Fourth Edition/Third Printing

To Mike and Annie, who are the best traveling companions anyone could ask for

MISSOURI

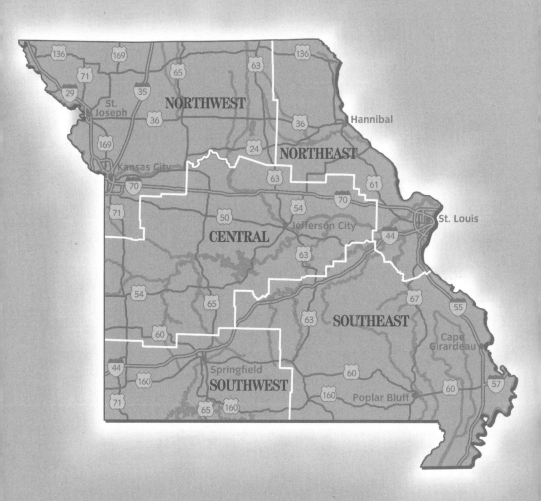

Contents

Acknowledgments

We would like to thank book editor Mimi Egan for her friendly and cooperative manner and professional editing and copy editor Lori Meek Schuldt and her yellow stickums for helping turn our marked-up copy into an informative and useful travel guide.

Introduction

We have lived in Missouri all our lives and have traveled across the state many times. Whether it was miniature golf at the Lake of the Ozarks, a float trip and campout on the Current River, or a visit to a Monet exhibit at the St. Louis Art Museum, we always found ways to entertain ourselves and get the most out of Missouri's magnificent natural wonders and commercial attractions.

Since the arrival of our son and daughter, we have revisited these destinations and found them as exciting as the first time because we now are able to share the fun with the kids. We also found ourselves pleasantly surprised as we sought out activities and attractions that would appeal to the whole family.

How would a ten-year-old react to Russian comedian Yakov Smirnoff's Branson show? With uncontrollable laughter. Do kids like swimming and fishing in a lake, any lake? Sure. Are the throwed rolls at Lambert's Cafe a big deal? You betcha. Can everyone find something to ride or do at Six Flags St. Louis or Worlds of Fun? Undeniably.

This book is the result of our family's travels, from St. Louis to Joplin, St. Joseph to Cape Girardeau, and all points in between. The book is divided into five regions, each of which is introduced by a map that highlights the towns and cities you'll want to visit. We've tried to include any and every attraction that appeals to kids. We also have tried to list restaurants that might not be among the ubiquitous chain franchises generally listed on signs near interstate highway exits throughout the state.

As you may know, Missouri is called the Show Me State. One theory says this nickname evolved when Missourians in the nineteenth century went west to work in the mines but had a bit of trouble catching on to new tasks. The story is that their employers said, "They're from Missouri; you've got to show them." We, however, prefer a second explanation involving a turn-of-the-twentieth-century state representative who supposedly said, "Frothy eloquence neither convinces nor satisfies me. I am from Missouri. You have got to show me."

We sincerely hope this guidebook is eloquent enough to help you explore Missouri, is informative enough to ensure hassle-free travel, and shows you the many good times waiting for your family in this beautiful state.

A Note about Missouri State Parks

The Missouri state parks system is currently moving toward a reservation-only procedure for campsites in state parks. But for the foreseeable future, while this new system is being implemented, the parks intend to set aside a limited number of first-come, first-served sites for campers without reservations. The majority of Missouri's state parks are setting aside approximately 30 percent of their campsites for campers who show up without reservations; about 70 percent of the sites will be reservations-only. If no one reserves a reservations-only site, then someone showing up without a reservation can have it at least for that night.

To reserve or not to reserve, that is the question! There is a non-refundable campsite reservation fee of $8.50 per campsite. This $8.50 per campsite fee is in addition to any other fees the individual parks may charge for camping or park use. You may feel bummed out if it turns out that your site would have been available anyway without the reservation. We tell you this so that you can make the decision that's right for you and your family.

We have listed two or more phone numbers for many of our state parks. The first number listed after the address is the direct line to that park. This is the best source of information about that particular park. The second number listed (800–334–6946) is the toll-free number for general information about Missouri state parks. The last number is the toll-free number for making campsite reservations: (877) 422–6766; it is only a reservations number. We hope this clarifies things and helps you organize your trip. Good luck and have fun!

Attraction, Lodging, and Restaurant Fees

In the attraction listings and the "Where to Eat" and "Where to Stay" sections, dollar signs indicate general price ranges. For attractions, the prices are per person, all ages, except where noted otherwise. For meals, the prices are for individual adult entrees. For lodging, the rates are for a double room, for a family of four, with no meals, unless otherwise indicated; rates for lodging may be higher during peak vacation seasons and holidays. Always inquire about family and group rates and package deals that may include amusement park tickets, discounts for area attractions, and tickets for concerts and other performing arts events.

Rates for Attractions

$	up to $5
$$	$5 to $10
$$$	$11 to $20
$$$$	more than $20

Rates for Restaurants

$	most entrees under $6
$$	most $7 to $12
$$$	most $13 to $20
$$$$	most over $20

Rates for Lodging

$	up to $40
$$	from $41 to $65
$$$	from $66 to $99
$$$$	$100 and up

Attractions Key

The following is a key to the icons found throughout the text.

SWIMMING		**FOOD**	
BOATING / BOAT TOUR		**LODGING**	
HISTORIC SITE		**CAMPING**	
HIKING / WALKING		**MUSEUMS**	
FISHING		**PERFORMING ARTS**	
BIKING		**SPORTS/ATHLETICS**	
AMUSEMENT PARK		**PICNICKING**	
HORSEBACK RIDING		**PLAYGROUND**	
SKIING / WINTER SPORTS		**SHOPPING**	
PARK		**PLANTS / GARDENS / NATURE TRAILS**	
ANIMAL VIEWING		**FARMS**	

Northeast Missouri

The central and northern parts of this region are primarily rural, offering a large lake for outdoor recreation and sleepy little towns along the Mississippi River where time seems to stand still. Chief among these is Hannibal, the onetime steamboat stop that today welcomes visitors to the formative places in the life of author Mark Twain. As you travel south in the region, you'll come upon St. Louis and its surrounding suburbs, which together form the largest metropolitan area in the state. From St. Louis's vibrant downtown to its many historic neighborhoods and the outlying suburban communities, there are dozens of family attractions, recreational opportunities, and entertainment options, many of them **free** or low cost. South and west of St. Louis you'll find small towns, nature preserves, and large parks offering outdoor recreation of all types.

Interstates 70, 55, 64, and 44 are the major thoroughfares in the northeast region of Missouri. It takes less than two hours to drive east along I–70, just south of Mexico, to the Gateway Arch in downtown St. Louis. The other three interstates branch out from downtown, leaving most destinations in the area less than thirty minutes away by car. Hannibal and Clarksville require a short trip off I–70 up Highway 79 in St. Charles County. Although drive times slow down once you're off the interstates, most state and local highways are in excellent condition.

Mexico

Founded in 1836, this small rural town has strong roots in agriculture, the firebrick industry, and world-famous saddle horses, as is proven by the American Saddle Horse Museum. Visitors with children likely will want to spend some time at the playground and picnic area in **Robert S. Green Park,** 501 South Muldrow, before moving on to other attractions.

NORTHEAST MISSOURI

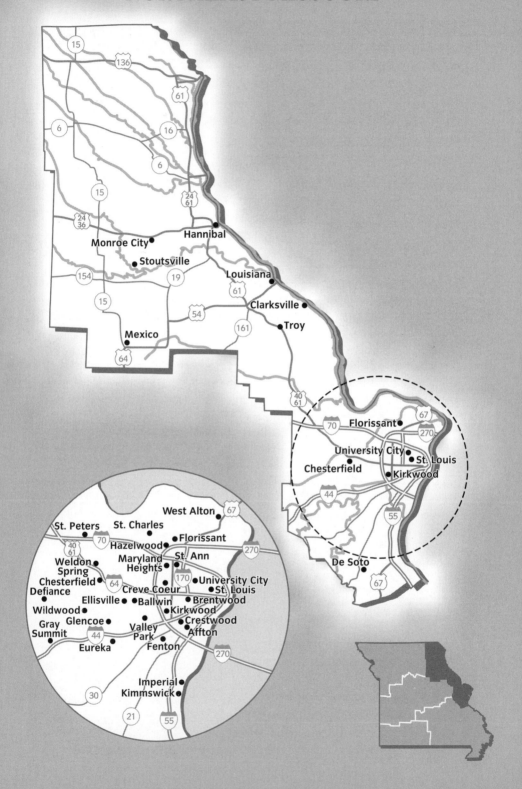

Missouri Military Academy (ages 6 and up)
204 Grand Avenue, Mexico 65265; (888) 564–6662; www.mma-cadet.org.

Free tours of the academy can be arranged by calling in advance. June is a popular month for tourists, who visit the school when it hosts the annual Miss Missouri Pageant, which attracts contestants from all over the state. August also is popular with college gridiron fans, who come to the academy to watch preseason workouts by the University of Missouri Tigers, who play their home games just south of Mexico in Columbia.

The Audrain Historical Society Museum Complex (all ages)
501 South Muldrow, Mexico 65265; (573) 581–3910. Open Tuesday through Saturday 10:00 A.M. to 4:00 P.M. and Sunday 1:00 to 5:00 P.M. year-round except January. $.

Antique dolls, dishes, tools, and clothing are displayed throughout a stately mansion once visited by Ulysses S. Grant. The Audrain Country School offers a glimpse of rural school life in the early part of the twentieth century with desks, books, slates, and games from schools throughout the county as well as an outhouse and an Akron-style country church that was completely disassembled at a rural site and then moved to the museum center, where it was reconstructed. The complex also houses the American Saddle Horse Museum, which is filled with equestrian memorabilia and paintings galore.

Randy and Jane's
TopPicks in Northeast Missouri

1. The Katy Trail, St. Charles to Sedalia
2. Gateway Arch and Jefferson National Expansion Memorial, St. Louis
3. Missouri Botanical Garden, St. Louis
4. City Museum, St. Louis
5. St. Louis Zoo, St. Louis
6. St. Louis Science Center, St. Louis
7. The Magic House, Kirkwood
8. Grant's Farm, Affton
9. Six Flags St. Louis, Eureka
10. Mark Twain Lake, Stoutsville
11. Purina Farms, Gray Summit
12. Hannibal

Scattering Fork Outdoor Center (ages 12 and up)

15559 Audrain Road, Mexico 65265; (573) 581–3003. Open April 1 through November 1 by appointment. $$$.

This nonprofit educational center uses the outdoors and a low-ropes challenge course to teach team building. Although principally targeted at larger groups, you can call ahead and arrange for a trained counselor to give your family a tour of the center, which has several trails. While there, you can take part in other activities, depending on your taste for adventure and excitement. Among the activities available are the Mohawk walk, which requires you to walk across a ditch on a cable with the aid of an overhead rope; the spider walk, during which you try to traverse a web of ropes without ringing a bell; and a rope swing that carries you from one platform to another. There also is a tepee on the property, which was a Sac Fox Indian campground as late as the early nineteenth century.

For More Information

Mexico Area Chamber of Commerce.100 West Jackson, Mexico 65265; (573) 581–2765 or (800) 581–2765; www.mexico-chamber.org.

Stoutsville

Mark Twain State Park (all ages)

R.R.1, Box 53, Stoutsville 65283; (573) 565–3440 or (800) 334–6946; www.mostateparks.com. The park is open daily 10:00 A.M. to 5:00 P.M. late April through November and 10:00 A.M. to 4:00 P.M. December through April. $. Call (877) 422–6766 at least forty-eight hours in advance for camping reservations. There is an $8.50 registration fee. Tent sites cost $8.00 per night. Campsites with RV hookups are $14.00.

The park overlooks the 18,600-acre Mark Twain Lake, which makes fishing and boating popular pastimes in these parts. The 2,775-acre park has hiking trails, ninety-eight developed campsites, 102 sites with electric, swimming beaches, picnic areas, and two full-service marinas. A waterfowl refuge along Middle Fork Salt River is an ideal location for bird-watching and wildlife viewing. The M. W. Boudreaux Visitor Center offers a good vantage point for bird-watching. The park also has a museum with the two-room log cabin where Mark Twain, whose given name was Samuel Clemens, was born. Exhibits feature personal belongings and books of the famous author-humorist and present information about his life.

Mark Twain Birthplace State Historic Site (ages 4 and up)

County Road U off Highway 107, near Florida; mailing address is 20057 State Park Office Road, Stoutsville 65283; (573) 565–3449 or (800) 334–6946; www.mostateparks.com. Open 10:00 A.M. to 4:40 P.M. year-round. $, children ages 5 and under **free.**

The two-room cabin where Samuel Langhorne Clemens was born now is surrounded by a modern museum that contains memorabilia of Mark Twain, the name Clemens adopted as a writer, and includes a handwritten manuscript of *The Adventures of Tom Sawyer.* Along with personal belongings, exhibits cover the writing career that brought him fame and a business career that often brought him pain.

Monroe City

The Landing (all ages)

42819 Landing Lane, Monroe City 63456; (573) 735–9422 or (877) 700–9422 toll free; www.marktwainlanding.com. Water park is open daily 11:00 A.M. to 7:00 P.M. but hours vary, so call ahead. Open Memorial Day through Labor Day. Adults $$$, kids ages 4 through 10 $$, children ages 3 and under **free.**

This resort offers everything a family needs or wants, including campgrounds, cabins, miniature golf, go-karts, a playground, and a water park with a giant wave pool, slippery slides, and a river.

Hannibal

As you travel east toward the Mississippi River, you'll come upon the little town that Mark Twain propelled to national prominence. Twain, who then was known as Samuel Clemens, grew up in this small hamlet on the banks of the river and featured it in some of his best-loved works of fiction. Today Hannibal offers activities and places of interest that take full advantage of its association with the famous American humorist. Before you visit, spend

Amazing Missouri Facts

By what name was American writer Samuel Langhorne Clemens better known?

Mark Twain

some time reviewing *The Adventures of Tom Sawyer* and *The Adventures of Huckleberry Finn* with your children. Kids who have read the Mark Twain stories or seen the movies based on his books will enjoy viewing the places where the "real" people lived.

Every July the town hosts Tom Sawyer Days and features the National Fence Painting Championships, a frog-jumping contest, the Tomboy Sawyer Competition, an arts and crafts show, Mississippi Mud Volleyball, live entertainment, and a huge fireworks display on the evening of July Fourth.

Walking is an excellent way to see the sights, but there also are several other ways to get around town while finding out everything you need to know about Twain's boyhood haunts.

Hannibal Trolley (all ages)
Board at Main and Bird Streets, Hannibal 63401; (573) 221–1161. Runs daily 9:00 A.M. to 5:00 P.M. April 15 through October. Adults and seniors $$, children ages 5 through 11 $.

This sixty-minute tour hits all of the important and memorable stops in town.

Twainland Express (all ages)
400 North Third Street, Hannibal 63401; (573) 221–5593. Runs daily April through October. $$.

The express, a shuttle made up to look like a train, offers one-hour sightseeing tours blending historical facts with humorous stories.

Mark Twain Clopper (all ages)
Starts in front of Grant's Drug Store on Main Street, Hannibal 63401; (573) 439–5054. Runs May through August. $.

This fun twenty-minute tour of downtown goes down to the river and back, all in a horse-drawn wagon.

Mark Twain Riverboat (all ages)
Landing at the foot of Center Street, Hannibal 63401; (573) 221–3222. Cruises daily at 1:30 P.M. May through October. Additional cruises at 11:00 A.M. and 4:00 P.M. from Memorial Day through Labor Day. $$.

You'll hear an hour-long narration of Twain's adventures and the history and legends of the river. You'll see sights along the river, and you can purchase refreshments at the snack bar. During special dinner cruises, beef sirloin and baked chicken top the menu, and live music is provided throughout the cruise.

Mark Twain Boyhood Home (ages 4 and up)

208 Hill Street, Hannibal 63401; (573) 221–9010. Open daily 9:00 A.M. to 4:00 P.M.; extended hours from spring to fall. Admission for all six buildings: Adults $$, children ages 6 through 11 $.

You'll see where the author grew up and find out about his childhood and the real people behind his characters. Next door is the Mark Twain Museum and Annex, where you can view memorabilia, displays, and a slide presentation on Twain's life. Across the street is J. M. Clemens Law Office, where Clemens's father presided as justice of the peace, and Pilaster House/Grant's Drug Store, where the Clemens family lived on the upper level for a short time.

Becky Thatcher Book and Gift Shop (ages 4 and up)

211 Hill Street, Hannibal 63401; (573) 221–9010. Open daily 9:00 A.M. to 4:00 P.M.; extended hours from spring to fall. **Free** admission.

Here you can visit two rooms from Laura Hawkins's childhood home. She was Twain's childhood sweetheart and the model for Becky Thatcher. A well-stocked bookshop offers a large selection of Twain's books in addition to children's classics and souvenirs for the whole family.

Haunted House on Hill Street (all ages, depending on level)

215 Hill Street, Hannibal 63401; (573) 221–2220. Open daily 8:00 A.M. to 5:00 P.M. March through November; open until 8:00 P.M. during summer months. $.

Guided tours include seeing twenty-seven wax figures, many of them from Twain's books. One level is devoted to the typical eerie, blood-and-guts fare so often associated with wax museums.

Optical Science Center and Museum (all ages)

214 North Main Street, Hannibal 63401; (573) 221–2020. Open Monday through Saturday 10:00 A.M. to 6:00 P.M., Sunday noon to 6:00 P.M. April through October 30. $.

This stop has hands-on exhibits about vision, optic lenses, and the optometry industry. You'll see optical illusions, lenses being made, and more than 500 pairs of glasses. You can also watch a puppet show and a computerized light show. Educational videos about vision are shown in a small theater.

Mark Twain Himself (ages 6 and up)

319 North Main Street, Hannibal 63401; (573) 231–0021. Open June 7 through August 1; shows at 5:30 and 7:30 P.M. but times might vary. $$$.

Chicago actor Richard Garey's one-man show captures the best of Twain's humor and satire and leaves no doubt that Hannibal native Twain was one of the funniest and clever- est men who ever lived. And the whole thing is staged in an 1849 barn on Dead Man's Alley in which Twain, when he still was Sam Clemens, is believed to have played. Since Twain is the reason you're going to Hannibal, you won't want to miss what he has to say.

Amazing
Missouri Facts

Who was the character on the M*A*S*H television series who claimed to be from Hannibal, Missouri?

Col. Sherman Potter

Molly Brown Birthplace & Museum (ages 6 and up)

Mark Twain Avenue, Hannibal 63401; (573) 221–2100. Open for tours daily from 9:00 A.M. to 6:00 P.M. June through August and weekends only from 10:00 A.M. to 5:00 P.M. in April, May, September, and October. $.

The restored birthplace of the Titanic's Unsinkable Molly Brown offers a gallery of *Titanic* information as well as a gallery of historical information on Brown's remarkable life.

Tom Sawyer Diorama Museum (all ages)

323 North Main Street, Hannibal 63401; (573) 221–3525. $; children ages 5 and under free.

Using sixteen hand-carved scenes, Art Sieving provides a window into what life in Hannibal might have been like in the 1840s. His dioramas include the whitewashing of the fence, Tom and Becky on Jackson's Island, and Tom and Becky in the cave.

Mark Twain Outdoor Theater (all ages)

Highway 61 South at Clemens Landing, Hannibal 63401; (573) 221–2945. Performances are held every evening from June through August and on weekends in the spring and fall. Adults $$$–$$$$, children ages 9 and under $$–$$$, without or with dinner.

In this two-hour pageant local actors bring to life Mark Twain and his famous characters with memorable episodes from *Tom Sawyer, Huckleberry Finn,* and *Life on the Mississippi.* Dinner also is available for an additional charge.

Mark Twain Cave (all ages)

Highway 79 South, Hannibal 63401; (573) 221–1656. Open daily 9:00 A.M. to 4:00 P.M.; extended hours April to October. Adults $$$, kids ages 5 through 11 $$, children ages 4 and younger free.

You'll relive an adventure of Tom Sawyer's with an hour-long tour, walking through chilly passageways, reading messages marked on cave walls by long-ago visitors, and learning about the outlaws that sometimes hid in this famous cave. The temperature is fifty-two degrees Fahrenheit year-round, so you might want to bring a jacket.

Cameron Cave (ages 5 and up)

Highway 79 South, Hannibal 63401; (573) 221–1656. Open daily, four tours a day Memorial Day through Labor Day. Adults $$$, kids ages 5 through 11 $$, children ages 4 and younger free. Combination ticket with Mark Twain Cave available: adults $$$$, children $$$.

Open for tours during the summer months, this cave is in a natural state and has no artificial lighting. You will make an exciting exploration by the light of lanterns carried by several of the people in your group.

Sawyer's Creek Fun Park (all ages)

Highway 79 South, Hannibal 63401; (573) 221–8221. Open daily 10:00 A.M. to dark. Closed in January and February.

A miniature amusement park with bumper boats, a miniature golf course, a kid-size train, and a shooting gallery and arcade. There is a cafe that offers a wonderful view of the river, and several shops (including a Christmas shop) are open year-round.

For More Information

Hannibal Visitors & Convention Bureau. 505 North Third Street, Hannibal 63401; (573) 221–2477; toll free, TOM AND HUCK (866–263–4825); www.visithannibal .com. Open daily 8:00 A.M. to 5:00 P.M. Call for visitor guide.

Missouri Division of Tourism Welcome Center. East side of Highway 61, 2 miles south of Highway 36; (573) 248–2420; www.visitMo.com. The center is open daily from 8:00 A.M. to 5:00 P.M. This is a place to load up on printed materials.

Louisiana

A leisurely drive south along Highway 79, which parallels the Missouri River, is a scenic delight. It reveals magnificent views along the river bluffs and winds through small, quaint river towns. In Louisiana, where the downtown business district is on the National Register of Historic Places, beautiful examples of Victorian architecture abound and Riverfront Park gives an unobstructed view of the Missouri River and boat access to it. Henderson-Riverview Park, at the crest of Main and Noyes Streets, has picnic facilities and a playground in full view of the river at its most magnificent.

Ted Shanks Conservation Area (all ages)

Highway 79, then 1 mile on County Road TT to area entrance; send mail to Box 13, Ashburn 63343; (573) 754–6171; www.mdc.state.mo.us (click on "Places to Go"). The area is always open.

Tucked between the Mississippi and Salt Rivers, you'll find a visitor center containing exhibits, displays, and an observation room highlighting the deer, waterfowl, turkeys, and

Amazing
Missouri Facts

In what play and musical do you find "Shoeless Joe from Hannibal Mo"?

Damn Yankees

other wildlife that live here. Hiking trails over the levees cross the marsh and wetlands at the junction of the rivers. Fishing, camping, hiking, and canoeing are available.

There is no fee for the area's primitive (no showers, electricity, or easily accessible water) campsites, available on a first-come, first-served basis.

For More Information

Louisiana Chamber of Commerce. 202 Third Street, Suite 120, Louisiana 63353-2057; (573) 754–5921; (888) 642–3800; www.louisiana-mo.com.

Clarksville

This small historic river town south on Highway 79 attracts tourists and wildlife with a magnificent location on 500-foot bluffs overlooking the Mississippi River.

Clarksville Visitor Center, River Heritage Center (all ages)
North of town on Highway 79, 302 North Second Street, Clarksville 63336; (573) 242–3132; www.clarksvillemo.com. Center open Wednesday though Monday 11:00 A.M. to 4:00 P.M.
Free.

This visitor center, once operated by the World Bird Sanctuary but now run by the city of Clarksville, has plenty of educational exhibits on everything from the eagles that have put the town on the map to the mussels found in nearby streams and rivers. A large number of eagles are attracted to the area in the winter because the Missouri River provides plenty of fish for them to eat. The center has a viewing platform with a spotting scope, but bring binoculars—they're better.

Birders Flock to **Eagle** Days

Every January and February Clarksville draws bird-watchers from all over who come to see the wintering bald eagles that live and fish along the river bluffs and around the locks. Eagle Days, held at the Clarksville Visitor Center and in town in late January, features special activities, guided eagle-viewing tours, and live eagle exhibits. **Free** admission. For more information, call (573) 242–3132.

Troy

Cuivre River State Park (all ages) 🏕️ 🚶 ⛺

Highway 47; send mail to 678 State Route 147, Troy 63379; (636) 528–7247 or (800) 334–6946; www.mostateparks.com. Center open daily 8:00 A.M. to 4:00 P.M.; admission to the park is free. Campsites are $14.00 for electric and water hookups, plus $3.00 for sewer, or $8.00 for a basic campsite April to October. Water for showers is turned off from October 1 through February 1. Call (877) 422–6766 at least forty-eight hours in advance for camping reservations. There is an $8.50 registration fee.

Rugged, wooded terrain and Big Sugar Creek are found among the 6,000 acres in the park, which includes a fifty-five-acre lake, more than 30 miles of trails, and a special campground just for equestrians. There are 110 regular campsites, thirty-two with full hookups available. A visitor center offers displays and trail maps.

Weldon Spring

August A. Busch Memorial and Weldon Spring Conservation Areas (all ages)

Highway 94; send mail to 2360 Highway D, St. Charles 63304; (636) 441–4554; www.mdc.state.mo.us. Both areas open daily 6:00 A.M. to 10:00 P.M.; fishing to 9:00 P.M.

This 14,000-acre wildlife preserve offers a mixture of timber, open fields, streams, springs, and lakes. An 8-mile self-guided automobile tour passes through several habitats that provide great opportunities for wildlife viewing. There are gun and bow ranges for target shooters and plenty of areas for fishing. Picnicking and limited hunting are allowed. A bait shop, open 6:00 A.M. to 9:00 P.M. from April 1 to September 30, rents boats, and a visitor center has exhibits and a naturalist on staff for anyone interested in the area's ecology. When combined with the adjacent Weldon Spring Conservation Area, the two preserves have more than 20 miles of hiking trails.

Defiance

Daniel Boone Home and Boonesfield Village (all ages)

1868 Highway F, Defiance 63341; (636) 798–2005; www.lindenwood.edu. Open daily 9:00 A.M. to 4:00 P.M. March through October and 11:00 A.M. to 4:00 P.M. November through February. Admission is $7.00 for adults, $4.00 for children ages 4 through 10, and includes a one-hour tour of Boone's home. A two-hour tour of all buildings on the site is $12.00 for adults, $6.00 for children.

This small town on the Missouri River is where the real-life American legend lived and died. Costumed guides give one-hour tour through the restored brick house Daniel spent seven years building after he moved here from Kentucky, completing it in 1810. Boonesfield Village, a collection of restored historic buildings surrounding the home, provides demonstrations of crafts and household chores of the nineteenth century and a full schedule of interpretive activities.

St. Charles

As you head east you'll start to notice the unmistakable signs of suburban sprawl, but there's more here than twentieth-century bedroom communities. When you stroll along historic Main Street in St. Charles, you'll feel as if you have been transported into the past. Here you'll find 13 blocks of charming, restored eighteenth- and nineteenth-century homes, stores, and taverns. This city was the first settlement on the Missouri River, and many of its old buildings are restored and open to the public. Lewis and Clark left for their historic journey from here.

St. Charles also is home to the Family Arena, located 1.75 miles south of Interstate 70 at 2002 Arena Parkway (St. Charles, 63303; www.familyarena.com). The arena, which seats from 8,000 to 11,400 depending on the musical or sporting event, is home to several minor-league sports teams. They include the St. Louis Steamers, who play October through April in the Major Indoor Soccer League (636–410–0388, ext. 501; www.stlsteamers.com; tickets $$–$$$); the Missouri River Otters, who play October through April

Amazing Missouri Facts

Where was the first Missouri state capital?

St. Charles

in the United Hockey League (636–946–0003; www.riverotters.com); and the Show Me Believers, who play March through July in the National Indoor Football League (636–916–0132; www.showmebelievers.com). Great tickets are always available at reasonable prices for these teams.

First Missouri State Capitol State Historic Site (all ages)

200 South Main Street, St. Charles 63301; (636) 940–3322; www.dnr.state.mo.us. Open Monday through Saturday 9:00 A.M. to 4:00 P.M., Sunday 11:00 A.M. to 5:00 P.M. Tickets $; ages 6 and younger free. There is a free slide show and small exhibit area.

This building was used by legislators immediately after Missouri became a state, while the permanent capital was being constructed in the middle of the new state in Jefferson City. The rooms have been restored to their condition during the 1820s, including the residences and store on the ground floor. Park rangers provide an excellent forty-five-minute tour that explores the lives of early legislators and inhabitants of the area.

Lewis and Clark Boat House and Nature Center (all ages)

1050 Riverside Drive, St. Charles 63301; (636) 947–3199; www.lewisandclark.net. Open 10:00 A.M. to 5:00 P.M. Monday though Saturday and noon to 5:00 P.M. Sunday. Admission $; children ages 2 and under free.

This museum uses diorama and artifacts to tell you about these famed explorers and one of the greatest adventures in American history. It is the permanent home of the replicas of Lewis and Clark's boats, and it showcases many of the plants and animals the Corps of Discovery found on its journey. It's a wonderful museum for school-age children and grown-ups who have an interest in the exploration and settling of the West.

St. Charles Princess (all ages)

233 North Main Street, St. Charles 63301; (636) 946–4995; www.saintcharlesprincess.com. Open April through November. Call for schedule of cruises; reservations required. Sightseeing cruise: adults $$$, kids ages 3 through 12 $$, children ages 2 and under free. Lunch cruise: adults $$$$, kids ages 3 through 12 $$$, children ages 2 and under free.

Boarding on the St. Charles riverfront, this 150-passenger craft provides ninety-minute sightseeing tours, with some narration; ninety-minute lunch cruises that include a box lunch; and dinner and specialty cruises.

Katy Trail State Park (all ages)

Trail parking is available at Boone's Lick Road and Main Street, St. Charles; (800) 334–6946; www.mostateparks.com. Bike rental: The Touring Cyclist, 104 South Main Street, St. Charles 63301; (636) 949–9630; tours of the trail, call TC Tours (314) 739–5180. Free.

This is the eastern end of the longest hiking and biking trail in the state. The tracks of the Missouri-Kansas-Texas Railroad have been replaced with hard-packed gravel, and the path now provides visitors with access to sleepy little rural communities, scenic views of the

A Cosby Family **Adventure**

One of our favorite forays is to pack up the family and take I–70 toward St. Charles en route to two boat rides, a fabulous family-style meal at the quaint Wittmond Hotel in Brussels, and a grand tour of several scenic roads north of St. Louis.

Wittmond's, located in a building that was an 1840s stagecoach stop, fills the table with plates of chicken, beef, sausage, green beans, potatoes, dessert, and drinks. The cost is $9.95 per person for anyone twelve and older, with younger children charged according to their age. Kids in high chairs eat **free.**

Because Wittmond's is on a peninsula in Illinois, you have to take a country road outside St. Charles to the *Golden Eagle* ferry, which for $5.00 one way or $9.00 round-trip transports cars across the Mississippi River. From here the restaurant is about 1½ miles farther on scenic Calhoun County Road; stay to the left at the fork. Once you've eaten strike out for the second leg of the journey, heading back toward the *Golden Eagle* but turning left instead of right at the fork in the road. This takes you to the **free** state ferry at Brussels, which carries cars across the Illinois River to the Great River Road near Grafton, Illinois, a quaint tourist-oriented town with a wide selection of shops, restaurants, and several nearby orchards.

Pick a bushel or two of peaches or pick out a collectible from one of the many interesting shops, and, if you stay long enough, perhaps grab a lighter bite at the Fin Inn Restaurant, where the turtle soup is tasty and three immense aquariums, as well as french fries and hush puppies, are capable of keeping most children occupied. If you passed on Wittmond's earlier, this is a great place for a substantial meal. You can find a lot more information about the Illinois side of the river at www.greatriverroad.com.

When interest and energy start to fade, head south on the incredibly scenic Great River Road to Alton, then continue south on Highway 3 to I–270 and west back into Missouri. You can start the trip on the Great River Road, but keep in mind that the *Golden Eagle* shuts down at 9:00 P.M. Sunday through Thursday, although it runs until 12:00 A.M. Friday and Saturday nights. The Brussels Ferry runs around-the-clock.

To reach the *Golden Eagle* (618–883–2217) take Highway 94 north to Highway B, turn west, and follow the signs to the ferry. For more information about the Brussels ferry, call (618) 786–3636. Wittmond's (618–883–2345) is open daily from 11:00 A.M. to 7:00 P.M. except during severe weather. The Fin Inn (618–786–2030) opens everyday at 11:00 A.M. and closes at 8:00 P.M. Sunday through Thursday and 9:00 P.M. Friday and Saturday. As always, in severe weather it makes sense to call ahead to ensure everything is open.

Missouri River bluffs, and opportunities to observe the wildlife living along the river corridor. The trail stretches more than 225 miles to Clinton, Missouri. It has a relatively easy grade and is perfect for family bicyclists or hikers. No motorized vehicles are allowed except for wheelchairs. Trail conditions vary with the season and the level of the river, so call before setting out on an extended trip.

Marais Temps Clair Conservation Area (all ages)

North on Highway 94, east on County Road H, north on Island Road for 2 miles to the area entrance; (636) 250–3674; www.mcd.state.mo.us (click on "Places to Go" at top left of screen). The area is closed during waterfowl hunting season, which runs for several weeks in October, November, and December. Free.

This 918-acre tract in the middle of the Mississippi River flyway is a great place for birdwatching. You can see large numbers of waterfowl, raptors, and other birds here.

Swing-A-Round Fun Town (all ages)

3541 Bogey Road, St. Charles 63303; (636) 947–4487; www.sarfun.com. Open 10:00 A.M. to 9:00 P.M. daily March through October, but call ahead because hours vary. Prices also vary from activity to activity. No general admission fee.

You can practice your stroke on an eighteen-hole miniature golf course, polish your swing at baseballs or softballs in one of nine cages, or explore Area 51 in a small arcade.

Grand Prix Karting (ages 5 and up)

3500 Highway 94 North, St. Charles 63301; (636) 946–4848. Open daily 10:00 A.M. to midnight March 1 through December 1. $$.

Go-kart rides are offered for everyone age five and up on a five-eighths-mile track that is billed as the Midwest's largest go-kart/sprint-kart track. Racing sprint karts are available for drivers age sixteen and older.

Edward "Ted" and Pat Jones–Confluence State Park (all ages)

1005 Riverlands Way, 2.7 miles off Highway 67 North at West Alton; P.O. Box 67, West Alton 63386; (636) 940–3322; (800) 334–6946; www.mostateparks.com. Open daily year-round sunrise to 30 minutes past sunset. Free admission.

Missouri's newest state park features a lookout point with an incredible view of the confluence of the Mississippi and Missouri Rivers. The 1,118-acre day park has hiking trails and several small interpretive exhibits with information about the rivers, the Lewis and Clark expedition, and Native Americans who once lived in the area.

For More Information

St. Charles Convention and Visitors Center. 230 South Main Street, St. Charles 63301; (636) 946–7776 or (800) 366–2427; www.historicstcharles.com.

St. Peters

Tilt (all ages)

1208 Mid Rivers Mall, I–70 and Mid Rivers Mall Drive, St. Peters 63376; (636) 279–2807. Open Monday through Saturday 10:00 A.M. to 9:30 P.M., and Sunday 11:00 A.M. to 6:00 P.M. Games are individually priced but generally range from 25 cents to $1.00 each.

A video arcade with nearly ninety games, including shooting and driving simulation programs. Games are rotated among three area Tilt stores. Tickets are awarded for prize redemption.

Hazelwood

When you head east and cross the Missouri River, you'll find several interesting stops in the northern suburbs of St. Louis.

Big Foot 4x4 Inc. (all ages)

6311 North Lindbergh Boulevard, Hazelwood 63042; (314) 731–8112 or (314) 731–2822; big foot4x4.com. Open Monday through Friday 9:00 A.M. to 6:00 P.M., Saturday 9:00 A.M. to 3:00 P.M. Free admission; $3.00 per child fee for Ride & Race Trax.

This is, simply put, the birthplace of monster trucks. You can see several versions of the original Big Foot; one is always on display so fans can take their pictures next to or underneath it. You can also see the factory where the trucks are built. With a little luck, you'll see a variety of the creatures parked while awaiting repairs or being readied for unleashing on the unfortunate derelict vehicles of the world. You also can shop for Big Foot souvenirs in the gift shop, which features monster truck wearables, toys, models, photos, and videos. While all of this is free—except for the souvenirs—kids also can pay $3.00 a head to spend time in the Ride & Race Trax. This play area allows kids to "drive" remote-controlled cars, drive large battery-powered vehicles, and bounce about in a bounce house, an inflatable plastic "house" made for jumping in.

James S. McDonnell Prologue Room (ages 5 and up)

Airport Road and McDonnell Boulevard, Berkeley 63134; (314) 232–6896. Open during June, July, and August only. Hours vary; reservations required. Free admission.

This museum provides a mind-boggling view of the role McDonnell Douglas and its relatively new parent, Boeing Corporation, have played in aviation history and space exploration. You can see full-size mock-ups of the *Mercury* and *Gemini* spacecraft and a full-size harpoon missile. There are models of the F-15 Eagle, F/A 18 Hornet, and the DC-3 airliner. It's a must-see for anyone interested in models, the space program, or military and commercial aviation.

Wet and Wild Respite

Raging Rivers Water Park, open from Memorial Day through Labor Day, is one of the best antidotes to St. Louis's sometimes notorious sweltering late-summer days. The only problem: It's in Illinois, so you have to "jump the creek" (the Mississippi River) to get there. Take Highway 367 north to Alton. The drive then is a short scenic one along the Great River Road, which you take north from Alton, Illinois, to Grafton, Illinois. The 20-acre park offers everything from a small pool for toddlers to a wave pool, swirl pool, and body flumes. Park hours vary, so call ahead (618) 786–2345; www.ragingrivers.com. $$$; children ages two and under **free.** Parking is $4.00.

Boeing Gift Shop (all ages)

5900 North Lindbergh Boulevard, Hazelwood 63042; (314) 233–2222. Open Monday through Friday 10:00 A.M. to 6:00 P.M., Saturday 10:00 A.M. to 3:00 P.M.

If flight is your fancy, spend some time browsing here. You'll find clothing, souvenirs, and decorative items emblazoned with the Boeing logo, an emblem of the most technologically advanced aircraft in the world.

St. Louis Mills Mall, Sportstreet (all ages)

5555 St. Louis Mills Boulevard (Highway 370, 1 mile west of Interstate 270), Hazelwood 63042; (314) 298–1500; wwww.stlouismills.com. Mall hours are 10:00 A.M. to 9:30 P.M. Monday through Saturday; 11:00 A.M. to 7:00 P.M. Sunday.

Kids and adults will find plenty to do on Sportstreet, a unique entertainment area in the newest mall in St. Louis. If sports, games, and kids' play areas are not to everyone's liking, you'll also find tons of shopping opportunities in this 1.1-million-square-foot mall.

- **ESPN X Games Skatepark:** *(314) 227–5630; www.xgamesskatepark.com. Open 10:00 A.M. to 11:00 P.M. daily* . The 40,000-square-foot indoor skatepark has twenty-five skate, board, and bike (BMX) ramps for athletes of all skill levels; a 6-foot half-pipe with sub box; a wall ride; a lounge; and a store selling skate- and bike-related items. Sessions alternate for skaters and bikers. $$$
- **Ice ZONE:** *(314) 513–1761; www.icezone.com. Call for public hours.* This NHL regulation-size ice-skating rink has several public sessions, including family nights and rock 'n' roll sessions. But it also is the official practice facility for the St. Louis Blues ice hockey team, which opens the 600-seat arena **free** of charge during Blues practices. $$
- **NASCAR SpeedPark:** *(314) 227–5600; www.nascarspeedpark.com. Open 10:00 A.M. to 9:00 P.M. Monday through Saturday, 11:00 a.m. to 7:00 p.m. Sunday.* There are five tracks, including simulated car racing indoors and gas-powered carts outdoors, as well as children's rides, miniature golf, bumper boats, a climbing wall, a soft play area, laser tag, a banquet area and state-of-the-art arcade games. $$

- **Putting Edge:** *(314) 291–7600; www.putting-edge.com. Open 10:00 A.M. daily, close midnight Friday and Saturday, 10:00 P.M. other days.* This challenging eighteen-hole indoor miniature golf course immerses players in a kaleidoscope of colors and themes. Billing itself as glow-in-the-dark minigolf and aided by an art gallery of more than 350 props and obstacles, the course puts players in scenarios ranging from a dense forest to the bottom of the ocean. $$; children ages three and under **free.**
- **PBS KIDS Backyard**: *www.ketc.org. Open during mall hours.* **Free** *admission.* Kids learn, play, and have fun in this area featuring computer kiosks, displays, jungle gyms, book nooks, and a small theater for PBS KIDS character events. PBS KIDS television programming also is provided by KETC-TV, the local PBS affiliate.
- **A Place to Grow:** *www.placetogrow.com. Open during mall hours.* **Free** *admission.* The artfully designed play space, based on the children's book of the same name, has a soft play area for kids ages two through four that is populated with the book's whimsical, oversize characters. For kids ages five through eight, touch-screen computer kiosks housed in huge veggies bring the tiny seed's exciting and inspirational adventure to life through engaging multimedia games and an interactive storybook.

Florissant

The first French fur traders came to this area in the mid-1700s, shortly before Pierre Laclede and Auguste Chouteau pulled their canoes ashore near the present site of the Gateway Arch on the St. Louis riverfront. Several buildings dating from the late 1700s still exist in Old Town Florissant.

Family Theater Series (all ages)

Florissant Civic Center, Waterford Avenue and Parker Road, Florissant 63033; (314) 921–5678.

Each season national touring companies are brought in to offer children's productions that the entire family can enjoy together. A regular schedule of concerts, musicals, and mysteries is also presented here. Call for a schedule of shows and ticket prices.

Sioux Passage County Park (all ages)

Old Jamestown Road, Florissant 63033; (314) 615–7275; www.st-louis countyparks.com. Open daily 9:00 A.M. to thirty minutes past sunset. No admission fee.

Five miles of wooded trails, campgrounds, and horse trails provide great opportunities for walks along the Missouri River. You'll also find athletic fields, fishing access to the river, picnic tables and shelters, a children's playground, and tennis courts.

River Heritage **Abounds**

The role the Mississippi River has played in the history and commerce of the region is brilliantly explained at two recently opened **free** museums just across the Lewis and Clark Bridge at Alton, Illinois.

The National Great Rivers Museum, a 7,000-square-foot beauty operated by the U.S. Corps of Engineers, is open daily from 9:00 A.M. to 5:00 P.M. Located adjacent to the Melvin Price Lock and Dam, it contains a replica of a towboat pilot house with an interactive video-steering program; a limestone cliff; nearly two dozen displays, several with video characters explaining life on the river; and a theater that shows a fifteen-minute film with some of the best video ever shot on the river.

Tours of the locks and dam are offered at the site; call (877) 462–6979; www.mvs.usace.army.mil/rivers/. To reach the museum, go north on Highway 367 in north St. Louis County, turn right at the end of the bridge, and go three stoplights to 2 Lock and Dam Way.

The other must-see attraction is the Lewis and Clark State Historic Site in Hartford, which is a little more than 5 miles south of Alton on Highway 3 at New Poag Road. The goal of the project is to re-create Camp River Dubois, the encampment that Meriwether Lewis and William Clark's famed Corps of Discovery used from December 12, 1803, until setting off for the unknown the following May 14.

The site contains a 55-foot-tall, 150-foot-long keelboat that is cut in half longways to show visitors how one might have been packed in 1804. Outside the building are five log cabins that have been built based on a sketch in one of the explorers' journals. The historic site even has a corps of reenactors who, during special events, do their best to demonstrate the activities that might have taken place at the encampment.

Among the annual events planned at the site are departure and arrival reenactments each May and December, a discovery event for kids each June, and an authentic period music festival each September. 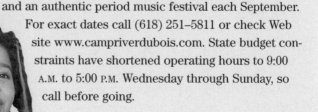 For exact dates call (618) 251–5811 or check Web site www.campriverdubois.com. State budget constraints have shortened operating hours to 9:00 A.M. to 5:00 P.M. Wednesday through Sunday, so call before going.

Birds **Galore!**

Birders and nature lovers in general will find plenty to watch at the River-lands Environmental Demonstration Area off Highway 367 in West Alton, on the Missouri side of the Clark Bridge across the Mississippi River from Alton, Illinois. The 2,200-acre tract, with viewing areas and exhibits open from 8:00 A.M. to 4:00 P.M. daily, is overseen by the U.S. Army Corps of Engineers. For more information about the area, call (888) 899–2602, or visit online at www.mvs.usace.army.mil/rivers/. $$$; children ages two and under **free.**

For More Information

Missouri Division of Tourism Welcome Center. I–270 at Riverview exit, just west of Missouri-Illinois state line; (314) 869–7100; www.visitmo.com. The center is open from 8:00 A.M. to 5:00 P.M. daily. This is a place to load up on printed materials.

St. Louis

Travel a little farther east and you'll hit the Mississippi River and the city of St. Louis, which was founded in 1764 by French fur traders. The city sits just below the confluence of the Mississippi and Missouri Rivers and is famous for its beer, baseball, historic neighborhoods, and original cuisine. This is where ice-cream cones, iced tea, hot dogs, and toasted ravioli originated. So don't leave town without sampling the local fare. Since Illinois is just across the river, you might want to check out some of the attractions on that side of the river, too. For information about attractions in the area, call (314) 421–1023 or (800) 916–0092; www.explorestlouis.com or www.stlouisfrontpage.com.

Amazing
Missouri Facts

What is the tallest national monument?

At 630 feet, the Gateway Arch in St. Louis

Gateway Arch (all ages)

11 North Fourth Street, St. Louis 63102, on the riverfront; (314) 655–1700 or toll-free, (877) 982–1410; www.stlouisarch.com. Open daily 8:00 A.M. to 10:00 P.M. from Memorial Day to Labor Day, daily 9:00 A.M. to 6:00 P.M. from September through May. Tickets to view Monument to the Dream and ride to the top are $11.00 for adults, $9.00 for children ages 13 through 16, and $5.50 for children ages 3 through 12. Individual tickets to ride the tram to the top are $8.00 for adults, $5.00 for children ages 13 through 16, and $3.00 for children ages 3 through 12; children ages 2 and under are **free.** Individual tickets to Monument to the Dream are $7.00 for adults, $4.00 for children ages 13 through 16, and $2.50 for children ages 3 through 12; children ages 2 and under are **free.**

Once you get anywhere near downtown you won't need directions, the arch dominates the skyline and makes downtown easy to navigate without a map. The arch grounds and the Old Courthouse across the street form the Jefferson National Expansion Memorial, a federal park dedicated to the president who purchased the Louisiana Territory and helped foster the westward expansion of our country.

Free City

St. Louis has many nicknames. The Gateway City refers to its role as a jumping-off point for westward expansion, a theme used when plans for the Gateway Arch were conceived. It is also known as Mound City, a reference to the many Indian mounds, such as those now found across the Mississippi River in Illinois at Cahokia, that were in the area when Europeans arrived. Still others have called St. Louis the River City, an obvious reference to its past prominence as perhaps the preeminent nineteenth-century steamboat port on the river.

Today, Free City might be an appropriate name. While economist Milton Friedman is correct in his assessment that "there's no such thing as a free lunch," admission to most of St. Louis's top-flight cultural institutions is **free** all the time. How can the institutions afford it? Years ago voters in the city of St. Louis and St. Louis County approved a special zoo-museum district supported by a property tax.

Consequently, there is no entrance fee to the magnificent St. Louis Zoo, certainly one of the best in the nation; the newly expanded St. Louis Science Center, one of the busiest in the United States; the St. Louis Art Museum, one of the leading institutions in the country; and the Missouri History Museum, which, among other exhibits, has a new permanent, interactive exhibition titled *Seeking St. Louis*.

The Missouri Botanical Garden, an incredible collection of plants and world leader in plant research, is **free** to children ages twelve and under. Adults pay $7.00 to get in.

Underneath the arch you'll find the Museum of Westward Expansion, an outstanding museum explaining the role of the people who conquered the West. The newest component of the museum is *Journey to the Top,* a two-part multimedia exhibit in what once were drab areas in the north and south legs of the monument where riders board trams to the top. In the south leg, you'll find *When Riverboats Ruled,* which offers a "tour" of St. Louis during the 1800s, enhanced by sights and sounds from the period, including the voice of Mark Twain. The north leg has *Fitting the Final Piece,* which explains the history of the arch and which, through the use of sights and sounds, gives you the feeling that you are on the arch during construction.

The rest of the museum has an unusual semicircular layout, so talk to a park ranger for a quick orientation before you begin browsing or it may be confusing to you and your children. The museum has fascinating exhibits illustrated with historic photographs of people and places and artifacts from the period. The rangers offer wonderful interpretive activities to spice up your experience and can answer all your questions.

There also are four animatronic figures, including Thomas Jefferson; William Clark, Lewis's coleader in the Corps of Discovery; an African-American "buffalo" soldier; and an 1846 Overlander woman who is preparing to head West. Each talk about personal experiences.

Be sure to purchase tickets to ride to the observation deck at the top of the arch when you first come in; you can visit the museum while waiting for your turn to go up. You'll ride in a very small conveyor car to reach the top where you can see all of the downtown area and, on a clear day, 30 miles beyond.

You won't want to miss *Monument to a Dream,* a fascinating film on the construction of the arch, or any of the rotating films shown in an IMAX theater.

The Old Courthouse (all ages)

11 North Fourth Street, St. Louis 63102; (314) 655–1700; www.nps.gov/jeff/. Open daily 8:00 A.M. to 4:30 P.M. Free admission.

This courthouse is steeped in history and has four galleries detailing the history of the city. You can see exhibits about the fur traders who founded the city, the transportation revolution during the Victorian era, and the city's heyday at the turn of the century. The Dred Scott case originated in this courthouse, and in the galleries on the west side you can learn about this monumental decision on slavery and the part it played in leading our country into the Civil War.

Laclede's Landing (all ages)

This business district area has preserved the feel of the nineteenth-century riverfront with restored century-old brick buildings and cobblestone streets. By night this is a principal entertainment district for adults, featuring a wide variety of bars and restaurants. But during the day children will love stopping in at one of several museums, and adults might want to spend a little time in some of the shops. Many of the restaurants are open for lunch and dinner. Check out a virtual tour at www.lacledeslanding.org.

Dental Health Theater (ages 4 and up)

27 North First Street, St. Louis 63102; (314) 241–7391. Shows Monday through Friday 9:00 A.M. to 3:00 P.M. Free admission, but reservations are required, so call ahead.

Young kids are treated to a forty-five-minute show that includes a short talk, a video, and a marionette performance, all of which explain the importance of proper dental hygiene. Don't miss the pink-carpet tongue surrounded by 3-foot-tall teeth.

Laclede's Landing Wax Museum (all ages upstairs)

720 North Second Street, St. Louis 63102; (314) 241–1155. Open daily April 1 through September 30 and shorter hours other times; best to call before going unless you're already in the area. Adults $$, children $ ages 12 and under.

More than 180 authentically costumed beeswax figures ranging from Richard Burton and Elizabeth Taylor as Antony and Cleopatra to a young, slim Elvis greet you here. Be forewarned not to go into the basement or take your young children down there unless you want to see the blood, guts, and gore that made wax museums so popular years ago.

Edward Jones Dome (all ages)

901 North Broadway Avenue, St. Louis 63102; (314) 342–5000 for information on events at the Dome; (314) 342–5201 for an operator. St. Louis Rams, (314) 425–8830; www.stlouis rams.com. $$$$.

Although a variety of events are held here throughout the year, the Edward Jones Dome is the home field of the St. Louis Rams professional football team. Tickets to Rams games go on sale in the summer for the following season.

Take the **Train**

Getting around downtown is easy and fun on Metrolink, the light transit railway that runs between downtown and Lambert St. Louis International Airport. Tickets are $1.25 for adults, 60 cents for children ages five through eleven and free for children ages four and younger. The only exception is a special $3.00 per person fare for riders leaving the airport. Everyone can ride free in the downtown area Monday through Friday from 11:00 A.M. to 1:30 P.M. For a schedule, route map, and ticket information call (314) 231–2345; www.metrostlouis.org.

Gateway Riverboat Cruises (all ages)

Riverfront, below the Gateway Arch, 50 South Leonor K. Sullivan Boulevard, St. Louis 63102; (314) 621–4040 or (800) 878–7411. There are several sightseeing cruises daily from April to October, weather and river conditions permitting. Adults $$, kids ages 3 through 11 $, children ages 2 and under free.

Kids and adults alike will love a one-hour sight-seeing cruise on the "mighty Mississippi" aboard the *Becky Thatcher* or *Tom Sawyer* paddle wheelers. The cruise is narrated by the boats' captains, who point out landmarks and entertain passengers with interesting local river lore. There also are music, dinner, and specialty cruises; call for information.

St. Louis Carriage Company (all ages)

1000 Cerre, St. Louis 63102; (314) 621–3334. Tours offered daily April through October from 6:00 to 11:00 P.M. $$$$.

Enjoy the charm of a leisurely tour of downtown on a horse-drawn carriage that will pick up guests from most major downtown hotels or can be boarded at the Old Spaghetti Factory, 727 North First Street; on Laclede's Landing; at the Adam's Mark Hotel, 1200 North First Street; and, during select times, on the riverfront below the Gateway Arch.

Busch Stadium (all ages)

300 Stadium Plaza, St. Louis 63102; (314) 421–3060; www.stlcardinals.com. Tickets $$$–$$$$. Cardinals team store, Gate 6; (314) 421–3263. Open daily year-round from 10:00 A.M. to 5:00 P.M. and during games.

Baseball always was big in St. Louis, but it got even bigger in 1998 when Mark McGwire clobbered seventy homers wearing a Redbirds jersey and phenom Albert Pujols came out of nowhere in 2001. If you're going to take in a game, wear something red. If you can't make it to a game, you can still pick up a souvenir year-round at the Cardinals team store, located at Gate 6. Tours also are available.

International Bowling Museum & St. Louis Cardinals Hall of Fame Museum (all ages)

Walnut and Seventh Streets, St. Louis 63102, across from Busch Stadium; (314) 231–6340; www.bowlingmuseum.com. Open daily 9:00 A.M. to 5:00 P.M. April through September, except Cardinals home games when closing is 6:30 P.M.; and 11:00 A.M. to 4:00 P.M. Tuesday through Saturday October through March. Admission to museums is $6.00 for adults, $4.00 for children ages 5 through 12. Stadium tours, when there's no day game, are $6.00 for adults; $4.00 for children ages 5 through 12. Children ages 4 and under are free for tours. Museums and tour combined are $9.50 adults, $7.50 children.

One admission price gives you two museums, two films, and four frames of bowling. The fact that bowling dates from ancient Egypt is one of the many bits of trivia you can pick up from some of the surprisingly interesting exhibits outlining the history of bowling. You'll see displays featuring the greatest players of the game, view a film titled *History of Bowling,* and bowl on computerized or old-fashioned lanes.

And when you've tired of bowling memorabilia, presto, you're right there gazing on the artifacts and learning about some of the greatest baseball players who ever lived. If you're not a baseball fan going in, you'll certainly come out knowing the names of Stan Musial, Bob Gibson, Lou Brock, Ken Boyer, Ozzie Smith, and, of course, Mark McGwire. The history of this proud franchise is presented nicely in the film *St. Louis Cardinals: A Century of Success.* Ask about the package that includes admission to both museums and a tour of Busch Stadium.

Eugene Field House and St. Louis Toy Museum (all ages)

634 South Broadway Boulevard, St. Louis 63102; (314) 421–4689; www.eugenefieldhouse.org. Open Wednesday through Saturday 10:00 A.M. to 4:00 P.M., Sunday noon to 4:00 P.M. March through December. Open January and February by appointment only. $.

The boyhood home of the famous children's poet is now a small museum housing antique toys and dolls in rotating displays with seasonal themes. Some of this museum's toys are loaned for display at the City Museum. The toy museum is planning an expansion in the near future.

Soulard Market (all ages)

730 Carroll Street, St. Louis 63104; (314) 622–4180. Open Wednesday through Friday 8:00 A.M. to 5:30 P.M., Saturday 6:00 A.M. to 5:30 P.M.

A farmers' market that has been in operation since 1779, Soulard Market has 150 stalls selling fruit and vegetables fresh from the farm, meat and fish, and numerous other items that change daily as merchants come and go.

Anheuser-Busch Brewery Tour Center (all ages)

Twelfth and Lynch Streets, St. Louis 63118; (314) 577–2626; www.budweisertours.com. Open Monday through Saturday; tours start at 9:00 A.M. and leave every forty-five minutes. Tours start at 11:00 A.M. on Sunday. Last tour leaves at 4:00 P.M. Free admission.

You don't have to be a beer drinker to enjoy a **free** tour that includes the historic Clydesdale stables, a short video on the making of beer, and a state-of-the-art bottling facility. The session ends with a short ride on a cable car and complimentary samples of beer and soft drinks. While this certainly is a tour aimed at adults, the awe shown by a young child standing a few feet away from a massive Clydesdale is a sight to behold.

Soldiers' Memorial Military Museum (all ages)

1315 Chestnut Street, St. Louis 63103; (314) 622–4550. Open daily 9:00 A.M. to 4:30 P.M. Free admission.

This memorial to fallen soldiers has an excellent display of handheld weapons, uniforms, photos, flags, and other items, primarily from World Wars I and II, but some dating from the Civil War. Anyone with an interest in weapons and military memorabilia will enjoy this stop. The museum also is across the street from the court of honor, an area with several memorials to those who lost their lives in wars.

Savvis Center (all ages)

1401 Clark Avenue, St. Louis 63103; (314) 531–7887 for automated calendar, (314) 622–5400 for operator. St. Louis Blues hockey, (314) 622–2500; www.stlouisblues.com. Tickets $$$–$$$$. St. Louis University Billikens basketball, (314) 977–3182; www.slu.edu. Tickets $$–$$$$.

This beautiful building is home to the St. Louis Blues professional hockey team and the St. Louis University Billikens basketball team, with a late fall and winter schedule. Savvis also regularly hosts other national sporting events, concerts by national entertainers, and family entertainment programs. Call for a calendar of events.

City Museum (all ages)

Summer hours are 9:00 A.M. to 5:00 P.M. Tuesday through Thursday, 9:00 A.M. to 1:00 A.M. Friday, 10:00 A.M. to 1:00 A.M. Saturday, and 11:00 A.M. to 1:00 A.M. Sunday. Closed Monday. Winter hours are shorter; closed Monday and Tuesday. Museum admission is $$, children ages 1 and under free. Admission to MonstroCity and Altered Skates Park $.

There is no better place in Missouri for a kid—or an adult—to expect the unexpected. Artist Robert Cassilly has created a monument to whimsy and flat-out fun exploration while elevating to a higher plane a wide range of art created from recycled materials. Add this to a healthy dose of local historical artifacts; MonstroCity, an unbelievable outdoor playground comprised of elevated enclosed walkways and play areas seemingly borne aloft by an airplane; Altered Skates Park, an indoor rink for the "wheeled" crowd; and many other nearly inconceivable constructions, and you have a destination worthy of several hours of your time. You'll know you are there when you walk up to the building and see the bus . . . about three stories above your head.

City (E)scape

Eclectic is almost too confining a word for St. Louis's newest and certainly most kid-friendly museum. The City Museum's promotional literature is right on when it calls itself "a place of fantasy, wonder, mystery, craft and whimsy." The brainchild of St. Louis artist Robert Cassilly, this constantly evolving and emerging environment is as tantalizing to adults as it is to children, and the latter, as you troop out the door on the way home, surely will be asking when they can come back. The attraction? Maybe 4,000 square feet of artificially created caves accommodating adults and children. Lost the kids? Look for them at the hidden stairway to the fort. Or maybe they're over at the Altered Skates Park. Stop in at the lizard lounge and try to figure out what the lizard columns are made of. How did Jonah feel when he was swallowed? Walk through the mouth of a 55-foot bowhead whale and find out. This is a one-of-a-kind experience. Don't let the kids miss it. Call (314) 231–2489 or check the Web site www.citymuseum.org.

Mount City **Meandering**

The Mound City, one of St. Louis's many nicknames, came from the Indian dirt mounds that were in the area when European settlers first arrived in the region in the late 1600s. Although many of the mounds on the Missouri side of the Mississippi River fell victim to "civilization" and "progress," the nearby Cahokia Mounds State Historic Site, 30 Ramsey Street, in Collinsville, Illinois, has managed to preserve part of what was one of the great prehistoric metropolises in the Americas. An interpretive center with life-size dioramas helps tell the story of the so-called Mississippian culture, the members of which farmed surrounding land and built the mounds from about A.D. 800 until 1400. At the settlement's peak, around A.D. 1000 to 1100, the city covered six square miles and had a population of nearly 20,000. You can still climb to the top of Monk's Mound, which is believed to be one of the largest—if not the largest—existing prehistoric structures built by man in the world. The site usually is open 9:00 A.M. to 5:00 P.M. year-round, but state budget cuts forced it to close for an extended period on Monday and Tuesday. Call ahead. Admission is **free,** but donations of $1.00 for children and $2.00 for adults are suggested. Take I–55/70 east to exit 6. Call (618) 346–5160 for more information; www.cahokiamounds.com.

Scott Joplin House State Historic Site (all ages)

2658 Delmar Boulevard, St. Louis 63103; (314) 340–5790; www.mostateparks.com. Open 10:00 A.M. to 5:00 P.M. Monday through Saturday, noon to 5:00 P.M. Sunday. Admission $; children ages 5 and under **free.**

The soundtrack of *The Sting,* a popular film that used Scott Joplin's compositions as background music, reacquainted the American public with the work of one of the country's most original composers. You can hear his music and see the house he lived in during the early part of the twentieth century in this National Historic Landmark.

Union Station (all ages)

1820 Market Street, St. Louis 63103; (314) 421–6655; www.stlouisunionstation.com.

This is a great place to shop, eat at the Hard Rock Cafe, (314) 621–7625, or just see a glorious railroad station that was once one of the busiest in the world. Visit the Grand Hall, which has been restored to its original condition and is now the lobby of a luxury hotel. Pick up a self-guided tour of the station at the information booth. When you hit the shops, don't miss The Best of St. Louis, with an unbelievably broad range of St. Louis memorabilia; The Disney Store, (314) 421–5050, where family-oriented videos are always playing; or Play and Learn, (314) 621–6266, with numerous educationally based toys. On the second level there is a food court where you can get a wide variety of fast, low-priced food. During the summer months there are regularly scheduled concerts and street performers at the station, and you can rent paddleboats on the artificial lake behind the station.

Bob Kramer's Marionnette Theater (all ages)

4143 Laclede Avenue, St. Louis 63108; (314) 531–3313; kramersmarionnettes.com. Tickets for a tour and show: adults \$\$, children ages 2 through 11 \$. You can also purchase tickets just for the show; call for a schedule.

Master puppeteer Bob Kramer has been practicing his craft since he was five years old; he started his studio in 1963. While you are there you can tour the workshop, see a one-hour demonstration of how the puppets are made, and watch a great puppet performance. The puppet shows change regularly and always include delightful seasonal productions.

Grand Center (age depends on event)

Branching out from the midtown intersection of Grand and Washington Avenues is an assortment of theaters and other buildings housing the headquarters of many of the arts organizations in St. Louis.

- **Fox Theater.** *527 North Grand Boulevard, St. Louis 63103; (314) 534–1111; www.fabulousfox.com.* This outrageous movie palace, with its enormous and ear-shattering Wurlitzer pipe organ, has to be seen to be believed. You can take a tour of the theater for a small fee or attend one of the Broadway-style shows or concerts staged here, or see one of the classic films occasionally shown.
- **St. Louis Symphony and Powell Hall.** *718 North Grand Boulevard, St. Louis 63103; (314) 534–1700; www.slso.org.* The symphony performs family concerts at magnificent Powell Hall, formerly the St. Louis movie theater, and at other locations throughout the area, with several summer concerts specifically for children.
- **Dance St. Louis.** *634 North Grand Boulevard, Suite 1102, St. Louis 63103; (314) 534–6622; www.dancestlouis.org.* The troupe performs several family programs every year, including *The Nutcracker* during the Christmas season.

Forest Park (all ages)

Kingshighway Boulevard and Highway 40 (I–64). The Boathouse Restaurant opens at noon daily, closes at 8:00 P.M. Sunday through Thursday and midnight Saturday and Sunday. Kids' menu available. Boat rental is \$12.00 per hour; open noon to 7:00 P.M.

The most popular park in the city, Forest Park covers more than 1,200 acres. It is home to several of the city's finest cultural institutions and contains a scenic 7.5-mile hiking and biking trail, as well as fishing, golf, tennis, and picnic facilities. You can get around inside the park during the summer months by hopping on the Forest Park Shuttle Bug, which stops at all the park museums. Catch the Shuttle Bug at the Central West End Metrolink station or one of the bus stops marked in the park (314–231–2345).

You can rent a pedal boat or rowboat at the boathouse as well as eat lakeside at the Boathouse Restaurant and fish or explore the lake (314–367–3423). You can skate at open-air Steinberg Memorial Skating Rink. During winter months you can ice-skate, and during the summer roller skating is offered. Bikes and fishing poles also can be rented there. Call (314) 367–7465. From June to August you can enjoy national entertainers and Broadway-style musicals at the Muny Opera theater, the largest outdoor amphitheater in the country and a St. Louis tradition for generations. Tickets range from $8.00 to $54.00. Call (314) 361–1900; www.muny.com.

St. Louis Art Museum (all ages)

Located at the highest point of Forest Park, Forest Park Drive, St. Louis 63110; (314) 721–0072; www.slam.org. Free admission. Open Tuesday through Sunday 10:00 A.M. to 5:00 P.M. (Friday to 9:00 P.M.); closed Monday.

The only building remaining from the 1904 World's Fair, this historic structure and its additions provide a beautiful setting for the wonderful art collection housed there. Reinstallation of the American Painting and Sculpture Garden is the newest project completed. Your children will most enjoy the small Egyptian room with an authentic mummy, the period rooms of furniture, the pre-Columbian collection, and the wild twentieth-century work on the top floor. The museum offers a wide variety of educational workshops and lectures for families and children, and it sponsors many special exhibits for which a fee is charged, except on Friday. Call for a schedule and prices.

Missouri History Museum (all ages)

5700 Lindell Boulevard entrance to Forest Park, St. Louis 63112; (314) 746–4599; www.mohistory.org. Open Wednesday through Monday 10:00 A.M. to 6:00 P.M., Tuesday 10:00 A.M. to 8:00 P.M. Free admission.

A fascinating midsize museum offering information relating to the history of the city, including the 1904 St. Louis World's Fair that was held in the park, the great fire of 1849, Charles Lindbergh's *Spirit of St. Louis* flight over the Atlantic, African-American music, and life in the city during the Gilded Age. The exhibits are engaging enough to capture the

Park **Call**

Missouri's excellent state park system is operated by the Department of Natural Resources. Call (800) 334–6946 around-the-clock for recorded information or during daily office hours to reach an attendant. Campsites also can be reserved by calling (877) 442–6766 at least forty-eight hours in advance. There is an $8.50 registration fee, in addition to the rental fee, for this service.

attention of all ages and include toys, tools, clothing, and photographs from the past. There also are many traveling or temporary exhibits.

St. Louis Zoo (all ages)

Hampton Avenue entrance to Forest Park on I–64 (Highway 40); 1 Government Drive, St. Louis 63110; (314) 781–0900; www.stlzoo.org. Open year-round 9:00 A.M. to 5:00 P.M., except Christmas and New Year's Day. Hours extended from 8:00 A.M. to 7:00 P.M. during the summer months. Admission to the zoo is free, although a few attractions carry fees for persons age 2 and older; children ages 1 and under are free. The fees are $4.00 to ride on the small-scale Zooline railroad, which takes you to four stations on a 1.5-mile trip around the zoo's perimeter; $2.00 to enter the Children's Zoo, a petting area and play space; for the children's zoo; $3.00 to enter the Insectarium; and $3.00 for the Sea Lion Show. An $11.00 Safari pass gains unlimited admission to these four attractions. There's also a $2.00 to ride the Conservation Carousel. The Children's Zoo, Insectarium and Conservation Carousel are free from 8:00 to 9:00 A.M. daily. Parking is $8.00 in the zoo's two parking lots, although there often is plenty of parking on park streets around the zoo, especially on the north side.

The hottest new attraction at the zoo is really cool, which can be very important during summer in St. Louis. At Penguin and Puffin Coast, visitors can see a group of Humboldt penguins' outdoor coastline home, featuring a 22-foot waterfall and misty tidal pool, and two indoor domed environments, one with penguins and another with puffins. The unique open design of the building gives a close-up experience with the birds and, as is always a sight to see, allows visitors to view these expert swimmers underwater.

Another new attraction that is designed to arouse children's interest in protecting the world's wildlife is the Conservation Carousel. It has sixty-four hand-carved animals representing endangered species.

The Jungle of the Apes, the zoo's natural habitat for gorillas, chimpanzees, and orangutans, also has been renovated, and you won't want to miss River's Edge. The ten-acre natural habitat houses Raja, the zoo's well-known young bull elephant, and several other elephants, as well as hippos, black rhinos, giant anteaters, cheetahs, hyenas, and dwarf mongooses. The Monsanto Insectarium is another popular stop in the eighty-three-acre zoo, which houses more than 6,000 animals. The sea lion show, offered only during the summer, is a must for children and adults.

Visit the Living World, a state-of-the-art education center that features interactive displays, computer games and activities, and a theater showing films about biodiversity. Live animal exhibits are interspersed with high technology and provide close-up looks at everything from one-celled organisms to birds, fish, and mammals. It's a great opportunity to closely examine various members of the animal kingdom, but try to avoid the busiest times of the day (10:00 A.M. to 3:00 P.M.), when you may have trouble getting up close to the exhibits.

Lions and tigers can be seen in Big Cat Country, nearly two acres of open-air cages designed to match the cats' home environments. You'll also see bear pits, enclosures for hoofed animals, and a sea lion basin that date from several decades ago at this easy-to-navigate zoo. Be sure to get a schedule of feeding times for the bears and sea lions. A charming walk-through birdcage, the largest free-flight aviary in the world, dates from the 1904 World's Fair and houses hundreds of birds you can see up close. A major renovation of the birdcage should be completed by summer 2004. A two-acre outdoor Bird Garden offers bird-watchers a natural setting with walkways, reflecting pools, and landscaped paths where they can see a large variety of bird species.

Turtle Playground (all ages)

Oakland and Tamm Avenues, south side of Highway 40 opposite south entrance to St. Louis Zoo. Open until 10:00 P.M. Free admission.

When was the last time your kids were able to slide down the back of a turtle the size of a semi truck? Well, this is the place to fulfill that fantasy. Artist Robert Cassilly (see City Museum and City(E)scape) has crafted three immense turtles—a snapping turtle, a soft-shelled turtle, and a red-eared slider—and four smaller ones here for climbing, standing, or simply sitting. There's also a snake curled in the shape of a bench and a serpent taking a bite out of the adjacent highway overpass. If you're visiting the zoo, this is a good way to spell the kids; it's only 2 short blocks from the south entrance to the zoo.

St. Louis Science Center (all ages)

5050 Oakland, St. Louis 63110; (314) 289–4444 or (800) 456–7572; www.slsc.org. Admission is free. Opens at 9:30 A.M. Monday through Saturday, closes at 5:30 P.M. Monday through Thursday and Saturday, 9:30 P.M. Friday. Open 11:30 A.M. to 5:30 P.M. Sunday. Omnimax the-ater tickets $$.

The new Boeing Space Station, with its magnificent view of the cosmos from the Star-Bridge, and the other activities on the StarBay level, and more exhibits created for the recently redesigned James S. McDonnell Planetarium, should top every visitor's must-see list.

This fantastic, fun science museum also has more than 500 interactive and hands-on exhibits covering such topics as the human senses, computers, flight, space, building, mining, medicine, weather, and prehistoric times. Two life-size animated dinosaurs pro-vide a frightening touch of realism; a laser show is flashed on the wall on the :45 of every hour; there's an underground tunnel that simulates a coal mine; and you can shoot cars passing underneath the walkway over the highway with a radar gun to see how fast they are traveling. One gallery explores the world of modern medicine and features a continu-ously running video of an actual operation for those who aren't too squeamish to watch. You'll want to budget plenty of time for exploration.

The science center houses several ticketed areas, with various admission prices. A Discovery Room with exhibits specifically designed for children ages two through eight offers science toys and tools to play with, a small cave and tepee to climb into, and small live animals to hold and watch. Tickets are sold for forty-five-minute sessions and cost

Amazing
Missouri Facts

What is the largest city in Missouri?

Kansas City

$3.00 per person. They must be purchased the day of your visit, so get them as soon as you arrive at the center. Then you can look around while you wait for your appointment to enter the room.

An Omnimax theater with a four-story-tall domed screen offers productions made specifically for the big, big screen. The theater has a 15,000-watt sound system that makes the nature and science films viewed here come alive. Call for show titles and times.

Cathedral Basilica St. Louis (all ages)

4431 Lindell Boulevard at Newstead, St. Louis 63108; (314) 533–0544; www.cathedral stl.org. Free admission to the church. Open daily 6:00 A.M. to 5:00 P.M. Tours run from 10:00 A.M. to 3:00 P.M. Monday through Friday. Admission to museum is $1.00.

On the surface, this might not be a lot of kids' first choice for fun. But any art lover—whether child or adult—must stop in to see the largest collection of mosaic art in the world adorning the walls and ceiling of the cathedral. A small museum in the lower level explains how mosaic art is created.

Exploring the Final Frontier

Visitors to the St. Louis Science Center now have a spectacular view of the great beyond from the Boeing Space Station's StarBridge in the James S. McDonnell Planetarium. The two-level space station, and a lower level Sky-Port—a sort of airport of the future—were installed in 2001 as part of a $13 million redesign of the thirty-seven-year-old planetarium. A powerful state-of-the-art Zeiss planetarium projector filling the dome with every star imaginable, and staff demonstrations and exhibits designed to enhance the stellar experience, give you the feeling that you are there. Visit the center online at www.slsc.org or call (800) 456–7572.

The Hill (all ages) 🔒 🍴

West of Kingshighway Boulevard from Southwest and Shaw Avenues.

Some of the city's finest, most expensive restaurants are here, but you can also find wonderful and reasonable family operations. Hungry families should check out Rigazzi's Restaurant, 4945 Daggett Avenue (314–772–4900), where the food is plentiful and the beer is served to adults in "frozen fishbowls." Order toasted ravioli and sample the appetizer that originated on the Hill. Amighetti's Bakery, 5141 Wilson Avenue (314–776–2855), is famous throughout the area for great sandwiches made on arguably the best bread in town. There is another Amighetti's at Manchester and McKnight Roads in Rock Hill (314–962–6030), but the original restaurant and bakery is located in the heart of the Hill across from St. Ambrose, the Catholic church that has been the center of this Italian community for decades.

A Cosby Family **Adventure**

We're always up for a day at the St. Louis Zoo, no matter what time of year. The trips are a little shorter in the winter and fall, but they're worth it even then because the World's Fair bear pits are one of our favorite stops. We love watching the polar bears, grizzlies, and Kodiak bears frolic and swim in the cold weather they like best. The penguins also always are among our favorites.

But spring, summer, and fall are the best times to plan a real daylong adventure around the zoo. We save a little time and money by packing a lunch and keeping it in a cooler in our car. And we like to park on the north side of the zoo—toward the St. Louis Art Museum—and eat lunch at the top or at Art Hill in front of the museum. On a sunny day the view is great.

When we were back in the zoo, and when our children were younger we would often duck out the south entrance and walk the block across Highway 40 to Turtle Playground. Children love climbing onto and sliding off the three immense turtles and four smaller ones. Adults like the winding serpent bench. Sometimes we would catch Turtle Playground as a last stop on the way home.

If things are moving quickly at the zoo, we'll add an hour or two at the nearby St. Louis Science Center, often parking outside the planetarium in Forest Park and taking the bridge across Highway 40 to the main building.

The best part about the whole day is that everything is **free,** unless we decide to ride the Zooline Railroad, visit the Children's Zoo, or watch an Omnimax movie at the science center.

Missouri Botanical Garden (all ages)

4344 Shaw Boulevard, St. Louis 63110; (314) 577–5100, (314) 577–9400, (800) 642–8842; www.mobot.org (click on "Just for Kids"; your children will love it). Open daily 9:00 A.M. to 5:00 P.M. Open until 8:00 P.M. Wednesday. Admission is $7.00 for ages 13 through 64, $3.00 for ages 65 and older; ages 12 and younger free with an adult. Admission for St. Louis City and County residents is $3.00 per person, $1.50 for seniors, and free on Wednesday and Saturday from 7:00 A.M. to noon. A tram-ride tour of the gardens is available for $3.00 per person; children ages 2 and under ride free.

One of the finest in the country, the Missouri Botanical Garden promises a fascinating time. More than eighty acres are planted in a variety of gardening styles that offer something for everyone:

- The **Climatron** dominates the landscape, and all ages will enjoy seeing this geodesic dome sheltering a living tropical rain forest complete with towering trees, a waterfall, and winding paths overrun with exotic plants and greenery. There is an interactive education center about ecology and the environment as you exit the dome.
- The **Japanese Garden,** one of the largest in North America, is an enchanting setting with graceful bridges over a lake, mini-waterfalls, giant koi fish to feed, a beautiful pebble beach, and rock-stepping paths to follow.
- The **Victorian maze** in the back of the garden provides your children with confusing turns to wander through while you watch the action from atop a Victorian viewing cupola.
- The **Kemper Center for Home Gardening** is adjacent to twenty-three demonstration gardens covering 8.5 acres to give you ideas for your own backyard.
- **Spoehrer's Children's Garden** combines all the fun of colorful, uniquely textured plants with topiary, rainbow colors, and unusual names to entertain and teach your children. This wonderful collection of gardens will delight your children with its scented garden of herbs to scratch and sniff, bell tower of chimes to play, sheep statuary to sit on, grass to walk on, and fountain to walk through for relief from the heat on summer days.

Tower Grove Park (all ages)

4255 Arsenal Street (immediately south of the Missouri Botanical Garden), St. Louis 63116; (314) 771–2679; www.towergrovepark.org.

Modeled after a Victorian walking park of the nineteenth century, its 289 acres are filled with ornate gazebos and statuary and provide an excellent place for hiking or picnicking.

Miniature Museum of Greater St. Louis (all ages)

4746 Gravois, St. Louis 63116; (314) 832–7790; miniaturemuseum.org. Open 11:00 A.M. to 4:00 P.M. Wednesday through Saturday, 1:00 to 4:00 P.M. Sunday; closed Monday and Tuesday. A parent must accompany young people ages 15 and under. Admission is adults $$, youths ages 2 through 17 $; children ages 1 and under free.

The museum is loaded with furnished dollhouses and other miniature vignettes, many crafted by local and nationally known artisans, which have been donated or acquired by

Amazing
Missouri Facts

Who designed the Climatron at the Missouri Botanical Garden?

Buckminster Fuller

its more than 200 members. This entertaining stop proves that it can be a small world after all.

Black World History Museum (all ages)

2505 St. Louis Avenue, St. Louis 63106; (314) 241–7057. Open Wednesday through Saturday 10:00 A.M. to 5:00 P.M., Sunday Memorial Day through Labor Day 2:00 to 5:00 P.M. Adults $$, young people ages 17 and under $.

The museum features wax figures of George Washington Carver, Dred and Harriet Scott, and other famous African-American Missourians.

Hop on **Amtrak**

If you happen to be traveling from St. Louis straight through to Kansas City, or to any city along the Amtrak right-of-way, consider taking the train. By traveling the old-fashioned way, you can sit back and watch the scenery go by when you ride the rails. The St. Louis–Kansas City route takes you through the Missouri wine country and follows the Missouri River halfway across the state. There are nine more stops along the way, many in charming, historic towns that offer visitors pleasant diversions on their trip and it ends within walking distance of Kansas City Union Station. Call (800) 872–7245; www.amtrak.com.

University City

Just outside the St. Louis city limits sits this suburb built around Washington University and featuring many small unique stores, bars, and restaurants along Delmar Boulevard. Don't forget to stroll the St. Louis Walk of Fame, lining sidewalks on both sides of the street, with star-shaped plaques honoring famous St. Louisans and their achievements.

Center of Contemporary Arts (all ages)
524 Trinity, University City 63130; (314) 725–6555; www.cocastl.org. $$$–$$$$.

A performing arts school, COCA offers the Frank Fowles Family Theatre Series, a children's theater series that is guaranteed to entertain the entire family. Call for a series schedule, which generally includes five or six productions between September and March.

St. Ann

Tilt (all ages)
76 Northwest Plaza, St. Charles Rock Road and Lindbergh Boulevard, St. Louis 63074; (314) 298–3440; www.tilt.com. Open Monday through Saturday 10:00 A.M. to 9:30 P.M., Sunday 11:00 A.M. to 6:00 P.M. Games are individually priced. Golf is $3.00 for adults before 5:00 P.M. on weekdays, $5.00 for adults after 5:00 P.M. and on weekends and holidays, $2.00 for children ages 12 and under.

This full-blown arcade with nearly 200 games, including shooting and driving simulation programs and Gauntlet, among others, is the largest in St. Louis. It also has an eighteen-hole indoor miniature golf course.

Maryland Heights

Maryland Heights Aquaport (all ages)
2344 McKelvey Road, Maryland Heights 63034; (314) 434–1919; www.maryland heights.com. Open 11:00 A.M. to 7:00 P.M. daily. Admission for nonresidents of Maryland Heights $$.

Activities at this water park include a lazy river, rapids ride, racer slides, zero-entry pool, and kiddie pool. Lap lanes also are available.

Amazing
Missouri Facts

What momentous baseball event took place in Missouri in 1944?

The all–St. Louis World Series; the Cardinals swept the Browns in four games.

Amazing
Missouri Facts

What Missourian won fame as a poet in England and won a posthumous Tony for the musical *Cats?*

T. S. Eliot

Creve Coeur

Creve Coeur Lake Park (all ages)

Marine and Dorsett Roads; send mail to 41 South Central, Clayton 63105; (314) 615–7275; www.st-louiscountyparks.com. Open daily 9:00 A.M. to thirty minutes after sunset. Free admission.

This 1,000-acre park has athletic fields, hiking trails, picnic and camping sites, tennis courts, a children's playground, and a paved path for biking, in-line skating, and running. The 300-acre lake is open for sailing, canoeing, and fishing.

Holocaust Museum and Learning Center (ages 11 and up)

12 Millstone Campus Drive, Creve Coeur 63146; (314) 432–0020; www.hmlc.org. Open 9:30 A.M. to 4:30 P.M. Tuesday through Thursday, 9:30 A.M. to 4:00 P.M. Friday, 10:00 A.M. to 4:30 P.M. Sunday. Free admission.

The story of this World War II–era catastrophe is told in photographs, artifacts, and audio-visual displays. The center also has a library and oral-history archives.

Chesterfield

Faust Park (all ages)

15185 Olive Boulevard, St. Louis 63017; (636) 532–7298; www.st-louiscountyparks.com. Park open daily from 9:00 A.M. to thirty minutes after sunset. St. Louis Carousel, (636) 537–0222, www.stlouiscarousel.com; and Butterfly House, (636) 530–0076, www.butterfly house.org; are open Tuesday through Sunday 9:00 A.M. to 4:00 P.M. Tickets to ride the carousel are $1.00 each. Admission to the Butterfly House is $5.00 for adults, $4.50 for children ages 3 through 11; children ages 2 and under free.

This has been a park in progress since it opened in 1968. Children will enjoy the beautiful Butterfly House and Education Center and the magnificently restored carousel. The 200-acre tract also includes an estate house and outbuildings designed by noted architect

Tom O. Barnett; Thornhill, the 1818 frontier home of the state's second governor; and a village composed of numerous other restored historic buildings brought to the site. One of the original buildings on the property is an unusual dairy barn with a Lamella roof, one that spans the entire 50-by-100-foot expanse of the barn without interior supports. Don't miss the visitor center; it's in a Queen Anne–style carriage house dating from the 1880s.

Piwacket Children's Theater (ages 10 and under)

Chesterfield Community Theater/YMCA, 16464 Burkhardt Place, Chesterfield 63017; (314) 963–8800. Open June through March. Ticket prices vary by event.

This theater has productions filled with rhythm, color, and song. The shows feature a minimum of props and sets and are designed to spark the imaginations of children ages ten and younger.

West St. Louis County

Queeny Park (all ages)

550 Weidman Road, Ballwin 63011; (636) 391–0900; www.st-louiscountyparks.com. Open daily 9:00 A.M. to thirty minutes after sunset. $ admission for swimming and skating: skate rental available. Admission to park is free.

Here you'll find a recreation complex with indoor/outdoor skating rinks and a swimming pool. The park also has tennis courts, one of the best children's playgrounds in the St. Louis area, and hiking trails that wind through the more than 500 acres of parkland.

Museum of Transportation (all ages)

3015 Barrett Station Road, Kirkwood 63122; (314) 965–7998; www.museumoftransport.org. Open daily 9:00 A.M. to 5:00 P.M. year-round. $; children ages 4 and under free.

This is a great opportunity for train buffs of all ages. Here you can see one of the most extensive collections of locomotives and railroad cars in the country as well as automobiles, buses, trucks, and an airplane. The collection of more than 300 pieces is primarily outdoors, and visitors take a self-guided tour that includes climbing into several of the locomotives and railcars. A towboat at the entrance to the museum is also fair game for climbing and exploring. A miniature train offers rides for a small fee from April through October.

Worldways Children's Museum (ages 1 and up)

15479 Clayton Road, St. Louis 63011; (636) 207–7008, (636) 207–7405; www.worldways.org. Open Monday through Saturday 9:00 A.M. to 5:30 P.M., Sunday 11:30 A.M. to 5:30 P.M. Closed Sunday during the summer. $; children under age 1 are free.

This children's museum, an interactive center where kids learn about other cultures with an "immersion experience," houses two permanent exhibits: Gateway to China and Oaxaca, Mexico. It also has periodic visiting exhibits from other countries. Children and their

parents learn about the cultures by dressing in colorful costumes, shopping in "foreign" stores, and tasting cuisine from the country they are experiencing. Museum educators give an introduction talk and remain on the floor to answer questions and otherwise assist visitors.

American Kennel Club Museum of the Dog (all ages)

1721 South Mason Road, St. Louis 63131; (314) 821–3647; www.akc.org. Open Tuesday through Saturday 9:00 A.M. to 5:00 P.M., Sunday noon to 5:00 P.M. $; children ages 4 and under free.

Art, books, artifacts, and changing exhibits are used to explain the history of the dog. Younger children probably will like all the "doggies" pictures and sculptures, but older children will get bored much quicker, unless you look up a video or other information about the type of dog you own.

Wildwood

Dr. Edmund A. Babler Memorial State Park (all ages)

Highway 109, between U.S. 40 and Highway 100; send mail to 800 Guy Park Drive, 63005; (636) 458–3813; www.mostateparks.com. Open daily 7:00 A.M. to 9:00 P.M. Visitor center open daily 8:00 A.M. to 4:00 P.M. Free admission. Camping is $8.00 for tents, $14.00 for RV hookup. Call (877) 422–6766 at least forty-eight hours in advance for camping reservations. There is an $8.50 registration fee.

The beautiful 2,400 wooded acres of this park on the Missouri River hills encompass seventy-seven campsites, a swimming pool, a horseback-riding concession for those who don't bring their own horses, a visitor center with exhibits about native wildlife, and 13 miles of hiking and equestrian trails.

A. P. Greensfelder Park (all ages)

Allenton and Hencken Roads; (636) 458–3801; www.st-louiscountyparks.com. Open daily 9:00 A.M. to thirty minutes after sunset. Free admission.

This park has 1,700 wooded acres offering picnic shelters, a children's playground, and miles of nature trails for hikers, mountain bikers, and horseback riders.

Glencoe

Rockwoods Reservation (all ages)

Highway 109 and Manchester Road, 2751 Glencoe Road, Glencoe 63038; (636) 458–2236; www.mdc.state.mo.us. Center open daily 8:00 A.M. to 5:00 P.M. Area open from sunrise to thirty minutes after sunset.

Rockwoods Reservation is a 1,900-acre forest and wildlife preserve that offers seven easy hiking-only trails through beautiful, unspoiled land. Start at the visitor center and pick up maps and brochures about the area and information about nature activities. There's a touch table with natural artifacts for curious little fingers.

Wabash Frisco and Pacific Steam Railway (all ages)

109 Grand Avenue, Glencoe 63038; (636) 587–3538; www.wfprr.org. Runs Sundays, May through October, with first trip leaving at 11:15 A.M. and last trip leaving at 4:15 P.M. $; children ages 3 and under free.

This steam-powered miniature railroad is operated by buffs who want to keep the mode of transportation alive. The 2-mile round-trip offers a scenic journey along Meramec River.

Ellisville

The Infield (all ages)

2626 Westhills Park Drive, St. Louis 63011; (636) 458–1144. Open daily 11:00 A.M. to 11:00 P.M. June through August. Call for off-season hours.

There's something here for everyone, including go-karts, an eight-stall batting cage with dual pitching machines, a miniature golf course, bumper boats, and an arcade with video games. Games and rides are individually priced. $–$$

Ballwin

Castlewood State Park (all ages)

1401 Kiefer Creek, Ballwin 63021; (636) 227–4433; www.mostateparks.com. Open daily 7:00 A.M. to thirty minutes after sunset.

This day park is located along the Meramec River and is part of the Meramec River Recreation Area, which stretches for 108 miles along the river. It's popular for canoeing and fishing and has 1,779 acres offering access to the river and 14 miles of trails for hikers, mountain bikers, and equestrians.

Amazing
Missouri Facts

Kirkwood

Powder Valley Conservation Nature Center (all ages)

11715 Cragwold Road, St. Louis 63122; (314) 301–1500; www.mdc.state.mo.us. Center and trails open daily 8:00 A.M.; center closes at 5:00 P.M., trails close at 8:00 P.M. in summer, 6:00 P.M. other seasons. Park closed Thanksgiving, Christmas, and New Year's Day.

Nature is great fun when you learn about it through interactive exhibits on the flora and fauna of this area. Feeding stations just outside the windows of a wonderful viewing room attract dozens of fine feathered friends and woodland wildlife. Several paved hiking trails through the surrounding wooded hills present plenty of opportunities for nature lovers to enjoy themselves. The center offers a wide range of nature programs and guided hikes for all ages on 112 acres.

Laumeier Sculpture Park (all ages)

12580 Rott Road, St. Louis 63127; (314) 821–1209; www.laumeier.com. Park open daily 8:00 A.M. to thirty minutes past sunset. Museum open Tuesday through Saturday 10:00 A.M. to 5:00 P.M., Sunday noon to 5:00 P.M. Free admission.

Walking in the woods becomes even more enjoyable when the natural landscape is scattered with freestanding works of art, many of them specifically designed for the setting. You can explore more than ninety-six acres of hiking trails and woodland paths featuring modern sculpture. There also is a museum in the center of the park with indoor exhibits. Even if your children don't like art, they'll enjoy running around the park. Every August tons of sand are brought in and a fantasy sand castle is created, weather permitting. The winter solstice is celebrated in mid-December with a fire and ice sculpture.

The Magic House: St. Louis Children's Museum
(school age and under)

516 South Kirkwood Road, Kirkwood 63122; (314) 822–8900; www.magichouse.org. Open Tuesday through Thursday 9:30 A.M. to 5:30 P.M., Friday 9:30 A.M. to 9:00 P.M., Saturday 9:30 A.M. to 5:30 P.M., Sunday 11:00 A.M. to 5:30 P.M. Open later between September and May. $$; children ages 1 and under free.

This wonderful collection of hands-on exhibits is housed in an old three-story mansion where your children can play with water, light, or sound; experiment with pulleys and wheels; experience optical illusions; work on computers; and enjoy the slide that shoots them from the top of the house to the first floor. There is a special area for children ages one to seven where they can explore at their own pace.

Brentwood

St. Louis Children's Aquarium (all ages)
416 Hanley Industrial Court, St. Louis 63144; (314) 647–9594; www.stlchildrensaquarium .com. Open daily 9:00 A.M. to 5:00 P.M. $$; children ages 2 and under free.

Although designed with kids in mind, folks of all ages will enjoy the displays about the ecology of the ocean, models and exhibits of the Amazon and Mississippi Rivers, and opportunities to touch numerous aquatic creatures. The petting pool features a changing cast but usually includes an iguana, turtles, hermit crabs, and a small horned shark. There's also a pool where visitors can pet large fish.

Crestwood

Tilt (all ages)
Watson Road and Sappington, 930 Crestwood Plaza, Crestwood 63126; (314) 963–8969; www.tilt.com. Open 10:00 A.M. to 9:00 P.M. Monday through Saturday, 11:00 A.M. to 6:00 P.M. Sunday. Games are individually priced. $–$$

This full-blown arcade with more than 100 games is one of the largest in the St. Louis area. It also is located in a large mall, which, when game time is over, should give parents time to pick up other items that might be needed on the trip. Tickets are awarded for prize redemption.

Amazing
Missouri Facts

St. Louis once was said to be "First in booze, first in shoes and last in___."

the American League (St. Louis Browns, now the Baltimore Orioles)

Fenton

Swing-A-Round Fun Town (all ages)

Highway 141 and Gravois, 335 Skinker Lane, Fenton 63026; (636) 349–7077; www.sarfun.com. Open daily generally 10:00 A.M. to 11:00 P.M. March through October and selected days November through February. Call ahead for hours and availability of specific rides.

This place has something for everyone to do. There are go-karts for big and little kids, bumper boats, three miniature golf courses, nine softball and baseball batting cages, an indoor Kids Town with a soft play environment, and a large arcade with more than eighty games.

Valley Park

Lone Elk Park (all ages)

Highway 141 at Highway 44, Valley Park 63088; (314) 963–9211; www.st-louiscountyparks.com. Center open daily 10:00 A.M. to 4:00 P.M. Park open 8:00 A.M. to dusk. Free admission.

At this wildlife sanctuary you can get close to free-roaming Rocky Mountain elk, American Plains bison, white-tailed deer, wild turkeys, and other creatures. To reach the park, take the service road west from the intersection of I–44 and Highway 141. The park has a drive-through area where the animals may come right up to your car. Other sections of the park offer picnicking and hiking trails, the longest of which is 7 miles and winds past views of the Meramec River. The Wild Bird Sanctuary (636–225–4390) operates a nature center where you can see live birds of prey being cared for and rehabilitated and talk to rangers about conservation work.

Eureka

Six Flags St. Louis (all ages)

Highway 44, exit 261, Eureka 63025; (636) 938–4800; www.sixflags.com. Open daily mid-May through August. Open weekends only in fall and spring. Operating hours vary, so call ahead. $$$$; children age 3 and under free. Parking is $8.00 per car, as are small storage lockers at the park's entrance.

Visitors flock to Xcalibur, which carries riders in sixteen gondolas hanging from a huge wheel. When the wheel spins, riders are catapulted 113 feet into the air before stopping momentarily and then repeating the procedure heading back toward earth. Ride this one before lunch.

The Boss, a massive, nearly mile-long wooden roller coaster with a top speed of 66 miles per hour and four drops—one of 150 feet—continues to pull in roller-coaster aficionados in general and wooden-coaster lovers in particular. In August 2001 a Brooklyn man set a record by riding the Boss for one hundred consecutive days. But the sweltering heat of St. Louis summers also has park-goers making a beeline for Hurricane Harbor, a twelve-acre water park with a Caribbean theme that is included in the price of admission. The water park has a 30,000-square-foot wave pool with 3- to 4-foot rolling waves, high-speed body slides, a raft ride that simulates a white-water experience, a five-story inner-tube slide, and a relaxing 1,000-foot inner-tube float.

The park has more than 100 rides and shows in several themed areas. In DC Comics, you'll find Mr. Freeze, a roller coaster that starts in a tunnel, climbs a vertical track, and then propels riders backward to their starting point. In Time Warner Studios you'll find Batman the Ride, a roller coaster on which riders in ski-lift-style chairs are pulled through loops, including a zero-gravity roll. The park has three other roller coasters: the Screamin' Eagle, which roars down a ¾-mile wooden track at speeds up to 62 miles per hour; the Ninja, featuring high-speed spirals, steep drops, and a double corkscrew; and the old reliable twisting but traditional Mine Train.

For the less coaster-conscious, more docile rides include the Colossus, a giant eighteen-story Ferris wheel that lets you survey the entire park from above; old-time cars to drive on a controlled track; and an authentic twenty-five-ton narrow-gauge steam locomotive that provides a tour around the park. Several water rides promise a thorough soaking on hot summer days, and excellent shows throughout the park provide great entertainment for everyone.

Looney Tunes Town has rides for little ones too small to ride the attractions with minimum height requirements located in other areas of the park.

Santa's Magical Kingdom (all ages)

Highway 44, north on Allenton Road, Eureka 63025; (636) 938–5925 or (800) 861–3020; www.eurekajellystone.com. Open daily after dark November through December. Call for admission price.

During the winter Yogi Bear's Jellystone Park Resort is transformed into a magical paradise that includes a thirty-five-acre display of animated scenes, spectacular special effects, and millions of lights celebrating the holiday season.

Hidden Valley Ski Resort (ages 5 and up)

17409 Hidden Valley Drive, Eureka 63025; (636) 938–5373; www.hiddenvalleyski.com. $$$$.

This beginner's slope has eight ski trails, two chairlifts, four rope tows, and a ski lodge. Season runs from December through March, with artificial snow providing continuous snow coverage.

Wild Canid Survival and Research Center (ages 4 and up)

Highway 44 at Beaumont Antire Road, west off exit 269, Eureka 63025; (636) 938–5900; www.wolfsanctuary.org. Tour $5.00 per person; $30.00 minimum. Admission by appointment only.

The center, founded by *Wild Kingdom* host Marlin Perkins, houses four species of endangered wolves and offers hour-long tours and special programs. Evening events include campfire storytelling and howling exhibitions. Call for a schedule of programs.

Gray Summit

Purina Farms (all ages)

Highway 44 to north on Highway 100 and left on County Road MM 1 mile to the entrance; send mail to 200 Checkerboard Drive, Gray Summit 63039; (314) 982–3232; www.purina.com. Open Tuesday through Sunday 9:30 A.M. to 2:00 P.M. late May through early September; shorter hours from mid-March to late May and early September to early November. Free admission, but reservations are required.

This free visitor center operated by the Ralston Purina Company and Purina Mills, Inc. has interesting educational displays, videos, and hands-on activities about the role domestic animals play in our lives. Several buildings house live animals for petting, including horses, cows, sheep, pigs, goats, chickens, and ducks. Smaller animals are in petting corrals that encourage visitors to get close and friendly. The cats and dogs have their own special house where you can see a variety of breeds. Visitors are permitted to pet selected animals. A hayloft equipped with ropes for swinging and hay bales for climbing provides the perfect play space for children. Special events are planned around holidays, and an outdoor theater hosts animal demonstrations and shows.

Shaw Arboretum and Nature Reserve (all ages)

Highway 100 and Interstate 44, Gray Summit 63039; (636) 451–3512; www.mobot.org /mobot/arboretum. The area is open daily 7:00 A.M. to thirty minutes after sunset. Center open Monday through Friday 8:00 A.M. to 4:30 P.M., Saturday and Sunday 9:00 A.M. to 5:00 P.M. $; children ages 12 and under free.

This is one of the best places in this region for nature walks. The 2,400-acre preserve has 14 miles of hiking trails that pass an oak-hickory forest, meadows, a floodplain, limestone bluffs, and the Meramec River. A four-acre wildflower garden, 100 acres of tallgrass prairie, a gravel bar on the river, and a boardwalk trail over wetlands provide a wide range of environments to see. The Manor House is an interpretive center that has exhibits on human land use and the various ways man relates to his environment.

Affton

Grant's Farm (all ages)

1051 Gravois Road, Affton 63123; (314) 843–1700; www.grantsfarm.com. Open Tuesday through Sunday 9:00 A.M. to 3:30 P.M. from mid-May to Labor Day; shorter hours from April to mid-May and Labor Day through October. Free admission. Reservations no longer accepted. Parking is $5.00 per car.

Operated by the Anheuser-Busch Company, this marvelous minizoo and animal refuge is located on the grounds of the Busch family's ancestral home. There is a petting zoo where you can hand-feed some of the animals, and several animal shows are offered. In the Bauernhof courtyard you'll find stables housing several Clydesdale horses as well as the family's collection of equestrian equipment and trophies. In this area visitors over the age of twenty-one can obtain a free sample of the company's products, or you can purchase soft drinks and snacks.

Your visit to the park ends with a twenty-minute ride through Deer Park, a nature preserve with more than thirty kinds of animals roaming freely. You'll also pass the historic cabin built by Ulysses S. Grant, for whom the property is named. If you love the Clydesdales, don't miss the stallion barn at the north edge of the parking lot, where you can see several breeders in their home stalls.

Ulysses S. Grant National Historic Site (all ages)

7400 Grant Road, Affton 63123; (314) 842–3298; www.nps.gov/ulsg. Open daily 9:00 A.M. to 5:00 P.M. Free admission.

This property, known as White Haven, was originally the family plantation of Grant's wife, Julia Dent. There are five historic buildings on the ten-acre site, including a two-story residence. Park rangers offer four-minute tours through the family home and programs about the Grants and the time period in which they lived.

South St. Louis County

Jefferson Barracks Historic Park (all ages)

533 Grant Road, Lemay 63125; (314) 544–5714; www.st-louiscountyparks.com. The park is open from sunup to thirty minutes after sunset. Powder Magazine Museum is open Wednesday through Friday 10:00 A.M. to 4:30 P.M., Saturday and Sunday noon to 4:30 P.M. Admission is **free.** Old Ordnance Room Museum is open Wednesday through Sunday noon to 4:30 P.M. $.

Learn about the U.S. military from the early 1800s to World War II at two park museums devoted to the proud history of this installation, which operated for more than 170 years and housed some of the greatest soldiers of our country. The Powder Magazine Museum chronicles the history of the fort, which operated on the site from 1826 to 1946, and rotating displays about various aspects of military history are exhibited in the Old Ordnance Room. The park also has several ideal overlooks of the Mississippi River, as well as picnic areas, archery fields, and bike and hiking trails. The National Association of Civilian Conservation Corps Alumni has its national headquarters in the park and also operates a museum here. Jefferson Barracks national cemetery is adjacent to the historic park.

Bee Tree Park (all ages)

Finestown at Becker Road, St. Louis 63129; (314) 615–7275; www.st-louiscountyparks.com. Open daily 9:00 A.M. to thirty minutes after sunset. **Free** admission.

Bee Tree Park offers fishing spots, hiking trails, picnic shelters, a wonderful children's playground, and a magnificent view of the Mississippi River on 198 acres.

Golden Eagle River Museum (all ages)

2701 Finestown Road at Becker Road in Bee Tree Park, St. Louis 63129; (314) 846–9073; www.st-louiscountyparks.com. **Free** admission. Open Wednesday to Sunday 1:00 to 5:00 P.M. May 1 through October 31. Tours of Nims Mansion are $1.00 per person.

This small museum tells the history and lore of area rivers and the steamboats that plied those waterways with boat models, pictures, artifacts, and memorabilia housed in a mansion perched on picturesque bluffs that provide a commanding view of the Mississippi River.

Amazing
Missouri Facts

What army officer destined for fame in the Civil War assumed command of Jefferson Barracks in south St. Louis County in 1855?

Robert E. Lee

Springdale Park and Pool and Miniature Golf (all ages)

2280 South Old Highway 141, St. Louis 63026; (636) 343–2123. Open 9:30 A.M. to 6:00 P.M. daily. Admission is $6.00; children ages 3 and younger **free.** Golf is $3.00 per person.

You'll find an enormous swimming pool, picnic grounds, and a miniature golf course open only on weekends. Every October the park turns into a 2,000-square-foot walk-through horror show that includes both indoor and outdoor exhibits and promises the fright of your life for Halloween. Halloween activities recommended for ages eight and older.

Suson Park (all ages)

Wells Road south of Highway 21; (314) 615–7275; www.st-louiscountyparks.com. Barns are open 10:30 A.M. to 5:00 P.M. daily from April through October and on weekends from November through March. **Free** admission.

One of the park's missions is to acquaint suburbanites and other urban dwellers with most breeds of farm animals. Three barns house a wide variety of animals, including cows, goats, horses, donkeys, chickens, ducks, and geese. The park, which is down the road from Jefferson Barracks National Cemetery, also has picnic tables, a children's playground, and three small fishing lakes that are regularly stocked by the state Department of Conservation.

Tilt (all ages)

Lindbergh and Lemay Ferry roads, 330 South County Centerway, Mehlville 63129, (314) 892–8756; www.tilt.com. Open 9:30 A.M. to 9:30 P.M. Monday through Saturday, 11:00 A.M. to 6:00 P.M. Sunday. Games are individually priced. $–$$.

This full-blown arcade has dozens of games and is located in a large mall, which, when game time is over, should give parents time to pick up other items that might be needed on the trip. Tickets are awarded for prize redemption.

Imperial

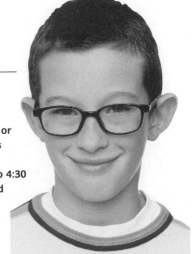

Mastodon State Historic Site (all ages)

1050 Museum Drive, Imperial 63052; (636) 464–2976 or (800) 334–6946; www.mostateparks.com. Park opens daily at 8:00 A.M., closes thirty minutes past sunset. Museum open Monday through Saturday 9:00 A.M. to 4:30 P.M., Sunday noon to 4:30 P.M. $; children ages 14 and younger **free.**

Known as the Kimmswick Bonebeds, this site is where the first evidence that mastodons and Ice Age people lived at the same time was unearthed. A museum displays a life-size mastodon skeleton replica and ancient artifacts excavated from the area. It also features a diorama and exhibits explaining the end of the last ice age and a fourteen-minute slide show about the site. The 425-acre site is ideal for hikes and picnics.

Kimmswick

This tiny town just off I–55 south of the St. Louis suburban area is often called a living museum. As you walk along the streets you'll feel as if you have stepped back in time and will find many small, unusual craft shops and stores. The **Apple Butter Festival,** held at the end of October, is a good time to visit, but expect to encounter crowds. There are demonstrations of pioneer skills such as broom making, candle making, and black-smithing, as well as a craft show, food booths, and a wide range of musical performances. All shops and restaurants are closed on Monday.

Kimmswick Visitors Center

314 Market Street, Kimmswick 63053; (636) 464–6464; www.discoverkimmswick.com. Open Tuesday through Friday 10:00 A.M. to 4:00 P.M., Saturday and Sunday 10:30 A.M. to 5:00 P.M.; shorter winter hours. Free.

Here you can see photos and displays of the town's history and pick up maps and information about shops and restaurants in the area.

Baseball Is Being Very, Very Good to St. Louis

St. Louis long has been known as one of the best baseball towns in America. And anyone who doesn't get his or her fill the Cardinals at Busch Stadium has two other sources of satisfaction. The River City Rascals and Gateway Grizzlies, both professional franchises in the independent Frontier League, offer up-close baseball on both sides of the Mississippi River. The Rascals play in 3,500-seat T. R. Hughes Ballpark (900 Ozzie Smith Drive in O'Fallon, Missouri), a half-hour west of St. Louis in St. Charles County. The Grizzlies, who fielded their first team in 2001, play across the river from St. Louis in GMC Stadium in Sauget, Illinois. For information about schedules and ticket prices, call the Rascals at (888) 762–2287 or visit on-line at www.rivercityrascals. com; or contact the Grizzlies at (618) 377–3000; www.gatewaygrizzlies.com.

De Soto

Washington State Park (all ages)

Highway 21; send mail to Route 2, Box 450, De Soto 63020; (636) 586–0322 for cabin reservations, (636) 586–2995 for interpretive center information; www.mostateparks.com. Camping sites for tents are $8.00; $12.00 for RV hookup. Call (877) 422–6766 at least forty-eight hours in advance for camping reservations. There is an $8.50 registration fee.

Nestled in the woods of this park is what once was a ceremonial burial ground for prehistoric native people. Today you can see the petroglyphs, or rock carvings, they left behind near the southern boundary of the park. Big River, a tributary of the Meramec River, borders the park and provides wonderful opportunities for recreation. You can rent a canoe and arrange to float from 3 to 22 miles. Tubing is a favorite activity on this small, shallow river, and the inner tubes can also be rented. Kitchen-equipped cabins and campsites are available as well as a lodge that is open from April through October. An interpretive center provides information and activities throughout the summer.

Festivals

MAY

The **St. Louis Storytelling Festival** (314–516–5948; www.umsl.edu/~conted/storyfes/) offers thirty to forty professional storytellers converging from across the nation on the first weekend in May to provide **free** performances in various locations throughout the St. Louis area. Don't miss this delightful opportunity to experience one of the oldest performing arts in human history.

The **Lewis and Clark Rendezvous** (636–946–7776 or 800–366–2427), held the third weekend in May in St. Charles, was a national signature event in 2004 during the Lewis and Clark Bicentennial. This living-history event offers great opportunities to see how people lived in the early days of this frontier settlement. Reenactors camp out for the weekend on the riverfront and play the parts of fur traders, mountain men, U.S. soldiers, and Native Americans. Booths sell handmade goods and crafts, and demonstrations include black-powder shoots, parades, fife and drum playing, and battle reenactments.

JUNE

Shakespeare Festival of St. Louis (314–361–0101; www.shakespearefestival-stlouis.com) provides two weeks of free evening performances of the Bard's work, just east of Art Hill in Forest Park. Performances are accompanied by a traditional "green show," which includes music, comedy, and specialty acts, such as jugglers and magicians.

Strawberry Festival (636–464–6464; www.discoverkimmswick.com), held the first weekend in June in City Park and the lot next to City Hall, Kimmswick, is a wonderfully entertaining family event with more than 200 crafts booths, food, and plenty of games for the kids.

JULY

Fair St. Louis (314–434–3434; fairstlouis.com), one of the nation's largest birthday parties, is held on the Gateway Arch grounds in downtown St. Louis over three or four days. Activities include several concerts by national entertainers, air shows with aircraft from hometown company Boeing (formerly McDonnell Douglas), activity booths, ethnic foods, and small stages with performances throughout the weekend. A downtown parade starts the event, and there are fireworks every night of the fair.

Riverfest (636–946–7776; 800–366–2427; www.riverfeststcharles.com) is a traditional Independence Day weekend celebration that includes great fireworks, a parade, food, beverages, a beer garden, carnival rides, and many booths.

National Tom Sawyer Days (573–221–2477). Held for nearly a half century during the July Fourth weekend in downtown Hannibal, this classic family event lets visitors simply watch or participate in events ranging from the National Fence Painting Championships to a frog-jumping contest. Food, music, crafts, and all types of entertainment are available during the four-day event.

AUGUST

The **Moonlight Ramble** (314–644–4660; www.moonlightramble.com), an 18-mile bicycle tour that starts in downtown St. Louis at 2:00 A.M., is held in August. For more than twenty years cyclists have been turning out in droves to participate in activities that include safety clinics and demonstrations the evening before.

SEPTEMBER

The **Japanese Festival** (314–577–5100; www.mobot.com), held every year on Labor Day weekend at the Missouri Botanical Garden in St. Louis, offers musical performances, ethnic food, cultural demonstrations, and vendors selling Japanese products. The highlight of the event is the night walk through the Japanese Garden with hundreds of lanterns lining the paths and floating on the water and Japanese performers and crafts throughout the garden. $; **free** for children ages 12 and under.

The **Great Forest Park Balloon Race** (314–821–6724; www.greatforestparkballoon race.com) takes place in September and features thirty to fifty hot-air balloons filling the sky in a hare-and-hound race in St. Louis Forest Park. The action starts the night before, when the balloons are tethered and lighted to create a spectacular drive-by sight, and continues the day of the race with the liftoff.

Big Muddy Blues Festival (314–241–5875; www.lacledeslanding.com). During Labor Day weekend numerous bands, performing on stages along the cobblestone streets of historic Laclede's Landing on the riverfront, play the music that is personified by the classic tune "St. Louis Blues."

St. Louis County Fair and Air Show (636–530–9386; www.stlcofair.org). Held during Labor Day weekend at the Spirit of St. Louis Airport in Chesterfield, this annual bash features a knockout air show; kids entertainment areas and carnival rides; demonstrations by everyone from experimental aircraft aficionados to traditional craftsman; food, and even Bud World, where adults can learn about the art of beer making. $$

Big River Days (573–242–3132; www.clarksvillemo.com). Clarksville's riverfront park comes alive on the third weekend in September when the focus is on history, nature, and fun. Boat and barge rides, raptor demonstrations, an enormous aquarium filled with indigenous fish, food, and other attractions celebrate the river that has played such a great role in this city's life.

DECEMBER

Las Posadas (636–946–7776 or 800–366–2427). During the first weekend in December this festival lights the entire historic downtown St. Charles area and offers special seasonal activities for the entire family, including this traditional reenactment of Joseph and Mary seeking shelter. The festivities include music, carolers, a tree-lighting ceremony, and a reception afterward. It's great fun for the whole family.

Where to Eat

MEXICO

G&B Steakhouse. Highway 54 South, Mexico 65265; (573) 581–0171. Open daily 11:00 A.M. to 9:00 P.M. Fabulous beef or chicken gyros, a catfish and pork chop special, and steaks, of course. $$

HANNIBAL

Cassano's Pizza & Subs. US–61 and Route MM, Hannibal 63401; (573) 221–5442. The name says it all, and the kids will love the pizza. Open daily 10:00 A.M. to midnight. $$

Mark Twain Dinette & Family Restaurant. 400 North Third Street, Hannibal 63401; (573) 221–5511. Open daily 6:00 A.M. to 9:00 P.M. Daily breakfast, with a super breakfast buffet Saturday and Sunday; burgers, tenderloin, and other sandwiches for lunch; and several delicious dinners, including scrumptious catfish. $$

Ole Planters Restaurant. 316 North Main Street, Hannibal 63401; (573) 221–4410. Owned by the same family for two generations and offering well-loved family recipes on the menu. Specialties include barbecue ribs, prime rib, and homemade pies. Open daily 11:00 A.M. to 3:00 P.M., 4:30 to 9:00 P.M. Monday through Saturday April through November. Shorter hours in December and March, closed January and February. $$

ST. CHARLES

Cracker Barrel Old Country Store. 901 Fairlane, St. Charles 63303; (636) 947–6566. Opens every day at 6:00 A.M. and closes Sunday through Thursday at 10:00 P.M. and Friday and Saturday at 11:00 P.M. A family-style restaurant with good food, healthy portions, and plenty of side dishes as well as an interesting store that is a great place for kids to wait if there is a line. $$

RT Weiler's. 201 Main Street, St. Charles 63301; (636) 947–1593. Open 11:00 A.M. daily; closes 1:00 A.M. Monday through Saturday, 11:00 P.M. Sunday. This kid-friendly bar and grill, with a name meant to mimic the name of a rather large breed of dog (Get it? Rottweiler), has a menu that adults and even the pickiest kid can live with. Peanut butter and jelly sandwiches, grilled cheese sandwiches, chicken strips, hamburgers, mini corn dogs, french fries and more are on the kids menu, and it's all served up to them in an authentic doggie dish. But don't worry; the kids' drinks come in a water bottle that they can take home, and the adults can get a real glass and plate. Kids meals for ages 10 and under are $3.50, otherwise $$.

ST. LOUIS

Hard Rock Cafe. 1820 Market Street, St. Louis 63103, Union Station; (314) 621–7625. Opens every day at 11:00 A.M. and closes

Monday through Thursday at 1:30 A.M., Friday and Saturday at midnight, Sunday at 11:30 P.M. Brimming full of rock-and-roll-related memorabilia and offering an eclectic menu with something for everyone. $$

John D. McGurk's Irish Pub. 1200 Russell Street, St. Louis 63104; (314) 776–8309. Open Monday through Saturday 11:00 A.M. to 1:00 A.M., Sunday 3:00 P.M. to midnight. Magnificent burgers make this landmark just south of downtown a great stop if you're anywhere near the Soulard neighborhood, and if you're not, it's worth the drive. $$

O'Connell's Pub. Kingshighway at Shaw Boulevard, 4652 Shaw, St. Louis 63110; (314) 773–6600. Open Monday through Saturday 11:00 A.M. to midnight, Sunday noon to 10:00 P.M. Head-to-head with McGurk's for the best burgers in St. Louis. Proximity to Forest Park makes it a good place to slip away to for a sandwich and fries at lunch. $

Rigazzi's. 4945 Daggett, St. Louis 63110; (314) 772–4900. Open Monday through Saturday 10:00 A.M. to 10:00 P.M., sometimes 11:00 P.M. Family dining in a boisterous setting, offering toasted ravioli, a perennial favorite of most kids, all types of pasta, and plenty of pizza as well as several luncheon specials served from a steam table. Try the onion rings. $$

Ted Drewes Frozen Custard. 6726 Chippewa, St. Louis 63109, (314) 481–2652; and 4224 South Grand, St. Louis 63111, (314) 352–7376. The Chippewa store is open daily Valentine's Day through December; the Grand store is open daily from Memorial Day through Labor Day. Hours generally are 11:00 A.M. to midnight, but they can vary, so call ahead if you're running late. You'll want to share this St. Louis tradition of eating what is arguably the best custard in the world. The famed Concrete shakes are so thick they're served upside down to prove the point. $

Several kid-friendly restaurant chains also have franchises throughout the city, most notably **White Castle** (serving small, kid-size hamburgers, cheese fries, shakes, and soda), **Steak n' Shake** (a more expensive hamburger, chili, shakes, and fries experience), **Krieger's Pub & Grill** (super-friendly kid places where hamburgers and fries are delivered on a take-home Frisbee and shakes comes in a take-home sports bottle), **Pasta House Co.** (pasta and meat dishes), and, of course, old standbys such as **McDonald's, Burger King, Taco Bell, Hardee's, KFC,** and **Church's Chicken.** Consult a telephone directory for nearest location.

UNIVERSITY CITY

Fitz's Bottling Co. and Restaurant. 6605 Delmar Boulevard, St. Louis 63130; (314) 726–9555. Open daily 11:00 A.M.; closing time varies from early evening to midnight in summer; call ahead. Root beer floats rule here for kids and adults, but there's a wide selection of burgers, pasta, and other food that kids will love to consume while they watch Fitz's root beer being bottled. $$

Creve Coeur

Fuddruckers. 12322 Dorsett Road, St. Louis 63043; (314) 434–5565. Open daily 11:00 A.M. to 9:00 P.M. This is a great place to keep the kids busy building their own burgers. $

Kirkwood

Massa's Restaurant. 210 North Kirkwood Road, Kirkwood 63122; (314) 965–8050. Open Tuesday through Thursday 11:00 A.M. to 11:00 P.M., Friday 10:00 A.M. to midnight, Saturday 5:00 P.M. to midnight, Sunday 5:00 to 8:00 P.M. Pizza, pasta, and sandwiches in the middle of a quaint little suburban downtown with many interesting shops. It's also a block from an Amtrak passenger train, so there's a possibility the children might be able to see a train stop to board passengers. $$

FENTON

Cracker Barrel Old Country Store. 1050 South Highway Drive, Fenton 63026; (636) 349–3335. Open Sunday through Thursday 6:00 A.M. to 10:00 P.M., Friday and Saturday 6:00 A.M. to 11:00 P.M. A family-style restaurant with good food, healthy portions, and plenty of side dishes as well as an interesting store that is a great place for kids to wait if there is a line. $$

KIMMSWICK

Blue Owl Restaurant and Bakery. Second and Mill Streets, Kimmswick 63053; (636) 464–3128. Generous portions are served during breakfast and lunch, and homemade desserts rule in a quaint setting provided by a nineteenth-century structure known locally as the Tavern. Open 10:00 A.M. to 3:00 P.M. Tuesday through Friday, 10:00 A.M. to 5:00 P.M. Saturday and Sunday. $$

Old House Restaurant. Second and Elm Streets, Kimmswick 63053; (636) 464–0378. Chicken and dumplings, prime rib, and homemade desserts are among the fare served during lunch and dinner in this renovated, two-story eighteenth-century log cabin. Open year-round 11:00 A.M. to 8:00 P.M. Tuesday through Sunday. Closed Christmas Eve through the Thursday after New Year's Day. $$

Where to Stay

STOUTSVILLE

South Fork Resort. Across from Mark Twain State Park, Stoutsville 65283; (573) 565–3500. Cabins and motel units are available, with boat rentals and boat ramps nearby. $$

HANNIBAL

Best Western—Hotel Clemens. 401 North Third Street, Hannibal 63401; (573) 248–1150 or (800) 528–1234. Checkout time is 11:00 A.M.; check-in time is 1:00 P.M. Seventy-eight rooms, indoor swimming pool, exercise room, whirlpool. Children ages 12 and under **free;** up to four people in a room. $$$

Comfort Inn. 123 Huckleberry Drive, Hannibal 63401; (573) 221–9988. Checkout time is 11:00 A.M.; check-in time is 2:00 P.M. Forty-eight rooms, outdoor pool, exercise room, hot tub, continental breakfast. Children ages 18 and under **free;** up to four people to a room. $$$

Howard Johnson Lodge. 3603 McMasters Avenue, Hannibal 63401; (573) 221–7950.

Checkout time is 11:00 A.M.; check-in time is 3:00 P.M. Sixty-three rooms, outdoor swimming pool. Children ages 18 and under **free;** up to four people to a room. $$$

Injun Joe Campgrounds. Highway 61 South at Clemens Landing; (573) 985–3581. With a wooded tent area, this campground has full hookups, laundry room, pool, water slide, canoe rental, miniature golf, go-karts, batting cages, fishing lake, and a picnic pavilion. $

Mark Twain Cave Campground. Highway 79 South; (800) 527–0304. Located adjacent to Mark Twain and Cameron Caves, the campground is open daily April 1 through November 1 and has RV and tent sites, laundry facilities, grocery, and camping supplies. $

ST. CHARLES

Comfort Suites. 1400 South Fifth Street, St. Charles 63301; (636) 949–0694. Checkout time is noon, check-in time is 3:00 P.M.; 171 rooms, fitness area, indoor pool, and continental breakfast. Children ages 17 and under are **free.** $$$

Fairfield Inn. 801 Fairlane Road, St. Charles 63301; (636) 946–1900. Checkout time is noon; check-in time is 3:00 P.M.; 80 rooms, indoor pool, hot tub, and continental breakfast. Up to five people in a room. $$$

Hampton Inn. 3720 West Clay, St. Charles 63301; (636) 947–6800. Checkout time is 11:00 A.M.; check-in time is 3:00 P.M.; 125 rooms, indoor swimming pool, exercise room, whirlpool, continental breakfast. Children ages 18 and under free; up to four people in a room. $$$

Travelodge. 2781 Veteran's Memorial Parkway, St. Charles 63301; (636) 949–8700. Checkout time is 11:00 A.M.; check-in time is 4:00 P.M.; 114 rooms, outdoor pool, continental breakfast. Children ages 17 and under are free. $$$

ST. PETERS

Holiday Inn Select–St. Peters. 4341 Veteran's Memorial Parkway, St. Peters 63376; (636) 928–1500. Checkout time is noon; check-in time is 3:00 P.M.; 195 rooms, continental breakfast, outdoor-indoor pool, game room. Children ages 12 and under are free. $$$

Florissant

Hampton Inn St. Louis-Northwest. 55 Dunn Road, Florissant 63031; (314) 839–2200 or (800) 426–7866. Noon checkout time; 2:00 P.M. check-in time; 132 rooms, outdoor pool, continental breakfast. Children ages 12 and under free. $$$

Red Roof Inn—Florissant. 307 Dunn Road, Florissant 63031; (314) 831–7900 or (800) 843–7663. Noon check-in and checkout; 108 rooms. Children ages 18 and under free. $$

ST. LOUIS

Adam's Mark Hotel. Fourth and Chestnut Streets, St. Louis 63102; (314) 241–7400 or (800) 444–2326. Checkout time is noon; check-in time is 3:00 P.M.; 910 rooms, indoor and outdoor pools, exercise room, breakfast. Children ages 18 and under are free. $$$$

Courtyard by Marriott. 2340 Market Street, St. Louis 63103; (314) 241–9111 or (800) 321–2211. Checkout time is noon; check-in time is 3:00 P.M.; 151 rooms, indoor pool, exercise room, Jacuzzi. $$$$

Drury Inn Union Station. 201 South Twentieth Street, St. Louis 63103; (314) 231–3900 or (800) 325–8300. Checkout time is noon; check-in time is 3:00 P.M.; 176 rooms, continental breakfast, indoor pool, exercise room, laundry room. Children ages 18 and under free. Suites with microwave and refrigerator. $$$$

Embassy Suites Hotel. 901 North First Street, St. Louis 63102; (314) 241–4200 or (800) 362–2779. Checkout time is noon; check-in time is 4:00 P.M.; 297 rooms, indoor pool, exercise room, Jacuzzi, cooked-to-order breakfast in atrium for up to six people per suite. $$$$

Hampton Inn–Gateway Arch. 333 Washington Avenue, St. Louis 63102; (314) 621–7900. Checkout time is noon; check-in time is 3:00 P.M.; 188 rooms, indoor pool, hot tub, continental breakfast Monday through Friday. $$$$

Hampton Inn Union Station. 2211 Market Street, St. Louis 63103; (314) 241–3200. Checkout time is noon; check-in time is 3:00 P.M.; 239 rooms, indoor pool, whirlpool, exercise room, continental breakfast. Children ages 18 and under free. $$$$

Hyatt Regency St. Louis. 1 St. Louis Union Station, St. Louis 63103; (314) 231–1234 or (800) 233–1234. Checkout time is noon; check-in time is 3:00 P.M.; 538 rooms, outdoor pool, health club with dry saunas. $$$$

Mayfair Wyndham Hotel. 806 St. Charles Street, St. Louis 63101; (314) 421–2500. Checkout time is noon; check-in time is 3:00 P.M.; 182 rooms and suites, outdoor pool in season, fitness room. $$$$

Millennium Hotel. 200 South Fourth Street, St. Louis 63102; (314) 241–9500 or (800) 325–7353. Checkout time is noon; check-in time is 4:00 P.M.; 780 rooms, indoor and outdoor pools, exercise room, Jacuzzi. $$$$

St. Louis Marriott Pavilion Hotel. 1 Broadway, St. Louis 63102; (314) 421–1776 or (800) 228–9290. Checkout time is noon; check-in time is 3:00 P.M.; 672 rooms, indoor pool, exercise room, Jacuzzi. $$$$

CREVE COEUR

Baymont Inn and Suites–Westport. 12330 Dorsett Road, St. Louis 63043; (314) 878–1212 or (800) 301–0200. Checkout and check-in times are noon; 145 rooms with no frills, continental breakfast. Children ages 18 and under **free.** $$$

Drury Inn Suites–Creve Coeur. 11980 Olive Boulevard, St. Louis 63141; (314) 989–1100 or (800) DRURYINN. Checkout time is noon; check-in time is 3:00 P.M.; 187 rooms. Indoor swimming pool, hot tub, exercise room, and inside parking. Suites with microwave and refrigerator. Children ages 18 and under **free.** $$$$

Holiday Inn West Port. 1973 Craigshire Road, St. Louis 63146; (314) 434–0100 or (800) 465–4329. Checkout time is noon;

check-in time is 3:00 P.M.; 329 rooms, indoor pool, Jacuzzi, exercise room. Children ages 12 and under **free.** $$$$

CHESTERFIELD

Doubletree Hotel and Conference Center. 16625 Swingley Ridge Road, Chesterfield 63017; (636) 532–5000 or (800) 222–8733. Checkout time is noon; check-in time is 3:00 P.M.; 223 rooms, indoor and outdoor pools, spa, exercise room. Children **free.** Special Friday through Sunday rate of $94.00 includes buffet breakfast for two in restaurant. Children ages 12 and under eat **free.** $$$$

EUREKA

Ramada Inn at Six Flags. Highway 44, exit 261; 4901 Six Flags Road, Eureka 63025; (636) 938–6661 or (800) 782–8108. This hotel next door to the park has an indoor recreation area with a swimming pool, sauna, whirlpool, and game room for unwinding after an exhausting day of having fun. $$$$

Yogi Bear's Jellystone Park Camp-Resort. Highway 44, north on Allenton Road, then left to 5200 Fox Creek Road, Eureka 63025; (636) 938–5925 or (800) 861–3020; www.eurekajellystone.com. In addition to RV and tent camping, there are air-conditioned cabins with kitchens, a general store, a self-service laundry room, and outdoor recreational facilities and planned activities. Opens March 1. $ (camping) to $$$ (for cabins).

Southeast Missouri

When you're traveling this region, I–55 to the east and I–44 to the north are the quickest, most direct routes to take around the perimeter of the southeast region of Missouri. Ste. Genevieve, Cape Girardeau, Sikeston, and New Madrid are just off I–55, and I–44 rolls through or close by Stanton, Sullivan, Leasberg, St. James, and Rolla. The best way to explore the interior of the region is along the north-south axis of Highway 67, or the meandering east-west route of Highway 60. Although both are slower than the interstates, the scenery is better and the drive more interesting.

Missouri's southeast region is rural, but it offers incredible outdoor recreational opportunities and many revealing insights into the past. The federal government is one of the biggest landowners, with jurisdiction over the Mark Twain National Forest, much of which is located in this region, and the Ozark National Scenic Riverways. The Mark Twain National Forest has more than 1.5 million acres of some of the most remote terrain in the state. The federally supervised forest and riverways offer visitors a beautiful, unspoiled natural environment to explore freely. Small historic towns dot the countryside and reveal the area's rich heritage. You also can find out a lot about this region from the National Forest Service at www.nps.gov/ozar/ and www.rosecity.net. The latter Web site is sponsored by several communities in the area.

Ste. Genevieve

Settled in 1735, this delightful historic town was the first permanent settlement west of the Mississippi River and promises tourists of all ages a great time. This is truly a living museum, with dozens of historic homes serving as residences. The numerous historic buildings here represent three time periods in the history of this area: the early French settlement of the 1700s, the coming of Americans during the early 1800s, and the later arrival of German immigrants. You and your children might enjoy discussing the differ-

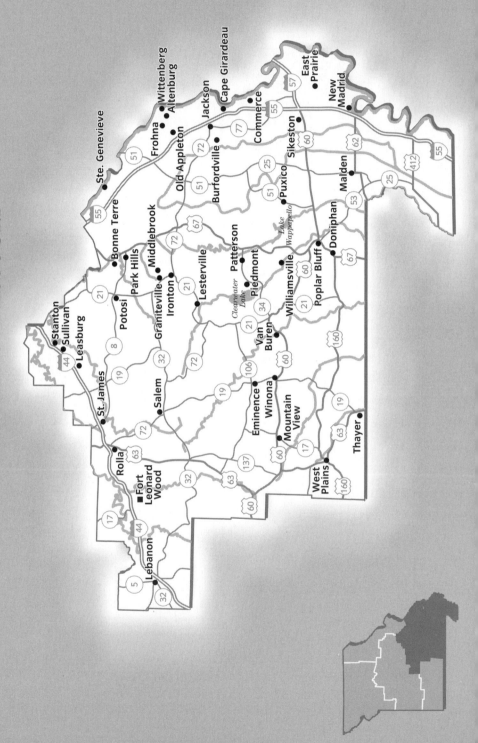

SOUTHEAST MISSOURI

ences. Even though the downtown no longer is on the riverfront because the river changed course years ago, you still can walk or drive to the river at several locations.

Great River Road Interpretive Center (all ages)

66 South Main Street, Ste. Genevieve 63670; (573) 883–7097 or (800) 373–7007; www.saintegenevievetourism.org. Open daily 9:00 A.M. to 5:00 P.M. Free admission.

This is the official visitor center and is loaded with information about the area. After you view the exhibits about the river and pick up the information you need, watch *Old Man River and Old Ste. Genevieve*, a seventeen-minute film that explains the important role the Mississippi River has played in the city's development. You can walk to many of the historic buildings and homes in historic downtown. The convention and visitors bureau Web site, www.saintegenevievetourism.org, is full of information about Ste. Genevieve's history, historical homes, and other points of interest for visitors.

Ste. Genevieve Museum (all ages)

Third and Merchant Streets on Dubourg Square, Ste. Genevieve 63670; (573) 883–3461. Open Monday through Saturday 9:00 to 11:00 A.M. and noon to 4:00 P.M., Sunday 11:00 A.M. to 4:00 P.M. $; children younger than kindergarten age free.

This museum, located on the town square, has an interesting collections of artifacts, including prehistoric Indian relics, old documents, and land grants.

Randy and Jane's
TopPicks in Southeast Missouri

1. St. Louis Iron Mountain and Southern Railway, Jackson

2. Mark Twain National Forest

3. Lake Wappapello

4. Elephant Rocks State Park, Graniteville

5. Johnson's Shut-Ins State Park, south of Graniteville

6. Bootheel Youth Museum, Malden

7. Bonne Terre Mine, Bonne Terre

8. Current and Jack's Fork Rivers

9. Eleven Point River

Honorable Mention: Fort de Chartres State Historic Site, Prairie Du Rocher, Illinois

Park **Call**

Missouri's excellent state park system is operated by the Department of Natural Resources. Call (800) 334–6946 or (800) 379–2419 (TDD) around the clock for recorded information, or during daily office hours to reach an attendant, or visit on-line at www.mostateparks.com. Campsites can be reserved by calling (877) 422–6766 at least forty-eight hours in advance. There is an $8.50 registration fee, in addition to the rental fee, for this service.

Bolduc House (all ages)

125 South Main, Ste. Genevieve 63670; (573) 883–3105. Call for hours. $; children younger than kindergarten age free.

Originally built south of town in 1770 by trader and miner Louis Bolduc and moved to the present site at 125 South Main in 1784, this is the best-known house in the region and an outstanding example of French colonial architecture, with a stockade fence, hip roof, galleries (porches), medicinal herb gardens, grape arbor, and authentic furnishings from the period. It is considered by many to be the first, most authentically restored Creole house in the country.

Felix Valle State Historic Site (all ages)

Merchant and Second Streets, Ste. Genevieve 63670; (573) 883–7102. Open 10:00 A.M. to 4:00 P.M. Monday through Saturday, noon to 5:00 P.M. Sunday. $; children younger than kindergarten age free.

This Georgian colonial–style limestone building built in 1818 has original mantels and interior trim and original brick and frame outbuildings in its garden and orchard. The partitioning of interior space into rooms and early Empire furnishings brought upriver by the first steamboats highlight the increasing sophistication of the village's well-to-do. The state also has restored the Shaw House, a neighboring building with a working 1830s kitchen.

Marina de Gabouri (all ages)

Located off Marina Avenue, Ste. Genevieve 63670; (573) 883–5599.

You and the children can watch the river traffic while you eat at the Eagle's Nest restaurant. Boaters who want to explore the river below the lock and dam system can access the river here.

A Cosby Family **Adventure**

Cosbys love boat rides and history. That's why we like to take the Modoc Ferry from Little Rock Landing just north of Ste. Genevieve to the Illinois side of the river and explore the remarkable French frontier sites in the area. After exiting the ferry, follow the bluff road to the intersection with Route 3, where a decision awaits you.

To the right, on Route 3 south, is the Pierre Menard Home (618–859–3031), the residence of Illinois' first lieutenant governor and one of the country's best examples of French colonial architecture, and the Fort Kaskaskia Historic Site, with the remnants of an early fort. Each gives you a vivid idea of what life was like on the American French frontier in colonial times.

But we turn left at the intersection to reach our favorite destination: the incredible Fort de Chartres State Historic Site (618–284–7230) and its partially restored stone fort dating from the mid-eighteenth century. You follow the bluff road into Prairie Du Rocher, Illinois' oldest town, and the fort is about 4 miles west of town.

The northern approach from the parking lot to the fort is breathtaking, with 15-foot walls protected at the corners by even taller bastions and accented in the center by a towering gatehouse. Inside are reconstructed barracks, a museum, and a restored powder magazine that is the only surviving structure from the original fort. Kids and adults love to climb the walls and share a vantage point similar to what French soldiers once had. It's mind-boggling to think a massive stone structure like this one—it replaced an earlier wooden fort—was here before the American Revolution. The restoration is particularly impressive to anyone who might have visited the site several decades ago, when only the stone foundations were present.

But the area is teeming with historic French colonial sites. If you don't want to cross the river, you can simply drive south from Ste. Genevieve about 10 miles to Kaskaskia Island, where a shrine houses the 650-pound bronze-and-silver Liberty Bell of the West, a gift from the king of France to the area's early 1700s French settlers.

Ste. Genevieve–Modoc Ferry (all ages)

Little Rock Landing, follow Main Street north of downtown, Ste. Genevieve 63670; (573) 883–7097; (800) 373–7007. Operates Monday to Saturday 6:00 A.M. to 6:00 P.M., Sunday 9:00 A.M. to 6:00 P.M., river and weather conditions permitting. Fee is $7.00 per car one-way; $12.00 round-trip.

This is the easiest way to get to the French colonial sites on the Illinois side of the river, but it's also a nice little boat ride for the kids. This is a good place to cross if you're planning a round-trip from St. Louis and other points upriver and intending to drive back up the Illinois side. If you plan to include the ferry in your trip, always call ahead to be sure it is running.

Maison Guibourd–Valle House (all ages)

1 North Fourth Street at Merchant, Ste. Genevieve 63670; (573) 883–7544. Open 10:00 A.M. to 5:00 P.M. daily April 1 through October 31. Admission is $; children ages 5 and under **free.**

Built in 1806, this elegantly furnished home offers costumed guides, changing exhibits, and dried herb displays in an attic featuring an incredible Norman truss and hand-hewn oak beams secured by wooden pegs. A beautiful courtyard contains an old stone well and rose garden.

Amoureux House (all ages)

St. Mary's Road, Ste. Genevieve 63670; (573) 883–7102. Seasonal hours; call ahead. $; children ages 5 and under **free.** Also **free** with the purchase of a ticket to the Felix Valle State Historic Site.

The poteaux-en-terre (post in the ground) method of setting upright log walls directly in the earth was well known when this house was built in 1792, although only five such structures now exist, and three of those are in Ste. Genevieve. The secret? Apparently indestructible cedar logs. The historic home overlooks Le Grand Champ agricultural fields, where much of the settlement's early farming took place.

Hawn State Park (all ages)

12096 Park Drive, Ste. Genevieve 63670; (573) 883–3603; (800) 334–6946; www.mostateparks.com.

One of the most beautiful parks in the state, this 4,800-acre preserve has native pines, hardwoods, and numerous dogwoods, redbuds, and wild azaleas. An 11-mile hiking trail takes you to Pickle Creek and the River Aux Vases. Picnicking and camping facilities are available; naturalists offer guided hikes and programs in the summer, with expanded programs planned for fall and spring.

Amazing
Missouri Facts

What is the state bird?

Eastern Bluebird

Fifty campsites, twenty-six with electrical hookups, are served by modern rest rooms, hot showers (water off from November 1 to April 1), laundry facilities, a dumping station, and playground equipment. Campsites with electrical hookups are $14.00 per day; others are $8.00 per day. Call (877) 422–6766 at least forty-eight hours in advance for camping reservations. There is an $8.50 registration fee.

Jackson

St. Louis Iron Mountain and Southern Railway (all ages)
Highways 61 and 25; send mail to P.O. Box 244, Jackson 63755; (573) 243–1688 or (800) 455–7245; rosecity.net/trains. Day excursions at 11:00 A.M. and 2:00 P.M. Saturday, 1:00 P.M. Sunday April through October, 1:00 P.M. Wednesday and Friday June through August. Dinner train is at 5:00 P.M. Saturday. Admission for day excursion is $15.50 for adults, $8.50 for children ages 3 through 11; children ages 2 and under free. There's a $2.00 additional fee to ride in an air-conditioned coach. Admission for dinner train is $26.50 for adults, $18.00 for children ages 3 through 11; children ages 2 and under are free. Call for schedule of special murder mystery tours.

The regular excursion is an eighty-minute, 10-mile amusement ride into the past between Jackson and Gordonville. You board authentic passenger cars from the 1920s and set off pulled by steam or diesel locomotives. Then the fun begins. There's always plenty of excitement on board, from visits by members of the Jesse James gang to strolling magicians and even a murder during a special four-hour trip. Two-hour, 14-mile-long dinner tours and three-and-one-half-hour, 16-mile-long mystery trips also are available. But whatever trip you choose, nothing beats the sound, feel, and smell of a train chugging down the tracks with you and the kids aboard. The kids might get to ride up top in the caboose or up front with the engineer; ask one of the attendants.

Lickitysplit Water Slide (ages 4 and older)
3925 Old Cape Road Circle, Jackson 63755; (573) 243–7202. Open daily 10:00 A.M. to 7:00 P.M. Memorial Day through Labor Day. $.

Is there a better way to get a respite from the southeast Missouri summer heat than sliding down one of two 600-foot-long slides into a 3-foot deep pool of cool water? Even if there is, this still is a lot of fun. However, be aware that your younger and smaller kids will need your help in the water.

There also is a video game room and a concession stand, which serves pizza and snacks.

For More Information

Jackson Chamber of Commerce.
125 East Main Street, Jackson 63755;
(573) 243–8131; www.jacksonmo.com.

Burfordville

Bollinger Mill State Historic Site (all ages)
113 Bollinger Mill Road, Burfordville 63739; (573) 243–4591 or (800) 334–6946;
www.mostateparks.com. Open Monday through Saturday 10:00 A.M. to 4:00 P.M., Sunday
noon to 4:00 P.M. $; children ages 5 and under free.

You can step back in time during a forty-five-minute tour of this five-story operating mill. In
addition to the tour, there are exhibits about the history of the mill. Next to the mill is a
covered bridge where outdoor exhibits explain the role of covered bridges in the state.

Cape Girardeau

Take a drive around the downtown area of this college town to see eight murals depicting
the heritage of the area. You can get a map and other literature at the Convention and Visitors Bureau office at 100 Broadway; it's open from 8:00 A.M. to 5:00 P.M. Monday through
Friday and 10:00 A.M. to 4:00 P.M. Saturday and Sunday from Memorial Day through Labor
Day. Founded in 1792 by the Spanish but greatly influenced by the French who later domi-
nated the region, the city is named for French trader Jean Baptiste Girardot. You can get a
good view of the modern "mighty Mississippi" simply by driving downtown and walking
through the gates in the flood wall. But a spectacular scenic view of the river, one the
early settlers certainly were more familiar with, can be found at the overlook at Cape Rock
Park. To get there, take Main Street until it ends, then turn right and drive for several miles
directly to the park.

Cape River Heritage Museum (all ages)
538 Independence Street, Cape Girardeau 63703; (573) 334–0405. Open Friday and Saturday 11:00 A.M. to 4:00 P.M. March through December. $.

The Cape River Heritage Museum has exhibits about the town's history in an old building
downtown that once housed the city hall and the fire and police stations. A full-size fire
engine is among the hands-on displays for children.

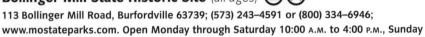

Amazing
Missouri Facts

Name the state musical instrument.

Fiddle

Amazing
Missouri Facts

What is the state song?

"The Missouri Waltz"

Southeast Missouri State University (all ages)

Located between Henderson Avenue and Pacific Street in the central part of the city. University Museum; (573) 651–2260. Open 9:00 A.M. to 4:00 P.M. Monday through Friday, noon to 4:00 P.M. Saturday and Sunday. Show Me Center; (573) 651–2297.

Walk around the campus and visit the **free** University Museum, which has historical exhibits and displays artwork by regional artists. Hours vary, so call before you visit. The Show Me Center on campus offers a full schedule of performances and productions, from concerts by national musicians and groups to rodeos, children's shows, and musicals. Call for ticket prices and a schedule.

Trail of Tears State Park (all ages)

Highway 177, about 10 miles north of Cape Girardeau; send mail to 429 Moccasin Springs 63755; (573) 334–1711; for camping reservations (877) 422–6766. Tent sites are $8.00; RV hookups are $14.00. Web site www.mostateparks.com. Open 9:00 A.M. to 5:00 P.M. Monday through Saturday, noon to 5:00 P.M. Sunday April through October. Closed Monday and Tuesday from November through March. Interpretive center hours vary; call for times.

This is a 3,415-acre park along the river with towering limestone bluffs and hillsides covered with mixed hardwood forests. An interpretive center documents the region's natural history, as well as the tragic story of the Cherokee Indians' forced march through this area, with photographs, maps, memorabilia, personal testimonies, and a video presentation. The park, which is in pristine condition, much like it was when the Cherokees made their march, also has picnic areas, campsites, hiking trails overlooking the river, and a lake with a boat ramp and a sand beach.

Fort D (all ages)

Fort and Locust Streets, Cape Girardeau 63703. **Free** admission.

This is the last existing fort of four ordered built during the Civil War by General John C. Fremont, who later made a name for himself during California's brief bid for national independence. The forts were to protect the town from assault by either land or water. Fort D, which can be viewed only from the outside, sits in a city park on a bluff overlooking the Mississippi River. It's another great river view.

Rocky Holler USA (all ages)

County Road 303; send mail to P.O. Box 686, Jackson 63755; (573) 243–6440. Open 10:00 A.M. to 6:00 P.M. Saturday and Sunday April through October. $; children ages 5 and under **free.**

Kids will go for the miniature golf, pony rides, panning for gold, and a petting zoo. Wagon rides, tram rides, and a blacksmith also are available.

Big River Family Fun Park (all ages)

610 Commercial Street, Cape Girardeau 63703; (573) 334–2278. Opens at noon daily, closes at 10:00 P.M. weekdays, midnight weekends, March though November. $–$$.

This quarter-mile road course is a good place to give the kids a chance to take the wheel, of a go-kart, that is. If they don't measure up to the 48-inch height limit, they can ride with you in a double cart. There's also an arcade, an eighteen-hole miniature golf course, and, for the big kids with drivers' licenses and Mom and Dad, souped-up "Super Single" carts that run only against each other.

Cape Skate (ages 3 and up)

620 Commercial Street, Cape Girardeau 63703; (573) 334–7655. Hours for sessions vary; call for schedule. You can use their side-by-side skates for **free** or rent in-line skates for $2.00. $

This is a family-oriented roller-skating rink with themed sessions ranging from Christian music to rock 'n' roll. There's a concession stand loaded with snacks.

The Ice (all ages)

Independence Street in Plaza Galleria, Cape Girardeau 63703; (573) 335–9048. Open 6:00 to 9:00 P.M. Thursday, 5:00 to 9:00 P.M. Friday, noon to 9:00 P.M. Saturday and 1:00 to 5:00 P.M. Sunday, October 1 through March 30. Bring your own skates or rent theirs for $2.75. $$.

This large rink, which bills itself as the only rink between St. Louis and Memphis, will be completely renovated when it opens for the 2004 season. A concession stand sells snacks and refreshments.

Red House Interpretive Center (all ages)

100 South Main, Cape Girardeau 63703; (573) 204–2331. Call for hours. $.

This museum contains interpretive information on many local historical topics, from African Americans and Indians to settlers in the area, including the four men who returned here after being members of Lewis and Clark's famed Corps of Discovery. But the principal attraction is a stocked trading post built in the vertical-log style used by French settlers in the early 1800s, when Lewis and Clark, on their way to St. Louis to start their trip, stopped for dinner at the "red house" of Louis Lorimier.

Tilt (all ages)

288 West Park Mall, Cape Girardeau 63701; (573) 334–5846; www.tilt.com. Open 10:00 A.M. to 9:00 P.M. Monday through Saturday, noon to 6:00 P.M. Sunday. Games are individually priced. $–$$.

This full-blown arcade has dozens of games. It also is located in a mall, which, when game time is over, should give parents time to pick up other items that might be needed on the trip. Tickets are awarded for prize redemption.

Arena Park Golf and Putt Putt (all ages)

2901 Hawthorne Road, Cape Girardeau 63701; (573) 332–0860. Open daily from 8:30 A.M. to 10:00 P.M., weather permitting, April 1 through October 30; 9:00 A.M. to 6:00 P.M. other times. $.

You can putt over a bridge and through a church on an eighteen-hole miniature golf course, hit a bucket of balls on a driving range, or prove your baseball skills in batting cages. There's even a pro shop if Dad or Mom need to pick up any golf equipment. Soda and snack machines on site.

For More Information

Cape Girardeau Convention and Visitors Bureau. 100 Broadway, Cape Girardeau 63701; (573) 335–1631 or (800) 777–0068; www.capegirardeaucvb.org.

Commerce

Tiny Commerce sits just a few miles south of Cape Girardeau. This town was established in 1790 and was once a bustling river town. It is directly on the banks of the river and boasts "the best view of the river between St. Louis and Memphis," according to locals. There are no river bluffs, swampy areas, or levee walls separating the town from the river. You can walk right down to the banks of the river to fish or watch the river go by. But, of course, that's not always good news. "Commerce is going to have floods," says Dixie High.

Commerce Museum (all ages)

201 Missouri Street, Commerce 63742; (573) 264–3900. Open by appointment only. Suggested donation of $2.00 per person.

This quaint museum chronicles Commerce's exceptionally bustling past with artifacts and photographs donated by local residents and displayed in an old church.

A Cosby Family **Adventure**

One of our favorite family adventures was a serendipitous encounter during a roundabout trip from St. Louis to Cape Girardeau. The unexpected surprise was the River Ridge Winery (573–264–3712; www.riverridgewinery.com), a family-run operation that produces 4,000 gallons of wine a year. It is nestled on gentle, rolling slopes less than 2 miles north of the small town of Commerce on County Road 321. Winemaker Jerry Smith and his wife, Joannie, have been selling wine only since 1994 and have four acres of vineyards planted in French hybrid grapes.

Although we first thought this would be a stop for adults only—we almost bypassed it—it turned out to be a pleasant and satisfying day for the kids, who have frequently asked when we will be going back. Part of its appeal to kids is the storybook setting, located in a small four-room farmhouse built in 1894. It sits right off the shaded two-lane road and serves as a tasting center and gift shop. A 200-year-old catalpa tree shades the gingerbread-trimmed house, which sports wooden porch posts with actual wine bottles built in. The winery produces the same continental-style wines grown in California and France. Eight varieties of dry and semidry wine are offered for sale and tasting.

But another attraction to the kids was the well-stocked gift shop offering small items they bought as gifts for friends. The gift shop also is loaded with dinnerware, baskets, wine accoutrements, Christmas ornaments, and gourmet food from all over the world. There are more food selections now than in the past, and music is provided from 2:00 to 6:00 P.M. Saturday and Sunday from March through September. Still, at times it is difficult to believe this quaint little business is so well connected to the rest of the world.

Picnic tables and chairs scattered over the property and a pavilion invite visitors to sit a spell. After plenty of warm conversation with the owners, we chose a bottle of wine for lunch and a couple to take home and bought soft drinks for the kids and a special picnic basket with bread, cheese, and sausage for a picnic. It's a short walk to the vineyards and a slightly longer hike to a great bluff view of the Mississippi River, providing it's the right time of the year and the trees have shed some foliage.

The kids protested when we finally had to get back on the road, but the winery, a nearly three-hour stop, went on our list of great places for a return visit.

Yule Log Cabin (all ages)

Highway N, 2 miles west of Commerce; send mail to P.O. Box 118, Commerce 63742; (573) 264–2747 or (573) 264–3712. Open 10:00 A.M. to 6:00 P.M. Monday through Saturday, 11:00 A.M. to 6:00 P.M. Sunday from mid-September to the first full week after New Year's Day.

This may be the most fascinating Christmas shop you'll come across anywhere. Located in a log cabin built by Jerry and Joannie Smith, who also run the River Ridge Winery, the Yule Log Cabin has one of the largest selections of Christmas ornaments and Yankee candles imaginable for sale. The Smiths pride themselves in the quality Christmas trees they grow and sell on the property, but it is the remarkably wide collection of Christmas ornaments that excites and entertains kids and adults alike.

Old Appleton

Highway 61 winds around through rural countryside to reveal rustic Old Appleton. This tiny village of eighty-two people presents a pretty-as-a-picture sight on the banks of Apple Creek, with a reconstructed iron bridge that originally dated from 1879.

Altenberg, Frohna, and Wittenburg

These three small towns near the river along Highway A help you understand the early German influence in the region. They remain a window into the culture transplanted to southern Missouri by a group of more than 500 immigrants from Saxony who, seeking religious freedom, settled the towns in 1839. The settlers were part of a group of about 800 people who left Germany bound for southeast Missouri, which a land agent in St. Louis

Amazing Missouri Facts

What is the state flower?

Hawthorn

said was very similar to Saxony. One of the seven ships they sailed on was lost at sea, and another 125 or so members of the group settled in St. Louis. Much of what was Wittenburg was inundated in the floods of 1993 and 1995.

Concordia Log College and Seminary (all ages)
Altenberg 63732; (573) 824–5542. Inside tours by appointment only. **Free** admission but suggested donation of $1.00.

Opened in 1939 by immigrants from Saxony, this is the first Lutheran seminary west of the Mississippi River. The site contains a log hut built in 1839, a small stone church built in 1845 that now serves as a museum, and Trinity Lutheran Church, a larger stone building built in 1867 that still is in use.

Saxon Lutheran Memorial Site (all ages)
Frohna 63748; (573) 824–5404. $.

A visitor center and museum tells the story of the original German immigrants. Visitors also can explore several vintage log cabins, barns, and outbuildings.

Sikeston

Sikeston Bootheel Rodeo (all ages)
Rodeo grounds, north of town; from March through August call (800) 455–2855. Alcohol-free seating available. $$$–$$$$

People come from all over the Midwest each August to attend the state's largest rodeo, and contenders come from all over the United States to compete for $100,000 in prize money. The big event for this part of the state features big-name entertainers, some of the top cowboys in the country, clowns, horse competitions, roping events, and bullfights.

East Prairie

Towosahgy State Historic Site (all ages)
I–55 south from Sikeston, east on Highway 80, south on Highway 77; send mail to Route 2, Box 343, East Prairie 63845; (573) 649–3149 or (800) 334–6946; www.mostateparks.com. Open 10:00 A.M. to 4:00 P.M. daily. **Free** admission.

This scenic drive into the delta area of Missouri takes you to the remains of a fortified Indian village from the Mississippian culture. There is an informational kiosk, a walking trail, and Indian mounds—one more than 20 feet high—to climb.

Big Oak Tree State Park (all ages) 🌲

I–55 to East Prairie turnoff, then south to 13640 South Highway 102, East Prairie 63845; (573) 649–3149 or (800) 334–6946; www.mostateparks.com. Park is open 6:00 A.M. to 10:00 P.M. daily. Visitor center is open 8:00 A.M. to 4:30 P.M. June through August, or at other times by asking at park office. Free admission.

Majestic trees tower over more than 1,000 acres of rich delta land. A boardwalk through the park lets you see the remnants of the vast swamp forest that once covered this part of the state. There are picnic areas, shelters, and a small lake for fishing. A visitor center is loaded with information about the region's history.

New Madrid

Called New "Mad-rid" by locals, this small town was founded to be the capital of Spain's holdings in the New World, but it since has developed an unsettling reputation: It is the epicenter of the New Madrid Seismic Zone, a web of earthquake faults that reaches into five states. In December 1811 it was the site of the strongest earthquake ever recorded in North America. During the wave of shocks that occurred over eight weeks, crevasses swallowed buildings, enormous trees were uprooted, and the Mississippi River even ran backward for a short spell. If you want to give your children a marvelous look at one of the widest points of the modern Mississippi River running in the right direction, take Main Street south to the levee, where an observation deck that juts into the river affords an 8-mile view. For more information, contact the new Madrid Chamber of Commerce, 560 Mott, P.O. Box 96, New Madrid 63839; (573) 748–5300 or (877) 748–5300; www.new-madrid.mo.us.

New Madrid Historical Museum (all ages) 🏛️

1 Main Street, New Madrid 63869; (573) 748–5944; www.new-madrid.mo.us. Open Monday through Saturday 9:00 A.M. to 5:00 P.M., Sunday noon to 5:00 P.M. $; children ages 5 and under free.

The small museum has an interesting collection of exhibits that explain how earthquakes work in general, including firsthand accounts and other information about the tragic quakes of 1811 and 1812, which rang church bells in distant Boston, Massachusetts. There also are exhibits about a critical Civil War battle that was fought in New Madrid as well as about the overall conflict.

Hunter-Dawson Home State Historic Site (all ages)

112 Dawson Road (also Highway U), New Madrid 63869; (573) 748–5340; www.mostateparks.com. Open Monday through Friday 8:30 A.M. to 5:00 P.M., Saturday 10:00 A.M. to 4:00 P.M., Sunday noon to 4:00 P.M. $; children ages 5 and under free.

This fifteen-room, yellow cypress mansion on the north side of town was built in 1858 by a local merchant. During special events, costumed guides aptly demonstrate the Southern charm and other mannerisms one might expect from Southern gentry who lived in this part of the state before the Civil War.

Higgerson School Historic Site (all ages)

300 Main Street, New Madrid 63869; (573) 748–5716. Open Monday through Saturday 9:00 A.M. to 5:00 P.M., Sunday noon to 5:00 P.M. Memorial Day through Labor Day. Tours by appointment only at other times. $; children ages 5 and under free.

This restored one-room schoolhouse operated at nearby Higgerson Landing until 1967 and is thought to have been the last one-room schoolhouse in use in Missouri. Moved to downtown New Madrid in 1998, its current furnishings represent the 1948 schoolroom that served thirty-two students in first through eighth grade.

Missouri Tourist Information Center

Exit 42 on Highway 55, P.O. Box 246, New Madrid 63869; (573) 643–2654; www.visitMo.com. Open 8:00 A.M. to 5:00 P.M. daily. Free admission.

Here you'll find plenty of hands-on printed material with information about attractions in this area or anywhere else in the state.

Malden

Bootheel Youth Museum (all ages)

700-A North Douglas Road, Malden 63863; (573) 276–3600. Open Tuesday through Saturday 10:00 A.M. to 4:00 P.M., Sunday 1:00 to 4:00 P.M. Adults $, kids ages 3 through 17 $$, children ages 2 and under free.

Don't be misled by the name: This hands-on, interactive discovery place will delight children of all ages. In 10,000 square feet of display space kids can climb on a 1927 fire truck and wear a real firefighter's uniform, check out a full-size Saturn automobile, see a seismograph monitoring earthquake activity, simulate an earthquake on a computer, build structures with huge plastic blocks, create life-size shadows in the shadow room, and shop in a kid-size grocery store. A Children's Village with interactive exhibits also includes a firehouse, recycling center, post office, and other stores or community-service providers.

Amazing
Missouri Facts

What is the extreme southeast section of Missouri called?

The boot heel

Poplar Bluff

If you drive to the northwest from Malden, you'll enter the beautiful foothills of the Ozark Mountains and find the small town of Poplar Bluff. For more information, visit the Poplar Bluff Chamber of Commerce Web site, www.poplarbluffchamber.org.

Moark Regional Railroad Museum (all ages)
303 Moran Street, Poplar Bluff 63901; (573) 785–4539. Call for hours; open year-round. **Free** admission; donations accepted.

An interesting collection of railroad memorabilia is displayed in an old depot. Items include pictures, railroad tools, books, and a model train layout.

Epps-Houts Memorial Museum (all ages)
Off Highway PP on County Road 451, Poplar Bluff 63901; (573) 785–2734. The museum is open by appointment only, with admission ranging from $2.00 to $5.00 depending on the length of the tour.

You can tour an extensive personal collection of travel memorabilia at this private museum. It is filled with items from Korea, Saudi Arabia, Iran, and Africa purchased by the owners during thirty-five years spent traveling around the world.

Poplar Bluff Historical Museum (all ages)
1010 North Main Street, Poplar Bluff 63901; (573) 785–2220. Call for hours; open year-round. **Free** admission.

The focus here is primarily local—history, sports, schools, and veterans—but there also are displays on the U.S. Postal Service, Boy and Girl Scouts, and the U.S. Forest Service.

Puxico

Mingo National Wildlife Refuge (all ages)

Highway 60 east, then go north on Highway 51 to the area entrance; send mail to 24279 Highway 51, Puxico 63960; (573) 222–3589; www.fws.gov/r3pao/ming_nwr. Stop at the visitor center for information and directions. Open approximately one hour before sunrise to thirty minutes after sunset. Free admission.

At Mingo you'll find a 1-mile boardwalk trail where you can see muskrats, beavers, wood ducks, tree frogs, turtles, water snakes, woodpeckers, and songbirds. Observation towers in several locations provide a panoramic view of the marsh. On Sundays in April, October, and November, you can go on a 25-mile auto tour featuring glimpses of deer, raccoons, wild turkeys, owls, and hawks. Hiking trails abound throughout the 40,000 acres of bottomland and cypress forest that have been preserved here and in the Duck Creek Wildlife Area.

Duck Creek Wildlife Area (all ages)

Highway 60 east, then go north on Highway 51 to the area entrance; send mail to Route 1, Box 186, Puxico 63960; (573) 222–3337. Open 24 hours a day. Stop at the visitor center for information and directions. Free admission.

More than 40,000 acres of bottomland forests and cypress swamp rich in wildlife and fishing and accessible via beautiful hiking trails through natural areas have been preserved here and at Mingo National Wildlife Refuge. Be sure to visit Pool 1 to see waterfowl from October through March and bald eagles, especially in the winter.

Williamsville

The 8,500-acre Lake Wappapello is surrounded by large tracts of public land and undeveloped areas. Because it is a shallow lake, it is not as popular with powerboaters as other lakes in the state. But it offers great fishing, sailing, and swimming areas in a natural, unspoiled state. Several national trails, including the Ozark Trail, pass through this area.

Lake Wappapello State Park (all ages)

Highway 172, at the southern end of the lake, Route 2, Box 102, Williamsville 63967; (573) 297–3247 or (800) 334–6946; www.mostateparks.com. Tent sites with electric hookups are $14.00, $8.00 for others. Call (877) 422–6766 at least forty-eight hours in advance for camping reservations. There is an $8.50 registration fee. Cabins range from $50 for two bedrooms to $70 for three bedrooms. Children ages 4 and under stay for free.

This state park has eighty campsites, several housekeeping cabins, a 150-foot sand beach, and three boat ramps. A 15-mile trail is available for hiking, backpacking, and all-terrain bicycling, and a shorter trail provides wonderful lake views.

Piedmont, Patterson, Middlebrook, and Lesterville

Just west of Piedmont is Clearwater Lake, a gorgeous 1,600-acre lake in a wilderness setting. Although the area is primarily rural, there are numerous resorts, campgrounds, and marinas to provide boating, swimming, skiing, and fishing throughout the lake area. Canoeing is available on the Black River north of the lake. For more information on local attractions, call the Piedmont Chamber of Commerce at (800) 818–4046.

Clearwater Lake Information Center (all ages)

Highway HH at the dam; (573) 223–7777. Open Friday through Monday 9:00 A.M. to 4:00 P.M. Memorial Day through Labor Day. Free admission.

The center provides information about five public recreation areas on the lake and gives you directions to beautiful Lon Sanders Canyon, a narrow rocky gorge that is worth a visit.

Sam A. Baker State Park (all ages)

Highway 143, northeast of the lake, R.F.D.1, Box 114, Patterson 63956; (573) 856–4223 or (800) 334–6946; www.mostateparks.com. Camping fees are $8.00 for tent sites, $14.00 for RV hookups. Call (877) 422–6766 at least forty-eight hours in advance for camping reservations. There is an $8.50 registration fee.

Located in the St. Francois Mountains, one of the most ancient ranges in North America, geologically speaking, the park has more than 5,000 wilderness acres surrounding Mudlick Mountain and a 15-mile trail providing access to the mountain. The park has a dining lodge, cabins, more than 200 campsites, and a clear stream for swimming. A nature center has exhibits about this mountain area.

Taum Sauk Mountain State Park (all ages)

Highway CC off Missouri Highway 21-72; send mail to HC Route 1, Box 126, Middlebrook 63656; (573) 546–2450 or (800) 334–6946; www.mostateparks.com. Campsites are $8.00 per night.

Encompassing the highest point in the state, this rugged park covers more than 6,000 acres and has picnic grounds, primitive campsites, and a paved hiking path to the high point.

Johnson's Shut-Ins State Park (all ages)

Highway N, 8 miles north of Lesterville; send mail to HC Route 1, Box 126, Middlebrook 63656; (573) 546–2450 or (800) 334–6946; www.mostateparks.com. Campsites are $14.00 per day for sites with electrical hookups; $8.00 a day for tent camping. Registrations only. Call (877) 422–6766 at least forty-eight hours in advance for camping reservations. There is an $8.50 registration fee.

In this incredible park the swift Black River runs around huge exposed boulders to create gorges, or "shut-ins." The result is a series of pools, chutes, and waterfalls that form a kind of natural water park. If you want your children to learn to appreciate the joys of nature, this is the place to bring them. The 8,500-acre park has fifty campsites, picnic areas, and 13 miles of hiking trails and is primarily wilderness area. It's also one of the most popular in the state system, so you must make a reservation if you're camping in the park.

Ozark Trail (adolescents and up)
For trail information and maps call (800) 334–6946, then dial "O" for operator and ask for the trail coordinator.

Johnson's Shut-Ins State Park is a major trailhead of the Ozark Trail, which winds through Missouri and Arkansas in some of the remotest areas of the Ozark Mountains.

Ironton

Fort Davidson State Historic Site (ages 5 and up)
North of Ironton on Highway V; send mail to P.O. Box 509, Pilot Knob 63663; (573) 546–3454 or (800) 334–6946; www.mostateparks.com. Open Monday through Saturday 10:00 A.M. to 4:00 P.M., Sunday noon to 5:00 P.M. Free admission.

Civil War buffs won't want to bypass this thirty-seven-acre site, where remnants of the bloody battlefield's earthworks are still visible. There are picnic areas and a small museum with exhibits that use fiber optics to demonstrate the troop movements during the battle, and you can go on a self-guided walking tour of the battlefield.

Silver Mines Recreation Area (all ages)
Take Highway 72, then turn south on Highway D; (573) 438–5427 or (573) 783–3769. Tent campsites are $8.00, RV hookups $14.00. Call (877) 422–6766 at least forty-eight hours in advance for camping reservations. There is an $8.50 registration fee.

Silver Mines is one of four recreational areas with campsites, picnic areas, and hiking trails in the beautiful, secluded wilderness that makes up this district of the Mark Twain National Forest. The trails here offer magnificent views of the St. Francis River and the bluffs and shut-ins along the river.

Amazing
Missouri Facts

What is Missouri's nickname?

The Show Me State

Graniteville

Elephant Rocks State Park (all ages)

Highway 21 at the northwest edge of Graniteville; send mail to Fort Davidson Historic Site, P.O. Box 509, Pilot Knob 63663; (573) 546–3454 or (800) 334–6946; www.mostateparks.com. Open 10:00 A.M. to 4:00 P.M. Monday through Saturday; 10:00 A.M. to 5:00 P.M. Sunday. Free admission.

This park lives up to its name with giant granite boulders a billion years old standing end to end. Follow a trail through the rocks and see Dumbo, the largest of the rocks at 27 feet tall and 35 feet long. Picnic grounds and a fishing lake are also available.

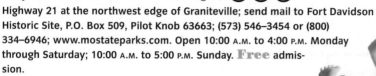

Park Hills

This area to the north of Park Hills was lead-mining country in the 1800s, and the remains of that industry, specifically how it has contoured the landscape, now provide recreation for tourists.

St. Joe State Park (all ages)

2800 Pimville Road, Park Hills 63601; (573) 431–1069 or (800) 334–6946; www.mostateparks.com. Open 7:00 A.M. to 8:00 P.M. daily. Camping fees are $14.00 per day for sites with electrical hookups; $8.00 per day for others. Call (877) 422–6766 at least forty-eight hours in advance for camping reservations. There is an $8.50 registration fee. Showers operate April 1 through October 31.

This is the second-largest park in the state system, and it has 1,600 acres designated for off-road vehicles. During the mining process pulverized limestone was dumped throughout the area, creating acres of sand flats that are now open for motorcycles, dune buggies, and four-wheel-drive vehicles. The entire park covers more than 8,000 acres and includes 108 campsites, horseback-riding and hiking trails, picnic areas, and four clear lakes, two with sand beaches.

Missouri Mines State Historic Site (all ages)

Highway 32 adjacent to St. Joe State Park; send mail to P.O. Box 492, Park Hills 63601; (573) 431–6226 or (800) 334–6946; www.mostateparks.com. Open Monday through Saturday 10:00 A.M. to 4:00 P.M., Sunday noon to 6:00 P.M. $; children 5 and under free.

You'll feel like you've entered a ghost town as you drive around this old lead-mining facility comprising twenty-eight separate structures owned and operated by the St. Joseph Lead Company until 1972. The Powerhouse Museum has three galleries with pieces of restored mining equipment and exhibits on geology and mineral resources.

Bonne Terre

Bonne Terre Mine (all ages)

Highways 67 and 47, 29 Allen, Bonne Terre 63628; (573) 358–2148. Open daily 10:00 A.M. to 4:00 P.M. April through October. Open Friday, Saturday, and Sunday from November through March. Walking tour $12.00 for adults, $6.00 for children ages 11 and under; pontoon boat tour is $17.50 for all ages.

Tours lead into the bowels of the earth and through an 80-square-mile cavern created during more than a century of mining. When the mine closed and the pumps were shut off, the underground area filled up with water and is now used by diving enthusiasts. For a schedule of scuba-diving tours, call West End Diving in St. Louis (314–731–5003).

Potosi

This district of the Mark Twain National Forest has more than 100 miles of hiking trails through a variety of Ozark topographies.

Council Bluff Recreation Area (all ages)

State Highway DD, about 25 miles south of Potosi, P.O. Box 188, Potosi 63664; (573) 438–5427; www.fs.fed.us/r9/marktwain/recreation/camping/camp_council_bluff.htm. Single campsites $8.00, doubles $16.00. Call (877) 422–6766 at least forty-eight hours in advance for camping reservations. There is an $8.50 registration fee.

This recreation area surrounds a lake with a sand beach and has picnic areas, several boat-launch sites, and fifty-five campsites, including thirty-nine singles, seven doubles, and seven walk-ins. Primitive camping is available along the Ozark Trail, which runs through this district.

Trout Lodge/Camp Lakewood (all ages)

Route 2, Box 240, Potosi 63664; (573) 438–2154 or (314) 241–9622; www.ymcaoftheozarks.com. Open year-round. Prices range from $101 and up per adult for doubles in summer (Memorial Day through Labor Day) and $84 other times, $50 per night for ages thirteen to sixteen, $45 per night for ages five through twelve April through October and free other months. Children ages 4 and under free year-round.

Operated by the YMCA, this family resort offers lodge rooms and private cabins with all meals, facilities, and most activities included in the price of the room. Activities include tennis, sailing, archery, fishing, volleyball, canoeing, and soccer. A complete fitness center, movies, campfires, and stocked ponds are also available. This is an ideal place for families that demand a physically active vacation.

Sullivan

Meramec State Park (all ages)

2800 South Highway 185, Sullivan 63080; (573) 468–6072; camping reservations (800) 334–6946; www.mostateparks.com. Cabins rent for $75.00 to $90.00 per night; call (888) 637–2632. Campsites are $14.00 with electrical hookup, $8.00 without. Call (877) 422–6766 at least forty-eight hours in advance for camping reservations. There is an $8.50 registration fee. Fisher Cave tour is $6.00 for adults, $5.00 for teenagers, $4.00 for ages 5 through 12, ages 4 and under are free.

A 6,700-acre park along the scenic banks of the Meramec River that encompasses rugged forested hills, river bluffs, several springs, and more than thirty caves. There are 200 campsites, cabins, canoe rentals, a motel and a dining lodge, which is open April through October. Nature programs are offered year-round, and the visitor center includes a 3,500-gallon aquarium and life-size diorama. Ninety-minute guided tours through Fisher Cave with handheld lights are available April through October.

Stanton

Meramec Caverns (all ages)

Highway 44, exit 230; send mail to Box 948, Stanton 63079; (573) 468–2283 or (800) 676–6105; www.americascave.com. Open daily 9:00 A.M. to 4:00 P.M., until 7:00 P.M. during spring, summer, and fall. Adults $$$, kids ages 5 through 10 $$, children ages 4 and younger free. No strollers allowed on tour.

This incredible cave has been attracting tourists since 1935 and is one of the most popular in the state. Guided tours last approximately eighty minutes. The guides explain geologic and historical aspects of the cave and even point out the hideout site of outlaw Jesse James. A motel, campgrounds, a gift shop, and scenic boat rides are available at the cave during the summer.

Jesse James Wax Museum (all ages)

Highway 44, exit 230; send mail to Box 948, Stanton 63079; (573) 927–5233. Open 9:00 A.M. to 5:30 P.M. May to Labor Day. Some off-season hours; call ahead. Adults $$, kids ages 6 through 10 $, children ages 5 and under free.

Anyone fascinated by the James gang and the mark they left on American outlaw lore, or by desperadoes in general, can see members of this notorious gang modeled in wax and set in life-size dioramas. The museum also includes an extensive collection of guns and dolls.

Leasburg

Onondaga Cave State Park (all ages)

7556 Highway H, Leasburg 65535; (573) 245–6576 or (800) 334–6946; www.mostateparks.com. Open daily 7:30 A.M. to 10:00 P.M. Camping fees are $14.00 per day for sites with electrical hookups; $8.00 without. Call (877) 422–6766 at least forty-eight hours in advance for camping reservations. There is an $8.50 registration fee.

The 1,300-acre park has seventy-two campsites, 3 miles of hiking trails, swimming, canoeing, and fishing areas on the Meramec River. It also has two caves you can visit, as described in the next two entries.

Onondaga Cave (all ages)

Onondaga Cave State Park, 7556 Highway H, Leasburg 65535; (573) 245–6576. Open daily 9:00 A.M. to 5:00 P.M. March through October. Adults $$, kids ages 6 through 11 $, children 5 and under **free.**

If you can visit only one cave in the area, this is your best bet—it's one of the most outstanding caves in the country. A visitor center has exhibits about the cave's ecosystem, and seventy-five-minute guided tours teach about the cave formations and the wildlife living inside the cave.

Cathedral Cave (ages 5 and up)

Onondaga Cave State Park, 7556 Highway H, Leasburg 65535; (573) 245–6576. Adults $$, children ages 12 and under $. Tours leave at 1:00 P.M. Saturday and Sunday Memorial Day through Labor Day, and Saturday only in April, May, and September.

Guided tours using handheld lights are available at Cathedral Cave. This tour is strenuous, with a quarter-mile hike to the cave entrance, and is available on weekends only.

St. James

Maramec Spring Park (all ages)

Highways 8 and 68, 6 miles south of St. James, 320 South Bourbeuse, St. James 65559; (573) 265–7387; tigernet .missouri.org/~tjf/maramec.html. Open daily during the daylight hours. A $3.00 per car admission fee to the park covers entry to the two museums.

This is a private park with campsites, picnic areas, a playground, hiking trails, a trout-fishing stream, and the Pick N Shovel Restaurant, which serves hamburgers, hot dogs, and other sandwiches. There also are two museums, one featuring old tools used in agriculture and a second that explains the history of the Maramec Ironworks, which oper-

ated on the site until 1876. The company was the first ironworks west of the Mississippi River, and a driving tour takes you through the remnants of the mining community.

Rolla

This city is the home of the University of Missouri–Rolla campus, the state's principal engineering school. For an interesting tour of the campus, go to the admissions office in Parker Hall or call (573) 341–4164, and take a few minutes to look over the partial replica of Stonehenge at Fourteenth Street and Bishop Avenue.

Mineral Museum (ages 5 and up)

125 McNutt Hall, UM–Rolla campus, Rolla 65409; (573) 341–4616. Open 8:00 A.M. to 4:30 P.M. Monday through Friday. Free admission.

The university was once known as the Missouri School of Mines, and this small museum chronicles that past. The exhibits include many mineral specimens from the region and a collection from throughout the world that was displayed at the 1904 World's Fair in St. Louis and later donated to the university.

Phelps County Museum (ages 5 and up)

302 West Third Street, Rolla 65401; (573) 341–4874. By appointment only; (573) 364–5977. Free admission.

Historic items from all over the county are on display here. You'll find Civil War items recovered from a nearby fort of that time, Indian projectile points dating from hundreds of years ago, and many photographs from the past.

Memoryville USA (all ages)

I–44 and Highway 63 North; (573) 364–1810; www.memoryvilleusa.com. Open 8:00 A.M. to 5:30 P.M. Monday through Friday, 9:00 A.M. to 5:00 P.M. Saturday and Sunday. $; children ages 6 and under free.

You can literally stroll down memory lane on a re-creation of the city's main street at the turn of the twentieth century. A collection of sixty antique and classic automobiles can be viewed, and the site also has an art gallery, an antiques store, and a restoration shop where visitors can watch vintage autos being repaired.

Salem

Located south of Rolla, Salem is the gateway to some of the most beautiful and pristine natural areas in the country. The combination of superlative floating streams at every level of difficulty, trails for beginning and advanced hikers, and camping opportunities make this a paradise for families seeking adventures outdoors. Highway 19, running north and south in this region, provides sensational scenery as it crosses three streams and passes through the national forest.

Ozark Information Center and Museum (all ages)

702 South Main Street, Salem 65560; (573) 729–5707. Open daily, usually 8:00 A.M. to 5:00 P.M. Free admission.

This is the best place locally to get printed information about the Ozark National Scenic Riverways, the web of floating streams and other waterways that crisscross this region of Missouri. A building housing a small museum on the area's history, and a bus parked outside the building, have information about camping facilities in the area and on the many area outfitters who provide the rafts and canoes used to float the streams.

Dillard Mill State Historic Site (all ages)

142 Dillard Mill Road, northeast of Salem on Highway 49; send mail to Davisville 65456; (573) 244–3120 or (800) 334–6946; www.mostateparks.com. Open Monday through Saturday 10:00 A.M. to 4:00 P.M., Sunday 11:00 A.M. to 5:00 P.M. $.

Located at the junction of Indian and Huzzah Creeks, the site features spring-fed creeks, a rock dam, and a waterfall cascading into a millpond in one of the most picturesque settings in the state. There are picnic areas and hiking trails in the park. Huzzah Creek is a favorite float stream, and you'll find many canoe outfitters and campgrounds in this area and to the north.

Montauk State Park (all ages)

Highway 119; send mail to R.R. 5, Box 279, Salem 65560; (573) 548–2201 or (800) 334–6946; www.mostateparks.com. Camping fees are $14.00 per day for sites with electrical hook-ups; $8.00 per day for others. Call (877) 422–6766 at least forty-eight hours in advance for camping reservations. There is an $8.50 registration fee. Call (573) 548–2434 for motel and cabin reservations, which run $63.00 per room with two double beds.

Montauk Springs and Pigeon Creek form the headwaters of the Current River. The park

Springs, **Springs** Everywhere

The northernmost access to the Current River is just southeast of Montauk State Park. When traveling by river on the upper Current, you can see Cave Spring, where you paddle inside the cave for approximately 100 feet; Welch Spring and the ruins of a nineteenth-century hospital; and historic Akers Ferry, which takes visitors across the river. The ferry operates daily 7:00 A.M. to 9:00 P.M. during the summer months, with shortened hours during the rest of the year. Call (800) 333–5628 or (573) 858–3224. The fare is $3.00 per car.

The beautiful, aquamarine Round Spring, off Highway 19, can be accessed by water or land. A cave on the site can be explored with handheld lights during an hour-long tour. There is an admission fee for the tour of the cave, which is open from Memorial Day through Labor Day. Call (573) 323–4236.

has an old gristmill you can tour, 1,300 acres with 156 campsites, and a motel with eighteen units, twenty-three housekeeping cabins, and a modern lodge. The stream is stocked with rainbow trout and attracts anglers during the season from March through October.

Eminence

This town lies close to the junction of the Current and the Jack's Fork River, which starts near the tiny town of Mountain View to the west. On this part of the Jack's Fork River you'll find Alley Spring and the three-story Alley Spring Grist Mill Historic Site, which is a museum. The historic red mill dating from 1894 is located on Highway 106 and is open daily from 9:00 A.M. to 4:00 P.M. from Memorial Day through Labor Day. This area of the riverway has hiking trails, a one-room schoolhouse open to the public, campsites, and swimming and picnic areas.

Winona

The Winona District of the Mark Twain National Forest is traversed by the Eleven Point and Current Rivers and is particularly popular for water recreation. The Eleven Point River, one of the most scenic rivers in the state, is part of the **National Wild and Scenic River System,** which aims at preserving rivers in their natural state. **Greer Spring,** off Highway 19, is a 1-mile hike from the highway parking lot. Benches along the path provide rest stops as you go. Some of the campsites in the area are accessible only by water. The district has numerous picnic areas, river access points, trails, and historically significant buildings and sites. For camping information, call (573) 325–4233.

Van Buren

Ozark National Scenic Riverways Headquarters (all ages)
Located off Highway 60; (573) 323–4236; www.nps.gov/ozar. Open Monday through Friday 8:00 A.M. to 4:30 P.M.

Information about this national treasure and maps of the system of waterways are available throughout the region, but you also can find what you need at a small visitor area here. The Ozark National Scenic Riverways encompasses more than 130 miles of shoreline along the banks of the Current and Jack's Fork Rivers. It is managed by the National Park Service and open to the public for swimming, camping, canoeing, rafting, and enjoying nature. This is Big Spring country, with the world's largest concentration of natural springs. From this area to the Arkansas border you'll find numerous clear, fast-running, spring-fed streams offering superb scenery and numerous opportunities for outdoor recreation. You can camp on gravel bars or in established campsites at numerous points along the rivers.

The area also has countless outfitters ready to rent you a canoe or raft. During summer months the streams turn into "canoe highways" filled with floaters. But don't shy away for fear of crowds; floating on an Ozark stream lined with limestone bluffs and lush forests is an experience not to be missed. If you go during the week, you may have the stream all to yourself. Another way to avoid crowds is to float during the spring or fall, but be aware that these spring-fed streams have extremely cold water. Call for flooding information before you go during either of these seasons. Make sure you visit the riverways Web site at www.nps.gov/ozar.

The streams in this area are Classes I and II, meaning they provide an easy float and are suitable for novices and families with children.

Hidden Log Cabin (all ages)

305 West John, at Ash Street, Van Buren 63965; (573) 323–4563. Open Monday through Saturday 9:00 A.M. to 5:00 P.M. April through November. $.

The family will enjoy taking a look at this 1872 home, the oldest building in Van Buren, and the primitive furnishings used at that time.

Doniphan

Current River Heritage Museum (all ages)

101 Washington Street, Doniphan 63935; (573) 996–5298. Open daily 9:00 A.M. to 4:00 P.M. Free admission.

This collection of displays on the heritage of the river valley since the early 1800s includes logging, military, and Civil War artifacts and information on early settlers in the area.

West Plains

Visitors can get a lot of information about the area by stopping at the Ozark Heritage Welcome Center at 2999 Porter Wagoner Boulevard. Call (417) 256–8835 or (888) 256–8835; www.westplains.net/areaattractions.html.

Civic Center (all ages)
110 St. Louis Street, West Plains 65775; (417) 256–8087.

West Plains is a hub for the surrounding rural area, which makes the Civic Center the perfect venue for stage shows with big-name entertainers, athletic events, and cultural productions. Call for a schedule of events.

Harlin Museum (all ages)
505 Worcester, West Plains 65775; (417) 256–7801; www.westplains.net/
areaattractions.html. Open Tuesday through Saturday noon to 4:00 P.M. mid-April through
October. Free admission.

This pocket museum is loaded with exhibits about people from the area such as musician Porter Wagoner and baseball great Preacher Roe, military memorabilia from World Wars I and II, and many artifacts from the late nineteenth and early twentieth centuries.

West Plains Motor Speedway (ages 6 and up)
Highway 63, 6 miles south of West Plains 65775; (417) 257–2112; www.westplains-
speedway.com. Races every Saturday night April through September. Adults $$, kids ages
7 through 11 $, children ages 6 and under free.

If your family wants some faster-paced action, check out the stock-car races on this ⅜-mile oval dirt track.

Thayer

Grand Gulf State Park (all ages)
Highway W, 6 miles west of Thayer; send mail to Route 3, Box 3554, Thayer 65791; (417)
264–7600 or (800) 334–6946; www.mostateparks.com. Open 8:00 A.M. to dusk.

Often called the Little Grand Canyon, this day park, located almost on the southern state line, has a marvelous river gorge that was created when a huge cave collapsed. The river winds for a mile through vertical cliffs as high as 120 feet. Picnic sites, hiking trails, and magnificent overlook areas are available.

Mountain View

This little city offers three parks worthy of a rest stop. West Park (Pine Street) has a beautiful walking trail; Wayside Park (Sixth and East Streets) offers a short, scenic walk past a log cabin, a railroad caboose, and three botanical gardens filled with native flowers; and Veterans Park (Sixth Street) has a new playground. For more information about the area, call (417) 934–2794 or (877) 266–8706; www.mountainviewmo.com.

You and the kids also will love the specialties served up at the old-fashioned soda fountain at Wildwood Art Gallery and Antiques downtown on First Street. Everything ice-cream-like, from fizzies to ice-cream sodas and sundaes, is available, and the gallery has jewelry, baskets, pottery, wooden items, dolls, and other crafts made locally. The gallery is open 8:30 A.M. to 5:00 P.M. Monday through Saturday; call (417) 934–6363.

Calico Cupboard (all ages)

116 North Oak Street, Mountain View 65548; (417) 934–6330. Open 10:00 A.M. to 5:00 P.M. Monday through Friday, 10:00 A.M. to 3:00 P.M. Saturday. Admission free.

This quilt store has more than 350 children's sewing machines, and several full-size highly collectible antiques, including one dating from 1854 by Eli Howe, who was one of the earliest inventors of the sewing machine. If you had a toy sewing machine, you'll probably see one like it here.

Fort Leonard Wood

An active army training installation, Fort Leonard Wood has provided training for more than three millions soldiers since it was established in 1940.

John B. Mahaffey Museum Complex (ages 5 and up)

Located at the fort, 495 South Dakota Avenue, Fort Leonard Wood 65473; (573) 596-0780; www.wood.army.mil/ccmuseum/index.htm. Open Monday through Friday 8:00 A.M. to 4:00 P.M., Saturday 10:00 A.M. to 4:00 P.M. Free **admission.**

The museum complex, which combines the U.S. Army Chemical Corps Museum, the Fort Leonard Wood Museum, the U.S. Army Engineer Museum, and the U.S. Army Military Police Museum contains an amazing array of exhibits on all sorts of military-related themes. There are exhibits on land-mine warfare, tactical bridging, demolition and explosives, arms and armaments, chemical warfare from World War I to the present, military police tactics and activities, and more. One exhibit recreates World War I trenches; another exhibit, which is a compound of thirteen buildings, portrays life at the fort during World War II. Still other exhibits chronicle the phenomenal career of Maj. Gen. Leonard Wood, the fort's namesake who, among other achievements, won a Medal of Honor and commanded the famed Rough Riders in the Spanish-American War.

Lebanon

Bennett Spring State Park (all ages)

26250 Highway 64A, Lebanon 65536; (417) 532–4338 or (800) 334–6946; www.mostateparks.com. Trout-fishing season is March through October. Camping tent sites are $8.00, RV hookups $14.00. Call (877) 422–6766 at least forty-eight hours in advance for camping reservations. There is an $8.50 registration fee.

A spring-fed stream stocked with rainbow trout brings fishing aficionados of every age to this 3,000-acre park. A hatchery in the park adds fish to the stream daily. Tours of the hatchery are available. Also in the park are hiking trails, a large spring, a nature center that is open year-round, nearly 200 campsites, a rustic dining lodge, and cabins. You can canoe on the Niangua River, which borders the park.

Festivals

MAY

Big Spring Arts, Crafts Festival, Courthouse Square, Van Buren; (800) 692–7582. Memorial Day weekend. It's an old-fashioned country fair with games, artists and craftspeople, bluegrass music, and a street dance with square dancing and round dancing.

JUNE

Fort de Chartres Trappers and Traders Rendezvous, Fort de Chartres State Historic Site, 1350 State 155, Prairie du Rocher, IL 62277, 4 miles west of Prairie du Rocher, Illinois; (618) 284–7230; greatriverroad.com/stegen/randattract/fdcvous.htm. The first weekend in June hundreds of military and civilian reenactors set up camp and present authentic cooking, craftsmaking, dancing, and other activities from the French colonial period.

JULY

Cape Girardeau Air Festival, Cape Girardeau Regional Airport; (573) 334–6230. Mid-July. A variety of military and civilian aircraft are on display and take part in aerobatics in this two-day event, which runs from 1:00 to 6:00 P.M. Admission is $7.00 for adults, $4.00 for children ages six through twelve; children ages five and under are **free.** There are many food booths, and airplane, helicopter, and simulator rides are available for an additional fee.

AUGUST

Jour de Fete, downtown Ste. Genevieve; (573) 883–7097; www.saintegenevieve.com. Held in mid-August, this event has parades, folk dances, live entertainment, and one of the largest crafts fairs in the state, with exhibitors coming from all over the Midwest. Actors dressed as early French settlers also reenact frontier life.

SEPTEMBER

SEMO District Fair, Fairgrounds, Cape Girardeau; (573) 334–9250 or (800) 455–3247. Mid-September. Missouri's oldest outdoor fair offers all the trimmings—horse shows, tractor pulls, a carnival, livestock—and big-time country music acts to boot.

City of Roses Music Festival, riverfront and downtown Cape Girardeau; (573) 335–1631; www.cityofrosesmusic

festival.com. On the last weekend in September, more than 50 local and national bands play a variety of music. Admission is $12.00 for adults; $5.00 for children ages five through twelve; and **free** for ages 4 and under.

Pioneer Days, downtown Mountain View; (417) 934–2794. In late September you'll find a wide variety of events celebrating our pioneer past, plus musical performances, a

parade, an arts-and-crafts show, a talent show, a classic car show, trick roping events, and more.

DECEMBER

Country Christmas Walk, downtown Ste. Genevieve; (573) 883–7097; www.ste-genevieve.com. Held in early December, this walk invites visitors to a festively decorated downtown, enhanced by carolers and a live nativity scene; greet Mr. and Mrs. Santa Claus.

Where to Eat

STE. GENEVIEVE

Anvil Saloon & Restaurant. 46 South Third Street on the Square, Ste. Genevieve 63670; (573) 883–7323. Open from 11:00 A.M. to 8:00 P.M. Sunday through Thursday, 11:00 A.M. to 9:30 P.M. Friday and Saturday. The best onion rings in these parts, along with scrumptious hamburgers, homemade pies, and liver dumplings served up in a building dating from the 1850s. $

Cafe Genevieve, in the Hotel Ste. Genevieve, Main and Merchant Streets, Ste. Genevieve 63670; (573) 883–3562. Open 7:30 A.M. daily, close at 9:00 P.M. Monday through Thursday, 10:00 P.M. Friday and Saturday, 6:00 P.M. Sunday. Family-style service on Sunday. Steaks, chicken, and seafood are served up here, but don't shy away from the onion dip and chips appetizer; the kids will love it. $$

Jack Oberle Market. About ½ mile west of downtown at 21529 State Highway 32, Ste. Genevieve 63670; (573) 883–5656. Open 6:30 A.M. to 5:00 P.M. Monday through Saturday. Known locally as the "Oberle" dog, the hickory-smoked all-beef sausage is made by Jack from his grandfather's recipe and goes great with his garlic cheese. $–$$

Old Brick House. Third and Market Streets

on the Square, Ste. Genevieve 63670; (573) 883–2724. Open 8:00 A.M. to 9:00 P.M. Monday through Friday, 11:00 A.M. to 7:00 P.M. Saturday, 11:00 A.M. to 7:00 P.M. Sunday. Located in the oldest brick building west of the Mississippi, the Old Brick serves crispy fried chicken with delicious homemade mashed potatoes, sirloin steaks; it even has a buffet. $$

Sara's Ice Cream & Antiques. 124 Merchant Street, Ste. Genevieve 63670; (573) 883–5890. Open daily 10:00 A.M. to 8:00 P.M. mid-May through October. After November 1, weekends by chance. The kids won't go for the antiques, but they'll love the homemade drumsticks, phosphates (a soft drink made with soda water and flavored syrup, which, long ago, also had a few drops of phosphoric acid, but that ingredient no longer is used), and ice-cream sodas. A "must" stop during hot spells, long walks, or when you simply want something sweet. $

Sirros. 261 Merchant, Ste. Genevieve 63670; (573) 883–5749. Open 11:00 A.M. to 10:00 P.M. Monday through Thursday, 11:00 A.M. to 11:00 P.M. Friday and Saturday, 11:00 A.M. to 8:00 P.M. Sunday. This is where the locals get pasta, pizza, cheeseburgers, and spicy french fries. $

CAPE GIRARDEAU

BG's Olde Tyme Deli. 205 South Plaza Way, Cape Girardeau 63703; (573) 335–8860. Open daily 10:45 A.M., close Sunday through Thursday 10:00 P.M., Friday and Saturday 11:00 P.M. Killer potato skins, fantastic Reuben sandwich, other great sandwiches, several full meals, and a kids' menu. $$

Broussards. 120 North Main Street, Cape Girardeau 63701; (573) 334–7235. Open Sunday and Monday 10:00 A.M. to 9:00 P.M., Tuesday through Thursday 10:00 A.M. to 10:00 P.M., Friday and Saturday 10:00 A.M. to 10:30 P.M. Cajun is the specialty here, with fantastic gumbo and a long kids' menu. You'll also want to try the shrimp or crawfish étouffée, mushrooms, onions, peppers, and other tasty bits cooked with the fish in a creamy white sauce. $

El Torero. 2120 Williams Street in the Town Plaza Shopping Center, Cape Girardeau 63701; (573) 339–2040. Open daily 11:00 A.M., Sunday through Thursday close 10:00 P.M., Friday and Saturday close 10:30 P.M. Mexican specialties include tacos, fajitas, and a children's menu. $

My Daddy's Cheesecake. 111 North Main Street, Cape Girardeau 63701; (573) 335–6660. Open 7:30 A.M. to 5:30 P.M. Monday through Friday, 8:00 A.M. to 5:30 P.M. Saturday, closed Sunday. Mississippi Mud and Turtle are among more than a dozen varieties of cheesecake served. But the kids probably will prefer the Gooey Louie cookie wedge, an incredible chocolate, pecan, and graham cracker concoction, or the frozen chocolate-covered cheesecake on a stick. $

Paglia's. 1129 Broadway, Cape Girardeau 63701; (573) 335–0366. Open daily 4:00 P.M., Sunday through Thursday close 11:00 P.M., Friday and Saturday close midnight. Excellent thin-crust pizza, pastas, salads, and more. $$

Port Cape Girardeau Restaurant. 19 North Water Street, Cape Girardeau 63701; (573) 334–0954. Open 11:00 A.M. to 9:00 P.M. Monday through Thursday, 11:00 A.M. to 10:00 P.M. Friday and Saturday, 4:00 to 9:00 P.M. Sunday. During the Civil War, this historic 1830s building on the riverfront housed Gen. Ulysses S. Grant's headquarters. Now it's a great place to nab lunch or dinner from a menu offering great barbecue, catfish, pork, a variety of sandwiches, and a kids' menu. $$

ALTENBERG

Tric's Family Restaurant. 129 Highway C, Altenberg 63732; (573) 824–5387. Open 8:30 A.M. to 2:00 P.M. Wednesday, 8:30 A.M. to 8:30 P.M. Thursday through Saturday, 10:00 A.M. to 2:00 P.M. Sunday. Closed Monday and Tuesday. Home-style cooking is offered in a cafeteria setting, fabulous pie is served daily, and German specialties are served on Saturday at dinner. $

SIKESTON

Lambert's Cafe: Home of Throwed Rolls. 2515 East Malone Street, Cape Girardeau 63801; (573) 471–4261. Open daily 10:30 A.M. to 9:30 P.M. Lambert's promises a great meal and an entertaining time. During your meal, fresh-baked rolls are thrown to you and you can choose from "pass-arounds," side dishes that change daily and are provided **free** of charge. Expect huge portions, a menu with an extensive selection, and reasonable prices. $$

Where to Stay

When traveling in southeast Missouri, plan to stay at a hotel in or near one of the larger cities because accommodations between these points are few and therefore often full. Cape Girardeau has a good selection, many at exit 96 on I–55, but Sikeston, Poplar Bluff, Ste. Genevieve, and Dexter also are good places to plan a stop.

STE. GENEVIEVE

Family Budget Inn. I–55 at Ozora exit 143, 17030 New Bremen Road, Ste. Genevieve 63670; (573) 543–2272. Checkout time is 11:00 A.M.; check-in time is 1:00 P.M. Outdoor pool. Children ages ten and under **free**; up to four people in a room. $$

Hotel Sainte Genevieve. Main and Merchant Streets, Ste. Genevieve 63670; (573–883–3562). Squeaky-clean basic rooms in historic downtown. Children stay **free.** $

Microtel Inn & Suites. 21958 Highway 32, Ste. Genevieve 63670; (573) 883–8884 or (888) 771–7171. Forty-two rooms, six suites, and continental breakfast. $$

CAPE GIRARDEAU

Although you'll find several chain motels along I–55, especially at exit 96, here are a few of our suggestions:

Drury Suites. I–55 (exit 96) and Route K, 3301 Campster Drive, Cape Girardeau 63701; (573) 339–9500. Checkout time is noon; check-in time is 3:00 P.M.; Eighty-seven rooms, indoor pool, hot tub, **free** use of nearby health club, extended Quick Start breakfast. Two-room suite with microwave. Children ages 18 and under **free.** $$$

Hampton Inn. I–55 (exit 96) and Route K, 103 Cape West Parkway, Cape Girardeau 63701; (573) 651–3000. Checkout time is noon; check-in time is 3:00 P.M.; Eighty-two rooms, complimentary breakfast for one Monday through Friday. Children ages 18 and under **free.** $$$

Holiday Inn. William Street and I–55 (exit 96), P.O. Box 1570, Cape Girardeau 63702; (573) 334–4491. Checkout time is 11:00 A.M.; check-in time is 3:00 P.M.; 186 rooms, indoor pool, outdoor pool, whirlpool, sauna, full-service breakfast for one adult and children ages 12 and under. Children ages 18 and under **free.** $$$

SIKESTON

Days Inn. Junction of Highways 60 and 61, Sikeston, 1330 South Main, Sikeston 63801; (573) 471–3930. Checkout time and check-in time are noon; 127 rooms, indoor pool, continental breakfast. Children ages 18 and under **free.** $$

POPLAR BLUFF

Comfort Inn. 2528 North Westwood, Poplar Bluff 63901; (573) 686–5200. Checkout time is 11:00 A.M.; check-in time is 2:00 P.M.; fifty-eight rooms, outdoor pool, hot tub, use of nearby health club, continental breakfast. $$$

Pear Tree Inn. 2218 North Westwood Boulevard, Poplar Bluff 63901; (573) 785–7100. Checkout time is noon; check-in time is 3:00 P.M.; seventy-one rooms, outdoor pool, continental breakfast. Children ages 18 and under **free.** $$

Three Rivers Inn. 2115 North Westwood, Poplar Bluff 63901; (573) 785–7711. Checkout time is noon; check-in time is 2:00 P.M.; 143 rooms, outdoor pool, complimentary breakfast for one. Children ages 19 and under **free.** $$

Southwest Missouri

S outhwestern Missouri offers countless opportunities for families looking for fun. Starting in the northern part of the region you'll find several small towns and the city of Springfield offering first-class attractions, including the birthplace of a nation-ally acclaimed children's author, a drive-through animal park, one of the finest caves in the nation, and a sporting-goods store that takes shopping to a whole new level of experi-ence. As you travel southeast you'll find more than one million acres of federally protected wilderness land and two large lakes nestled in the Ozark Mountains. The ancient hills cov-ering the southeastern part of this region are renowned for scenic drives when the wooded hills are dotted with blossoming wild dogwood trees in the spring or turned into kaleidoscopes of color in the fall. The city of Branson in this area has lured vacationers for decades and now is a music-show mecca with more than thirty-five theaters providing every type of family fare. To the west the region is rich in Civil War history, limestone caves, and lakes and streams offering water activities of all sorts.

Mansfield

Laura Ingalls Wilder & Rose Wilder Lane Home and Museum (all ages)

3068 Highway A, 1 mile east of the town square, Mansfield 65704; (417) 924–3626; www.lauraingallswilderhome.com. Open Monday through Saturday 9:00 A.M. to 5:00 P.M., Sunday 12:30 to 5:30 P.M. March 1 though November 15. $–$$; children ages 5 and under free.

Anyone who has read and admired the *Little House* books or enjoyed watching the television series will want to visit the house where these wonderful classic children's books were written. It is preserved the way it was when the Wilder family lived there. Artifacts, family

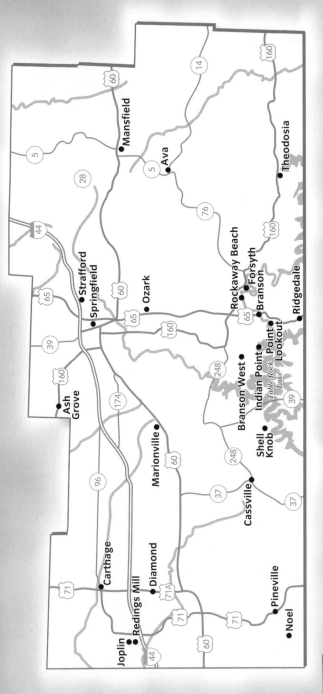

SOUTHWEST MISSOURI

pictures, and possessions belonging to the Wilders provide you with a glimpse into the life of the woman whose books have been enjoyed by generations of children. A museum next to the Wilder home features exhibits of pioneering history as described in the books.

Strafford

Exotic Animal Paradise (all ages)
I–44, 10 miles east of Springfield, 124 Jungle Drive, Strafford 65757; (417) 859–2016; www.exoticanimalparadise.com. Open daily 8:00 A.M. to 6:30 P.M., but off-season hours vary. $$–$$$; children ages 2 and under free.

More than 3,000 animals of sixty species are on display in this 400-acre game preserve. Visitors drive along a 9-mile trail to get an exciting, up-close look at the animals, most of whom are roaming free. Don't forget to purchase a couple of bags of feed at the entrance, because if you feed them the animals will come right up to your car window. The trickiest part—and the fun—is keeping their heads out of your car, which means children of any age who are afraid of animals won't be comfortable here because the close-up encounters are plentiful.

Halfway through your ride you reach **Safari Center,** where you can get out of the car, get something to eat, use the rest room, buy souvenirs, visit the petting zoo, and ride a pony. You can go through the park at your own speed, but plan on spending two or three hours if you have young children. They won't be rushed through this place.

Randy and Jane's
TopPicks in Southwest Missouri

1. Silver Dollar City, Branson

2. Shepherd of the Hills Homestead and Outdoor Drama, Branson

3. Discovery Center, Springfield

4. Lambert's Cafe, Ozark

5. Glade Top Trail, Ava

6. Bass Pro Shops Outdoor World, Springfield

7. Wonders of Wildlife Living Zooquarium, Springfield

8. Missouri Sports Hall of Fame, Springfield

9. Exotic Animal Paradise, Strafford

A Cosby Family **Adventure**

Our kids love the Exotic Animal Paradise on I–44 east of Springfield. It isn't fancy. Despite its name, the park has no exotic displays or settings, just hundreds of animals roaming about inside the fenced enclosures traversed by the road you follow. But the camels, ostriches, deer, and mules (or are they donkeys? we're not sure) come right up to your vehicle.

And that's where the adventure begins . . . as well as the shrieking. Our daughter was pitching feed out the window to some type of small deer when, unnoticed, she turned to find an ostrich head half inside the car looking for a handout. My son and daughter's whoops scared the poor, long-necked critter so badly it stepped away from the car as they rolled up the windows while throwing it a few pieces of the feed we purchased when entering the park. From that point on it was pandemonium, as the kids alternately left the window down long enough to attract a camel, or a mule (donkey?) with an offering and then shrieked and rolled the window up as the guest came too near.

There was excitement when this animal or that one blocked the road, seemingly intent on stranding us, and mock disappointment when an animal across the way wouldn't accept an offering and come closer. A stop at the Safari Center in the middle of the park allowed us to grab a soda, stretch our legs, and check out a small petting zoo before continuing on through the park. After a couple hours and a bag of feed—we should have bought two bags—we were back on the highway and heading to Lambert's in Ozark for some throwed rolls.

But over the years we have learned that every tourist destination is not for everyone. Relatives of ours with three children ranging from ages four to nine tried the park and came away dissatisfied. The problem? Their kids didn't like the pushy animals coming up to their van and begging for food; it scared them. Given the not insignificant admission fee to the park, this discomfort became a bit of a problem. Our daughter was seven and our son ten when we last did the park, and she was scared, too. But deliciously so, not enough to want to leave. I guess the trick is to know where your kids stand before shelling out the admission fee and buying the feed.

Springfield

The city of Springfield sits just north of the Ozark Mountains and is one of the fastest-growing areas in the state. Although for many vacationers this city is just a pit stop on the route to Branson, it deserves closer attention. There's plenty to do and see. Caves are big here: The area has 300 of the state's more than 5,500 caves. Begin your exploration of this gateway to the Ozarks by picking up information at the Tourist Information Center located on Highway 65 at the Battlefield Road exit. Call (417) 881–5300 or (800) 678–8767.

Fantastic Caverns (all ages)

I–44 to Highway 13; north 1 mile to Fantastic Caverns Road, then left for about 3 miles, Route 20, Box 1935, Springfield 65803; (417) 833–2010; www.fantasticcaverns.com. Open daily 8:00 A.M. to 7:00 P.M. $$–$$$; children ages 5 and under free.

In the only drive-through cave in the United States, the temperature remains a comfortable sixty degrees year-round. The driver of a Jeep tram gives you a fifty-minute spiel that combines history, ecology, conservation, and geologic information in a way that even kids will enjoy. The cave is magnificent, and its history is fascinating.

Crystal Cave (all ages)

Highway H off I–44 north of Springfield, 7225 North Crystal Cove Lane, Springfield 65803; (417) 833–9599. Open daily, weather permitting, 9:00 A.M. to 1:00 P.M. year-round. $$; kids ages 3 and under free.

Wannabe spelunkers will prefer the eighty-minute walking tour of this smaller cave and its beautiful cave formations and symbols that indicate Native American habitation.

Dickerson Park Zoo (all ages)

3043 North Fort Avenue, Springfield 65803; (417) 864–1800; www.dickersonparkzoo.org. Open daily 9:00 A.M. to 5:00 P.M. April through September. The zoo closes at 4:00 P.M. October through March. $–$$; children ages 2 and under free.

This zoo is designed to give kids an exciting look at the animals, yet it offers enough information to be educational and interest adults as well. Lovely walking trails lead visitors through carefully landscaped animal exhibits. There's a petting zoo where kids can purchase food and feed small animals. A "Missouri Habitats" area shows animals and habitats native to the Ozarks, including black bears, bobcats, and river otters.

Springfield Conservation Nature Center (all ages)

4600 South Chrisman Avenue, Springfield 65804; (417) 888–4237; www.mdc.state.mo.us/. Open Tuesday through Sunday 8:00 A.M. to 5:00 P.M. From April through October the trails are open until 8:00 P.M. Free admission.

Peace and tranquillity are in great supply in this eighty-acre natural oasis within the city limits. A visitor center provides interactive displays and activities for all ages. Even the youngest and wiggliest worm in your family will have fun playing with puppets, assembling a tree puzzle, or examining items in the extensive collection of "found" natural objects on display. Six hiking trails range in length from 1/5 mile to 2 miles, so all ages can be accommodated on a nature walk. An inside viewing area lets your family observe the mammals, birds, and other animals visiting the center's pond and feeders in any kind of weather. It's a great place to learn about and enjoy the natural beauty of the Ozark region.

Wonders of Wildlife Living Zooquarium (all ages)

500 West Sunshine Street, Springfield 65807; (417) 890–9453; www.wondersofwildlife.org. Open daily May through October 10:00 A.M. to 8:00 P.M., November to April 10:00 A.M. to 6:00 P.M. $$–$$$.

Springfield's newest attraction—featuring sharks, otters, and more than 160 other live species—is itself a whole new kind of critter. Its unique architecture uses a combination of wood beams and glass to give visitors the airy illusion of being in the Ozarks. Nature lovers will enjoy viewing the animals in their natural settings and will be amazed when taking an entertaining, informing, and tranquil Walk in the Ozarks—all indoors!

Stops along the way include an otter pool; a 150,000-gallon pond fed by a waterfall from an "underground" river that is home to a family of beavers and a community of fish; and Tumbling Creek Cave, with a colony of live bats. An exhibit on predators, such as the coyote, wolf, black bear, grizzly bear, and mountain lion, is near Bobcat Cave, with a pair of live bobcats.

Visitors are immersed in the various environments, from the waterfall, limestone bluffs, and sinkholes in the Ozark Hills Habitat to the numerous "underwater" vantage points in many exhibits. An enormous 220,000-gallon tank, filled with nurse sharks, rays, tarpon, sea bass, bluefish, mackerel, bonefish, and dolphinfish, is curved so that visitors can step into a central area and, accompanied by soothing sounds, feel like they are surrounded by these impressive species in the middle of their natural habitat.

Bass Pro Shops Outdoor World (all ages)

1935 South Campbell Avenue, Springfield 65898; (417) 887–7334; www.basspro.com. Open Monday through Saturday 7:00 A.M. to 10:00 P.M., Sunday 9:00 A.M. to 6:00 P.M. Free admission. Sportsmen's Gallery open 8:00 A.M. to 8:00 P.M. $–$$.

You'll know why this is the most popular tourist attraction in Missouri the second you walk in the entrance, which, by the way, happens to be modeled after a massive Adirondack Mountains lodge, with a gigantic fireplace, bookcases, and other furnishings. Then it's into the balance of the 290,000-square-foot store, where you'll find the expected hunting and fishing supplies and equipment in an unmatched variety as well as wildlife gifts, art, and jewelry; hiking and camping equipment; sports and outdoor clothing for men, women, and children; and a 40,000-square-foot boat and recreational vehicle center that will make you think you're back outdoors.

There is a theme park atmosphere in the store, which includes a four-story waterfall; indoor rifle, pistol, and bow ranges; fish-feeding shows in a 140,000-gallon aquarium—one of five huge aquariums—with divers and a video; a McDonald's restaurant; a barbershop; a driving range and putting green; and a great seafood restaurant, Hemingway's Blue Water Cafe.

When you go, if you also intend to visit Wonders of Wildlife next door, plan to stay at least half a day. If you've got the time, be sure to go upstairs to the Sportsmen's Gallery. this museum displays more than 700 mounted animals as well as a fantastic collection of antlers and horns. Designate a meeting place and time in case you get separated, and take a map from the person who greets you when you enter. You will need it. This isn't merely a store—it's an experience your family won't want to miss. Special holiday events are featured throughout the year.

PFI Western Store (all ages)

Highway 65 and Battlefield Road, 2816 South Ingram Mill, Springfield 65804; (417) 889–2668. Open Monday through Saturday 9:00 A.M. to 7:00 P.M., Sunday from 11:00 A.M. to 5:00 P.M.

The families of mothers who are going to let their children grow up to be cowboys won't want to miss the largest Western store in the state. It has a 16-foot video wall, Western fashions for all ages, and more than 10,000 pairs of boots on display.

Incredible Pizza Company (all ages)

2850 South Campbell Avenue, Springfield; (417) 887–3030. Open 11:00 A.M. to 9:00 P.M. Sunday through Thursday; 11:00 A.M. to 10:00 P.M. Friday and Saturday. Buffet $–$$; rides $–$$.

There's too much going on here to just call this a restaurant. There is a buffet loaded with pizza, pasta, desserts, and an 80-item salad bar; bottomless drinks are 25 cents But there also are go-karts, bumper cars, miniature golf, and dozens of interactive games.

Putt Putt Golf and Games (all ages)

3240 South Campbell Avenue, Springfield 65807; (417) 889–7888. Daily hours in summer but weekends only, weather permitting, in the winter. $.

Three—count 'em, three—eighteen-hole miniature golf courses, batting cages, and a video arcade offer a variety of family entertainment options.

Missouri Sports Hall of Fame (all ages)

3861 East Stan Musial Drive, Springfield 65809; (417) 889–3100; www.mosportshalloffame.com. Open Monday through Saturday 10:00 A.M. to 4:00 P.M., Sunday noon to 4:00 P.M. $–$$.

The interactive displays and authentic sports memorabilia here document Missouri's greatest sports heroes in a way that kids will love. They can peer through the open window of a real race car, listen to five recorded pep talks by former St. Louis Cardinals and Kansas City Royals manager Whitey Herzog, hear themselves call play-by-play with the best in the broadcasting business, or experience taking a fast one over the plate from a pitching machine simulating the pitching speeds of several of the greatest contemporary pitchers in baseball. St. Louis resident Bob Costas also narrates several films, including a seven-minute film about the Missouri Sports Hall of Fame.

Southwest Missouri State University Campus (all ages)

Hammons Student Center, 661 South John Q. Hammons Parkway, and Juanita K. Hammons Hall for the Performing Arts, 525 South John Q. Hammons Parkway, Springfield 65806; (417) 836–7678. Admission fees charged; call for schedules and prices.

Depending on the time of the year, you can watch the SMSU Bears play football, basketball, baseball, or soccer, in a new stadium, or you can catch one of the many theatrical performances or shows that play Hammons Hall.

Discovery Center (all ages)

438 St. Louis Street, Springfield 65806; (417) 862–9910; www.discoverycenterofspringfield.org. Open Tuesday through Thursday 9:00 A.M. to 5:00 P.M., Friday 9:00 A.M. to 8:00 P.M., Saturday 10:00 A.M. to 5:00 P.M., Sunday 1:00 to 5:00 P.M. $$; children ages 2 and under free.

This interactive, hands-on environment is a cross between science and children's museums that will appeal to kids from ages two to eighty. The goal is to bring an understanding of our world—from environmental and health issues to hometown economics—through a challenging environment composed of interactive exhibits. Paleolab uses fossils and other clues to explore the distant past; Energy Works shows you how energy works. In Wonderland children ages six and under can work with numbers, play with magnetic boards, and explore the unexpected power of a nearly unspoken word with a whisper tube. In Discovery Town, visitors pass through the facades of businesses to observe the inner workings of a television station, newspaper, bank, market, travel company, and other businesses found in any town anywhere.

Wilson's Creek National Battlefield (all ages)

Highways 182 and ZZ, 10 miles west of Springfield; send mail to 6424 West Farm Road 182, Republic 65738; (417) 732–2662; www.nps.gov.wicr. Open daily 8:00 A.M. to 5:00 P.M. $.

Here is a national park encompassing the rolling hills that were the site of a bitter struggle for control of Missouri that marked the state's entrance into the Civil War. The visitor center offers engaging displays that children will find fascinating and a video that provides a good background on the people and events of the battle.

Self-guided auto and walking tours of the park let your family set their own pace as

Park **Call**

Missouri's excellent state park system is operated by the Department of Natural Resources. Call (800) 334–6946 or (800) 379–2419 (TDD) around the clock for recorded information, or during daily office hours to reach an attendant, or visit online at www.mostateparks.com. Campsites can be reserved by calling (877) 422–6766 at least forty-eight hours in advance. There is an $8.50 registration fee, in addition to the rental fee, for the service.

they explore the now peaceful and serene site of this hallowed ground where in one day 500 men died, 2,000 were wounded, and Union Brigadier General Nathaniel Lyon became the first general in the war to lose his life in battle. You can follow the course of the battle as you read the maps and historical information along the tour trail. Guided tours, historic weapons firing demonstrations, and living-history events are held periodically. Call ahead to find out about scheduled activities.

General Sweeny's Museum of Civil War History (all ages)

Highway ZZ, north of Wilson's Creek National Battlefield; send mail to 5228 South State Highway 22, Republic 65738; (417) 732–1224; www.civilwarmuseum.com. Open Wednesday through Sunday 10:00 A.M. to 5:00 P.M. March 1 through October 31. $; children ages 4 and under free.

The museum has several thousand artifacts from the Civil War, primarily from the fighting in Missouri, Arkansas, Kansas, and the Indian Territory. Organized chronologically, fifty-plus exhibits take you from the violence in "Bleeding Kansas" in the 1850s to the surrender of the last Confederate troops of Gen. Stand Watie at Doakville Indian Territory on June 23, 1865. The story is told with a variety of artifacts, including rare photos, flags, medical instruments, swords, and guns.

History Museum for Springfield and Greene County (all ages)

Third floor of City Hall, 830 Boonville Avenue, Springfield 65802; (417) 864–1976; www.historymuseumsgc.org. Open Tuesday through Saturday 10:30 A.M. to 4:30 P.M. $.

Built in 1894, the City Hall building has great historical significance, having served as a United States Customs House and a post office. The museum collections include artifacts from all facets of life in southwest Missouri in the past two centuries. There are more than 15,000 antiques, china, dolls, and pieces of furniture; more than 30,000 books and documents; and nearly 7,000 historical photographs that are rotated through several exhibits each year.

Air & Military Museum (all ages)

2305 East Kearney Street, Springfield 65803; (417) 864–7997; www.ammomuseum.org. Open Tuesday through Saturday noon to 4:00 P.M. $.

This museum displays memorabilia and equipment of American and foreign armed forces. It also has a comprehensive archive on the history of aviation and United States military history, and it is headquarters of the Ozark Mountain squadron of the Confederate Air Force.

Gray/Campbell Farmstead (all ages)

2400 South Scenic Avenue (in Nathanael Greene Park), Springfield 65807; (417) 862–6293. Open Saturday and Sunday 1:30 to 4:30 P.M. May through September, by appointment in April and October Sunday only. Free admission.

The farmstead contains the oldest house in Springfield, a log house dating from 1856, and two crib barns. Costumed docents and others put on demonstrations of crafts and nineteenth-century living during Sheep and Wool Days, held the second Sunday in June, and the 1850s Lifestyle Exposition, held the third Saturday and Sunday in September.

Japanese Stroll Garden (all ages)

2400 South Scenic Avenue in Nathanael Greene Park, Springfield 65807; (417) 864–

1049; www.parkboard.org. Open Thursday through Monday only 9:00 A.M. to 7:30 P.M. April through October. $; children ages 12 and under free.

When you take a leisurely stroll along the manicured paths, you'll find a tea hut, arched bridge, and stepping-stones in this charming seven-and-a-half-acre walled garden. Come prepared for a lengthy walk across the park to the garden.

Tilt (all ages)

2825 South Glenstone Avenue, Springfield 65804, (417) 889–6755; www.tilt.com. Open 10:00 A.M. to 9:00 P.M. Monday through Saturday, 10:00 A.M. to 6:00 P.M. Sunday. Games are individually priced. $–$$

This full-blown arcade has dozens of games and is located in a mall, which, when game time is over, should give parents time to pick up other items that might be needed on the trip. Tickets are awarded for prize redemption.

Jordan Valley Ice Park (all ages)

635 East Trafficway Street, Springfield 65806; (417) 866–7444; www.icepark.org. Open daily; call for public hours. $–$$

Two indoor National Hockey League regulation-size skating rinks provide ice skating year-round for the entire family. Skate rental and a concession stand offering drinks and sandwiches are available at the park, which is the home rink for the Southwest Missouri State University hockey team.

Battlefield Station Family Hobbies (all ages)

220 West Battlefield Road, Springfield 65807; (417) 887–5592. Open 10:00 A.M. to 8:00 P.M. Monday through Saturday; 1:00 to 6:00 P.M. Sunday. Free admission.

A visual delight, this store is a nice diversion, with model railroad displays inside and out, railroad memorabilia, collectibles, and hobby supplies galore.

Ted E. Bear's Toy Factory (all ages)

1839 East Independence Street, Suite W, Springfield; (417) 823–7883. Open 10:00 A.M. to 7:00 P.M. Monday through Saturday, 1:00 to 5:00 P.M. Sunday. Free admission.

If you want to make a stuffed toy, you can choose from more than sixty animals and outfits, and choose the animal's eye color and the degree of softness, based on how much stuffing you put in. It doesn't cost anything to look, but if you want to make an animal, they cost from $9.00 to $35.00.

Richardson's Candy House (all ages)

3857 South Campbell Avenue, Springfield; (417) 883–3900; www.candyhouse.net. Open 9:30 A.M. to 8:00 P.M. Monday through Saturday; noon to 6:00 P.M. Sunday. Free admission.

You can watch candy makers at work and then buy from a delicious assortment that includes hand-dipped chocolates, fudge, brittle, caramel nut corn, English toffee, and more.

Ash Grove

Ozarks Afro-American Heritage Museum (all ages)

107 West Main, Ashgrove, 65604; (417) 672–3104; www.oaahm.org. Open 9:00 A.M. to 1:00 P.M. Tuesday through Thursday, 10:00 A.M. to 2:00 P.M. Saturday or by appointment. Admission free; donations accepted.

The museum documents local African-American life from slavery times to the present through a collection of everyday and unusual items. Exhibits include quilts and textiles created by slaves and their descendents, hand-built furniture and farm implements dating to the 1800s, and pastel portraits and photographs of local African-American families.

Ozark

This tiny town just south of Springfield celebrates its founding more than 150 years ago each June with **Village Days.** Festivities include live entertainment, canoe races, tug-of-war contests, reenactments of famous gunfights, a petting zoo, a street dance, and games for kids.

Later in the year, from November to early January, Finley River Park is dressed up with lights and displays for a **Festival of Lights,** and a Christmas festival, parade, and lighting ceremony are held to kick off the season. For hours and dates for either event, call the Ozark Area Chamber of Commerce, (417) 581–6139.

Doennig Sport Swings and Ozark Paintball (ages 10 and up)

Highway 65 South to Highway EE, then east to 671 Jackson Spring Road, Ozark 65721, where you'll find the barn with swings painted on the roof; (417) 443–6600. Swings open to public Friday and Saturday 7:00 to 9:30 P.M. and Saturday 10:00 P.M. to midnight. $$. Call for schedule of public paintball sessions and prices.

You probably won't find this place in many tourist guidebooks. This homegrown attraction features several buildings with swinging apparatus—for singles and doubles—rigged up for anyone brave enough to swing away. Parents are required to sign releases for children ages seventeen and younger. Hayrides, bonfires, horseshoe pitching, and paintball games are also provided. The paintball playing areas includes fields with hay fortresses and underground tunnels. This place is not for the faint of heart and is best suited for older children and teens. If you or your kids want to swing on the wild side, this is the place.

Ava

As you leave the Springfield area and travel southwest, you'll notice a change to rural, sparsely populated countryside, much of it natural and unspoiled. Across the southern half of the state, 1.5 million acres have been protected as national forest land. The Mark Twain National Forest provides recreation, nature study, and incredible opportunities for families wanting to get away from it all and enjoy natural splendor. Call the Ava district office (417– 683–4428) for information and directions before you visit, because you could easily get lost in these wilderness and semiwilderness areas.

Glade Top Trail (all ages)

From Springfield, Highway 65 South to State Highway 125, P.O. Box 188, Ava 65608; (417) 683–4428; www.fs.fed.us/r9/marktwain. Free admission. Open year-round.

This 17-mile gravel road designated a National Scenic Byway offers your family the chance to view spectacular vistas of mountains and glades and catch sight of wild turkeys, deer, roadrunners, lizards, and other wildlife in their habitats. This area is especially beautiful during spring wildflower season and when the leaves turn in the fall.

Hercules Glade (ages 5 and up)

From Springfield, Highway 65 South to Highway 160, then east to entrance; P.O. Box 188, Ava 65608; (417) 683–4428; www.fs.fed.us/r9/marktwain. Free admission. Open year-round.

This wilderness area offers more than 12,000 acres of isolated and challenging trails. Get directions before you go, and bring everything you will need.

Chadwick Motorcycle Use Area (ages 5 and up)

From Ozark, Highway 14 east to Sparta, 125 south to the City of Chadwick, Highway HH from Chadwick to the area; P.O. Box 188 Ava 65608; (417) 683–4428; www.fs.fed.us/r9/marktwain.

Daily permit fees for RVs are $5.00. Overnight camping fee is $5.00 per person.

If your family owns motorized recreational vehicles, you can use them on the 110 miles of trail. Several campgrounds, picnic facilities, and hiking trails are available in this area. There are no admission charges to national forest areas.

Bucks and Spurs Ranch (ages 5 and up)

South of Ava off Highway A, Route 4, Box 740, Ava 65608; (417) 683–2381; www.bucksand spurs.com. Three- and six-day packages are available. Children ages 3 and under **free.** Call for rates and availability.

This is a 1,000-acre working horse and cattle ranch open to city slickers and others who want to try their hand at the cowboy life. You and your kids can enjoy trail rides along Big Beaver Creek and in the surrounding countryside adjacent to the national forest and share in the chores necessary to keep the ranch running, such as driving cattle or riding fence with the ranch hands. Ranch-style meals are served on the trail or in the ranch house. An unforgettable vacation is waiting for you if you're looking for a tourist experience that hasn't been prettied up.

For More Information

Ava Area Chamber of Commerce.
P.O. Box 1103, Ava 65608;
(417) 683–4594;
www.avachamber.org.

Theodosia

In the southernmost part of the region, the tiny town of Theodosia sits on the shore of **Bull Shoals Lake**, known for great bass fishing and less developed than the two larger lakes farther west. This part of Bull Shoals is the most rugged and offers a more isolated, relaxed experience than the lake areas closer to Branson. The main activities here are fishing and enjoying the unspoiled scenery and abundant wildlife that live along the shoreline.

Theodosia Park (all ages)

Highway 160 at the bridge over Bull Shoals Lake, Theodosia 65761; (417) 273–4626; http://reserveusa.com; (877–444–6777 year-round for reservations). Park is open April through October. Campsites are $13.00 to $16.00 per day.

This park has clean rest rooms and a protected swimming area, and the campsites have hot showers.

Theodosia Marina-Resort (all ages)

Highway 160 west of the bridge, Theodosia 65761; (417) 273–4444. Cottages are $85 for up to four people, $6.00 each additional person. Motels rates for doubles range from $55 and up.

This is a full-service marina where you can rent fishing boats, ski boats, and tubes. The resort has a year-round motel and five housekeeping cottages as well as an outdoor swimming pool, tennis courts, and a playground.

For More Information

Theodosia Area Chamber of Commerce. P.O. Box 11, Theodosia 65761; (417) 273–4111; www.missourichamber.com/theodosia.

Bull Shoals Lake and White River Area. P.O. Box 344, Isabella 65676; (417) 273–4020; www.bullshoalslake.org.

Forsyth

As you travel to the west from Theodosia toward Branson you'll encounter many small towns nestled in the Ozark hills. Some are on the shores of one of the lakes in this area and offer great water recreation opportunities. The scenic river bluffs along Bull Shoals Lake are great for wildlife viewing.

For More Information

Forsyth Chamber of Commerce. P.O. Box 777, Forsyth 65653; (417) 546–2741; www.forsyth-mo.com.

Rockaway Beach

Rockaway Beach is a tiny resort community on the banks of Lake Taneycomo. This 22-mile lake has a dam at each end and has unusually cold water. It offers excellent fishing opportunities but because of the water temperature is not conducive to most water sports. The lake is renowned for trout fishing—more than 800,000 rainbow and German brown trout are taken from it every year.

Along Beach Boulevard downtown are marinas where you can rent paddleboats, canoes, pontoons, fishing boats, and fishing equipment, and hire guides. You can walk along the lakeshore and enjoy Rockaway Beach City Park, where you'll find picnic tables, a children's playground, **free** boat access, and a public fishing dock. Call (800) 798–0178 from 9:00 A.M. to 1:00 P.M. Monday through Friday.

For More Information

Rockaway Beach Bureau of Tourism.
P.O. Box 1004, Rockaway Beach 65740; (800) 798–0178; www.rockawaybeachchamber.com/tourism.htm.

Branson

You can't tackle this entertainment boomtown without a good city road map and a clear idea of what your family wants to do. There are too many choices and too many exciting attractions to wander around town without a plan. So make your first stop at one of the city's two visitor centers. They are both just off U.S. Highway 65—on Missouri Highway 248 and U.S. Highway 160. Here you can get lodging information, show times, prices and locations, and more tourist literature than you can carry. There is a wide range of ticket prices for adults and children. Most theaters offer three shows daily: early afternoon, late afternoon, and evening; many also offer a morning show. Organized family vacationers can call in advance and hit town ready to go. Call (417) 334–4136 or (800) 214–3661, or visit online at www.explorebranson.com.

Branson has become known as the live-entertainment capital of the world; the city has more theater seats than Broadway and more than forty theaters. More than five million visitors a year come for the family shows and entertainment. Every show in town is appropriate for children, there is no gambling in the area, and there are few nightclubs. The entertainers put on enthusiastic performances and always seem to be having as much fun as, if not more than, the visitors.

Downtown Branson also has a renovated lakefront with an embankment topped by wide sidewalks and green areas with park benches, public fishing docks, and picnic spots. In **North Beach Park** you can feed the flocks of birds that congregate there. You'll find Canada geese, mallard ducks, and other water birds ready and willing to accept any and all food offerings you bring. Several full-service marinas are available for boat rental or access to the lake.

Incredible Acrobats of China (all ages)

MGH Performing Arts Center, 464 State Highway 248, Branson 65616; (877) 212–4462. Shows at 8:00 P.M. daily May through November; many 3:00 P.M. shows but check for scheduling. $$$–$$$$; children ages 2 and under free if sitting on a parent's lap.

This internationally acclaimed troupe of thirty acrobats, magicians, and dancers performs seemingly impossible feats every day. Even after you see it, you won't believe some of it.

Hollywood Wax Museum (all ages)

3030 West Highway 76, Branson 65616; (417) 337–8277; www.hollywoodwax.com. Open daily 8:00 A.M. to midnight. $$–$$$; children ages 4 and under free.

Mark McGwire, Marilyn Monroe, Rambo, Charlie Chaplin, and even Elvis, of course, are among the more than 170 wax figures displayed on two floors.

Baldknobbers Hillbilly Jamboree (all ages)

2835 West Highway 76, Branson 65616; (800) 998–8908; www.baldknobbers.com. Shows at 8:00 P.M. Monday through Saturday March through December. $$–$$$; children ages 2 and under free if sitting on a parent's lap.

This must-see show—the first show in Branson—has been offering hillbilly music and laughs since Dwight D. Eisenhower was president and is still packing people in.

Presleys' Country Jubilee (all ages)

2920 76 Country Boulevard, Branson 65617; (417) 334–4874; www.presleys.com. Shows are 8:00 P.M. mid-March through mid-December. $$$–$$$$; children ages 2 and under free if sitting on a parent's lap. A family pass is available.

Four generations of the Presley family (no relation to Elvis) sing old country favorites, new country sounds, and gospel harmonies. They dance and cut up in a musical and comedy stage show that the whole family will enjoy. They also do a great Christmas show.

Lawrence Welk Show (all ages)

The Welk Resort Center and Champagne Theater, 1984 Highway 165, Branson 65616; (800) 505–9355; www.welkresortbranson.com. Shows are at 2:00 and/or 8:00 P.M., with the Christmas show starting in early November. $$$–$$$$; children ages 3 and under free.

If your family enjoys lavish stage shows with singing, dancing, and fancy costumes, not to mention the Lennon sisters and their singing daughters, and the amazing Joann Castle with her ragtime piano, you'll want to catch this show. Many kids also will love the beautiful and very entertaining Christmas show as well.

Braschler Music Show (all ages)

Braschler Theater, 3044 Shepherd of the Hills Expressway, Branson 65616; (417) 334–4363; www.braschlermusicshow.com. Open April through December; shows at 3:00 P.M. Monday through Friday, 8:00 P.M. Sunday. $$$; children ages 12 and under free.

This variety show offers enough country, gospel, and comedy entertainment to keep the whole family happy.

Dixie Stampede (all ages)

1525 West Highway 76, Branson 65616; (800) 520–5544. Closed January to mid-March. Afternoon and evening show times vary, so call for a schedule. Admission, including dinner, is $39.00 for adults, $23.00 for children ages 4 through 11; children ages 3 and under free if they sit on a parent's lap and share the parent's food.

In this unusual dining experience, you sit and eat rotisserie chicken, barbecue pork loin, soup, potato wedges, corn on the cob, biscuits, and dessert as the show takes place in an enormous arena in front of you. The ninety-minute show features thirty-two performing horses, relay and buckboard races, and plenty of silly audience participation. Kids will love arriving early to see the stars of the show—the horses—in their stalls surrounding the theater.

IMAX Entertainment Complex (all ages)

3562 Shepherd of the Hills Expressway, Branson 65616; (417) 335–4832; www.branson imax.com. Open daily 8:00 A.M. to 9:00 P.M. Call for show times. Admission for IMAX and Elite Cinema, $$; children ages 3 and under free. Admission to Little Opry Theatre, $$$–$$$$; children ages 12 and under free.

One of several IMAX movies starts every hour and is shown on a six-story-high movie screen with a 22,000-watt sound system. The movie *Ozarks: Legacy and Legend* tells about the history of the Ozark people; it plays on a regular basis and shouldn't be missed if you find these hills a fascinating place and want to know more about them. The movie is forty-eight minutes long, which is the general length of an IMAX film, and was created just for Branson tourists and can't be seen anywhere else. Other popular IMAX films rotate through the theater, which also periodically screens popular 35 mm films, such as *Titanic*. At five times the size of a normal theater screen, the effect is stunning and the sound unsurpassed. The complex also has Elite Cinema, which shows first-run theatrical films, and Little Opry Theatre, which shows musical and theatrical productions.

Shepherd of the Hills Homestead (all ages)

5586 West Highway 76, Branson 65616; (417) 334–4191 or (800) 653–6288; www.the shepherdofthehills.com. Park opens 10:00 A.M. Monday through Saturday April through October, closes 8:00 P.M. through mid-August, 7:00 P.M. thereafter. Shows daily at 7:30 P.M. A combination ticket that includes the drama, a meal, a tour, admission to the tower, and all attractions at the Homestead, except horseback rides and the Clydesdale wagon ride, is $37.50 for adults, $18.95 for children ages 4 through 15; children ages 3 and under free. Call for current price of a special family pass.

The tourist influx to Branson started with the publication in 1907 of Harold Bell Wright's novel *The Shepherd of the Hills*. One of the best values in Branson is this mini–theme park where the story is kept alive. During a fifty-five-minute tour you can see places where the author stayed while writing the book and ride up 225-foot Inspiration Tower to get a panoramic view of the Ozarks. The one-price admission lets you enjoy the hills, pony rides, a music show, and a great playground for the kids. Several shops and restaurants also are on the premises. Horseback riding ($14.00 per person) and a Clydesdale wagon ride ($5.00 per person) are available during the summer.

Christmas Is **BIG** in Branson

The entire city of Branson and the surrounding towns celebrate Ozark Mountain Christmas during the months of November and December. Almost every theater has a special Christmas show, and the streets, the Ozark hills, and most buildings are strung with lights and decorated with Christmas cheer. Several neighboring towns offer lighting displays, and bridges over the lakes are decked with lights that reflect off the quiet water for an enchanted atmosphere throughout the whole area. For information about special holiday events, lighting displays, and shows call (417) 334–4136 or (800) 241–3661.

Each night a spectacular drama based on the book is staged in an authentic outdoor setting, featuring powerful scenes of masked vigilantes on horseback and a burning cabin. It is definitely a must-see in Branson and a show you and your children will not soon forget. The Homestead hosts special events throughout the year and has the Trail of Lights, a wonderful drive-through lighting display from early November through early January.

Silver Dollar City (all ages)

Highway 165 southwest of Branson, 399 Indian Point Road, Branson 65616; (417) 338–2611 or (800) 952–6626; www.silverdollarcity.com. Open daily 9:30 A.M. to 7:00 P.M. late May through late August, but park opens in April with shorter hours. Call for off-season hours and prices. $$$$; children ages 3 and under free.

Dedicated to turn-of-the-century crafts, music, and memories, this forty-acre theme park is designed to resemble an 1890s mining town. The newest ride is Wildfire, an exhilarating looping roller coaster. But the range of activities also includes Buzzsaw Falls, a thrilling water ride with roller-coaster movements; ten other rides; Splash Harbor, a four-level structure with a variety of water-propelling gadgets; and Tom Sawyer's Landing, a fantastic children's play area with tunnels and climbing structures that could keep your kids busy for hours. Country music shows take place in nine theaters of various sizes, and more than one hundred resident craftspeople demonstrate their skills and sell their wares in shops throughout the park.

Every evening concludes with a two-hour extravaganza of country music at the outdoor Echo Hollow amphitheater. Shows throughout the day range from silly to serious and provide something for everyone's taste.

McHaffie's Pioneer Homestead is a living-history area inside the park where your family can tour authentic pioneer buildings and join in the activities of daily life during pioneer times.

A tour of Marvel Cave is included with admission to the park, and you'll want to see for yourself how this cave lives up to its name. It has a twenty-story Cathedral Room and is the deepest cave in the state, not to mention one of the largest caves in the country. As you descend all the stairs, don't worry about little ones climbing back up. Cable trains return you to the surface from the cave's deepest point.

Amazing
Missouri Facts

The Missouri Compromise admitted Missouri and what other state into the Union at the same time?

Maine

White Water (all ages)

3501 West Highway 76, Branson 65616; (417) 336–7100 or (800) 532–7529; www.silver
dollarcity.com. Open daily 10:00 A.M. to 6:00 P.M. from the end of May through the beginning of September. Extended hours June through August. $$$$; children ages 3 and under
free.

Water activities and wet rides are provided in a tropical-oasis atmosphere at this twelve-
acre water park. The twelve rides include the 207-foot triple-drop Paradise Plunge, a
500,000-gallon wave pool, the lazy Paradise River, and Splash Island with tunnels, slides,
waterfalls, nozzles, and pools just for the little ones. Life jackets and certified lifeguards
are on hand so you can relax and let your children run free.

Showboat *Branson Belle* (all ages)

4800 State Highway 165, Branson 65616 (near Table Rock Dam); (417) 336–7171 or (800)
227–8587; www.silverdollarcity.com. Cruises depart four times a day April through Decem-
ber. $$$–$$$$; children ages 3 and under **free.**

You can enjoy a quiet cruise on Table Rock Lake on the elaborate 650-passenger *Branson
Belle*. Each cruise includes a meal and a production in the three-story opera hall highlight-
ing the showboat era of entertainment. You have twenty minutes after the meal to
explore the boat, which may not be enough time for your kids. If you want to see the lake
views, leave the table a little early.

Celebration City (all ages)

399 Indian Point Road, Branson 65616; (800) 575-9370; www.silverdollarcity.com. Open 3:30
P.M. daily, close 11:00 P.M. in the summer; 10:00 P.M. in the fall. $$$$; children ages 3 and
under **free.**

Billed as "The Night Place for Families," this cousin to Silver
Dollar City is divided into three distinct sections: Cele-
bration Street, Electric Boardwalk, and Route 66. Celebra-
tion Street has a Victorian tint, with a carousel, water
sculptures, fountains, and plenty of shops. Electric Board-
walk is loaded with rides, ranging from the Scram-
bler and the Accelerator, a tower-drop experience,

to the Fireball, which flips riders all about and over and back, and Shoot D Chutes, a log-flume ride guaranteed to get you wet. This area also is where the *Celebrate!* Laser Show is performed. Route 66, as its name implies, celebrates moving vehicles, such as the automobile—and by extension, speed—and life in the 1950s and '60s, replete with drive-in restaurants. Top rides here are Ferris Wheel and the Ozark Wildcat Wooden Roller Coaster, an eight-story structure that achieves speeds of up to 45 mph. But there also are several rides here, including a traditional Tilt-A-Whirl and the Jack Rabbit, a coaster that provides a 52-foot drop. The park has twenty rides in all, seven of them for the small fry; several theaters; a number of themed restaurants; and many shops selling souvenirs and nostalgic items. Money-saving combination packages with Silver Dollar City and White Water also are available; call for details.

Ride the Ducks (all ages)

2320 West Highway 76, Branson 65616; (417) 334–3825; www.ridetheducks.com. Open daily 8:00 A.M. to 5:00 P.M. March through December, weather permitting. Call for departure details. $$–$$$; children ages 3 and under free.

These eighty- to ninety-minute tours in World War II amphibious vehicles go over the dam and up Baird Mountain and then finish with a twenty- to twenty-five minute cruise on Table Rock Lake. Breakfast, lunch, and special Christmas lights tours also are available; call for information.

Thunder Road (all ages)

Highway 76 at the intersection of Gretna Road; 3235 West Highway 76, Branson 65616; (417) 334–5905. Open daily 9:00 A.M. to midnight March through October. Call for off-season hours. $–$$

Two miniature golf courses, single and double go-karts, bumper cars, batting cages, a bungee trampoline ride, a gyro orbiter ride, and the largest video arcade in the Branson area provide enough entertainment to keep the family busy for hours. No admission charge; individual ride tickets sold.

Pirate's Cove Adventure Golf (ages 4 and up)

2901 Green Mountain Drive, Branson 65616; (417) 336–6606. Open 9:00 A.M. to 11:00 P.M. beginning March 1. $$

Kids' activities abound here, with two eighteen-hole miniature courses with a pirates' hideout theme, a small video entertainment center, and a gift shop.

Ozark Mountain Water Ducks (all ages)

1836 Highway 76, Branson 65616; 1½ blocks west of the Dixie Stampede; (417) 336–2111. Open 8:00 A.M. to 6:00 P.M. daily March through November. $$–$$$; children ages 3 and under free.

Promising "more duck for your buck," these reconditioned World War II amphibious vehicles take you on an eighty-minute narrated sightseeing tour along a route that includes a trip by the dam and a twenty- to twenty-five-minute ride on Table Rock Lake.

The Track Family Fun Parks (all ages)

Five locations along Highway 76; (417) 334–1612; www.bransontracks.com. Track 3 is open year-round, weather permitting; seasonal hours on other tracks. $–$$; ask about ticket package with half-price-ride card.

Each of the Track's five locations on Highway 76 offers a distinctly different assortment of go-kart tracks, miniature golf, bumper boats, and kids' parks with rides for small children. Track 4 is the biggest and, in addition to all the other activities, offers a track exclusively for licensed drivers. Tracks 3 and 4 also have several rides for beginners ages three and up.

Table Rock Helicopter Tours (ages 10 and up)

3309 West Highway 76, Branson 65615; (417) 334–6102. Tours available 9:00 A.M. to 9:00 P.M. during the summer, 10:00 A.M. to 7:00 P.M. during the spring and fall. $$$$.

Here is an excellent way to enjoy the breathtaking scenery in the Ozark Mountains and the Branson area. You'll fly over the White River, Table Rock Dam, and the beautiful, crystal-clear Table Rock Lake. In the fall, the mountain forest is painted magnificent colors.

Branson Scenic Railway (all ages)

206 East Main Street (downtown), P.O. Box 924, Branson 65615; (417) 334–6100 or (800) 287–2462; www.bransontrain.com. Box office is open daily 7:30 A.M. to 4:30 P.M. Train departs three or four times a day; call for times. $$$–$$$$; children ages 2 and under free.

This forty-minute round-trip train ride provides a relaxing view of Ozark Mountain valleys and ridges, many of which are inaccessible by road. You depart from the restored Branson railroad depot, which dates from the early 1900s, and travel in vintage luxury passenger cars complete with domed roofs.

Ruth and Paul Henning Conservation Area (all ages)

West Highway 76 just past the Branson city limits; (417) 334–3324 or (417) 895–6880; www.mdc.state.mo.us. (Click on "Places to Go" at the top left of screen.) Open 4:00 A.M. to 10:00 P.M. for walkers, 8:00 A.M. to dark for automobiles. Free admission.

This certainly is one of the best wildlife- and nature-viewing areas in the state. Start with a walk in the woods and go to the scenic lookout area where you can get a spectacular view of the countryside. Use the nature trails for leisurely walks over the rolling hills or for serious exercise. Walk along the Boulder Glade Trail and watch for broad-winged hawks on the overlook, or keep an eye out for tarantulas, scorpions, and lizards in the open glades.

Main Street Marina (all ages)

500 East Main Street, Branson 65615; (417) 334–2263; mainstreetmarina.com. Open daily 7:00 A.M. to 5:00 P.M.

This is a good place to rent fishing, bass, and pontoon boats for chasing the fish in Lake Taneycomo or simply taking a ride on it.

Branson Trout Dock (all ages)

305 Boxcar Willie Drive, Branson 65615; (417) 334–3703. Open daily 7:00 A.M. to 6:00 P.M.

You can rent a Bass Tracker boat, a new Sun Tracker pontoon, or a variety of other fishing boats, and take home some of the marvelous trout in Lake Taneycomo.

Ripley's Believe It or Not Museum of Amazement (ages 10 and up)

3326 West Highway 76, Branson 65616; (800) 998–4418, extension 2. Open daily 9:00 A.M. to 11:00 P.M. year-round. $$–$$$; children ages 3 and under **free.**

As you drive through town, your kids will notice a building that is falling apart—or at least appears to be—and they'll likely want to explore this strange combination of children's museum, freak show, and depository of oddball collections. It requires considerable reading and can be discomforting for the squeamish, so it's not appropriate for small children. But it features many wild and interesting things, some educational and some just weird. Older kids and teens will enjoy it the most.

Dick's Oldtime 5 & 10 (all ages) ⊜

103 West Main Street, Branson 65616; (417) 334–2410. Open 8:30 A.M. year-round, closes at 9:00 P.M. April through January, 5:30 P.M. otherwise.

This wonderful store features more than 50,000 items stocked floor-to-ceiling and overflowing in the aisles. Shopping here is like stepping into a 1930s dime store. This is one shopping trip your kids won't want to miss.

Grand Country Inn (all ages)

1945 West Highway 76, Branson 65616; (417) 335–3535 or (800) 828–9068. Checkout time is 2:00 P.M.; check-in time is 11:00 A.M. $$$; children ages 17 and under **free.**

This mall complex can provide a one-stop vacation destination for families. The 319-room hotel has its own small water park, Splash Country, two outdoor pools, one indoor pool, and a small laundry room. Next door you'll find a theater offering five country-music shows daily, a mall with twenty shops, an indoor tropical-style miniature golf course, the Aladdin Arcade with video games, and a game room with pool tables, and more.

Table Rock **Lake**

This 53,000-acre lake immediately southwest of Branson offers endless opportunities for boating, swimming, and fishing. Known as an excellent lake for bass fishing, it also has catfish, walleye, and bluegill in abundance. The exceptionally clear water makes it a favorite with scuba divers.

Shepherd of the Hills Fish Hatchery and Conservation Center

(all ages)

Located off Highway 165 below Table Rock Dam on Lake Taneycomo; 483 Hatchery Road, Branson 65616; (417) 334–4865; www.mdc.state.mo.us. Open daily 9:00 A.M. to 5:00 P.M. **Free** admission.

Fascinating exhibits from the Missouri Department of Conservation describe the process used to raise trout for release in the lakes. Guided tours, Monday through Friday from Memorial Day to Labor Day, and an introductory film provide a good overview of the area and the facility. Several aquariums will give your kids a close-up look at native Ozark fish. Trails beginning at the hatchery will lead you through a variety of natural settings, from the shoreline of the lake to the high rocky bluffs overlooking the White River Valley. The trails provide a great location for wildlife sightings and bird-watching. During the winter you can observe birds of prey, shorebirds, and aquatic wildlife feeding throughout the area.

Dewey Short Visitors Center (all ages)

Table Rock Dam, 4600 Highway 165, Branson 65616; (417) 334–4104. Open daily 9:00 A.M. to 5:00 P.M. April 1 through December 15. **Free** admission.

The center features *Taming of La Riviere Blanche* (Taming of the White River), a twenty-minute film that shows how the dam was built and what the area used to be like; four exhibits showing what the seasons look like in the Ozarks; and a looped nature trail. You also can take the kids on an educational tour of the powerhouse to see how the dam generates electricity.

Table Rock State Park (all ages)

5272 State Highway 165, Branson 65616 (¾ mile south of Table Rock Dam); (417) 334-4704 or (800) 334–6946; www.mostateparks.com. Tent campsites are $8.00 per day, electrical hookups are $14.00 per day. Call (877) 422–6766 at least forty-eight hours in advance for camping reservations. There is an $8.50 registration fee.

The park has 163 campsites for tents and recreational vehicles, an excellent day picnic area, and plenty of frontage on beautiful Table Rock Lake.

State Park Marina and Dive Shop (ages 5 and up)

Table Rock State Park, 380 State Park Marina Road, Branson 65616; (417) 334–3069; www.boatbranson.com. Open 7:00 A.M. to 8:00 P.M. daily during summer season, shorter hours in fall; closed November 1 through March 1. Call for rates and availability. For information about *Spirit of America*, see next entry or call (800) 867–2459.

You can rent a wide variety of water vehicles, including jet skis, pontoon boats, ski boats, canoes, paddleboats, and fishing boats. You also can parasail and scuba dive or take a ride on the catamaran *Spirit of America*.

Spirit of America (all ages)
Docked at State Park Marina and Dive Shop, 380 State Park Marina Road, Branson 65616; (800) 867–2459; www.sailbranson.com. Cruises from April through mid-September. Call for hours. $$–$$$; children ages 4 and under free.

You and the family can enjoy the lake in peace and quiet with a ninety-minute excursion on board this forty-nine-passenger catamaran. If you have a mind to, matey, you can help put up the sails that propel the craft. The captain says once you take this cruise, you'll return to do it again and again.

Jim Stafford Show (all ages)
Jim Stafford Theatre; 3440 West Highway 76, Branson 65616; (417) 335–8080; www.jim stafford.com. Shows Monday through Saturday at 8:00 P.M. and Wednesday at 2:00 P.M. $$–$$$$; children ages 6 and under free.

Comedian Jim Stafford, who came to everyone's attention years ago with the song "Spiders and Snakes," is as zany as ever. Your kids will love his hilarious comedy—including entertaining production numbers like "Don't Be Chicken When It's Time to Crow." The show is fun-filled from start to finish and has a spectacular segment with three-dimensional effects. He also has a great Christmas show, which starts in November.

For More Information

Branson/Lakes Area Convention & Visitors Bureau. (417) 334–8798 or (800) 214–3661; www.explorebranson.com.

Point Lookout

The drive south from Branson on U.S. Highway 65 offers a scenic view as you pass through rock outcroppings where the highway was blasted through the hills. Point Lookout, a tiny town just south of Branson, is home to the picturesque College of the Ozarks, or "C of O," as the students call it. This four-year liberal-arts college requires all students to work on campus to defray the cost of tuition. There are approximately eighty work areas located on campus, ranging from a theater and a radio station to a dairy farm and a bakery. Most areas on campus are open to the public, including Edward's Mill, where you can purchase whole-wheat flour, cornbread mix, and grits; a weaving studio featuring handwoven items from pot holders to clothing; and greenhouses where houseplants and flowers are sold. For information about the college, call (417) 334–6411.

Ralph Foster Museum (all ages)

College of the Ozarks campus; (417) 334–6411, extension 13407. Open Monday through Saturday 9:00 A.M. to 4:30 P.M. March through late November. $; children ages 18 and under free.

This museum houses a mind-boggling collection of 750,000 items pertaining to Ozark history and folklore. Some of the most popular items include the car from *The Beverly Hillbillies* television show, an enormous collection of weapons and firearms, a miniature circus, and life-size stuffed animals. There is a hands-on discovery room for children ages four through eight where kids can crawl through a cave, try on clothing, and examine a wide assortment of objects, such as stuffed animals, doctors' instruments, rocks, magnets, Braille documents, and drawing tools.

For More Information

Tablerock Lake/Kimberling City Chamber of Commerce. P.O. Box 495 NET, Kimberling City 65686; (417) 739–2564 or (800) 554–4444; www.tablerocklake.org.

Ridgedale

Big Cedar Lodge Resort, A Bass Pro Shop Property (all ages)

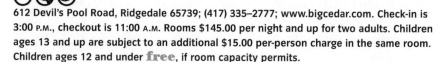

612 Devil's Pool Road, Ridgedale 65739; (417) 335–2777; www.bigcedar.com. Check-in is 3:00 P.M., checkout is 11:00 A.M. Rooms $145.00 per night and up for two adults. Children ages 13 and up are subject to an additional $15.00 per-person charge in the same room. Children ages 12 and under free, if room capacity permits.

Considered one of the best resorts in the country, Cedar Lodge is nestled in a fairly remote area of the Ozark hills on Table Rock Lake. It is a picturesque place with landscaped grounds and buildings designed in the grand style of wilderness hunting lodges of the past. The property was once a private vacation spot for two wealthy businessmen and has a rich history of stories as well as a resident ghost. Luxury accommodations are available in several lodge buildings or in private cottages and cabins. A full range of recreation options is offered, including horseback riding, carriage rides, hayrides, tennis, nature trails, a fitness center, golf, miniature golf, fishing, boat rental, and full marina services.

Port of Lights (all ages)

Off Highway 13 on a peninsula that juts into the lake, (800) 554–4444; www.tablerock lake.org/port_of_lights. Open daily dusk to midnight November and December. Admission is $5.00 per car.

This 3-mile, drive-through light extravaganza includes animated figures, holiday characters, and a 120-foot tunnel of snowflakes.

Slow Down and Take in the Scenery

The roads throughout this area provide beautiful panoramic views, but take them at a leisurely pace. You run the risk of you or your children getting extremely carsick. The rolling, dipping, twisting, turning roads are spectacular but can challenge even strong stomachs. For panoramic views of the lake, take Highway 86 west from Highway 65, then go north on Highway 13. The highway often follows the Old Wilderness Road used by Native Americans, early traders, and settlers.

Branson West (Lakeview)

The little town of Lakeview was renamed Branson West to take advantage of the publicity being lavished on the live-entertainment mecca just to the east. Branson West is close to many lakeside resorts, marinas, and campgrounds located directly on Table Rock Lake.

Talking Rocks Cavern (all ages)

South of Branson West off Highway 13 at 423 Fairy Cave Lane, Branson West 65737; (417) 272–3366, (800) 600–2283; www.talkingrockscavern.com. Open daily 9:00 A.M. to 7:00 P.M. June through August, closed in January; open daily 9:30 A.M. to 5:00 P.M. the rest of the year. $$–$$$; children ages 4 and under free.

One of the most beautiful caves in the state, Talking Rocks Cavern features a forty-five-minute tour dramatized by a light and sound show. Above the ground, a 400-acre nature preserve with hiking trails and a picnic area allows you to enjoy one of the most beautiful parts of the lake. You also can go gemstone panning, an activity in which you pay from $4.50 to $9.75 for a bag of minerals and other materials that you pour into a prospector's pan and "wash" until only your gemstones remain.

Indian Point

Tribesman Resort (all ages)

Six miles west of Branson, 416 Cave Lane, Branson 65616; (800) 447–3327; www.tribesman.nu. One-bedroom units start at $67 for four people, with an additional-person fee of $10 per person. Children ages 4 and under are free up to room limit.

This year-round resort has fifty-five family lodge units with full kitchens, three outdoor swimming pools, and an indoor swimming pool. A full range of activities for children during the summer months includes picnics, ice-cream socials, crafts, nature walks, and storytelling. There is a children's fishing hole, professional fishing guides can be hired, and pontoon, ski, and fishing boats can be rented.

For More Information

Indian Point Chamber of Commerce.
(800) 888–3313; www.indianpointchamber.com.

Shell Knob

As you leave the Branson area and travel west there are fewer attractions and vacation spots and more open spaces.

Timbers Resort (all ages)

Highway 39, at the foot of Shell Knob Mountain in the Mark Twain National Forest; send mail to Box 70, Shell Knob 65747; (800) 753–3082; www.shellknob.com. Cabins start at $80.00 for two adults; children ages 7 and under are free if within room's suggested capacity. There's a $10.00 per person fee for children ages 8 and over.

The resort is in a secluded, wooded setting on the main channel of Table Rock Lake. It has fifteen completely furnished cabins with fireplaces located about 150 feet from the water. A year-round facility, it has a heated pool with a vinyl dome, a playground, an outside hot tub, and a dock.

For More Information

Shell Knob Chamber of Commerce.
(417) 858–3300; www.shellknob.com.

Cassville

Roaring River State Park (all ages)

South of Cassville on Highway 112; Route 2, Box 2530, Cassville 65625; (417) 847–2539 or (800) 334–6946; www.mostateparks.com. Campsites are $8.00 for tents, $14.00 for electrical hookups. Cabins are $89 per night for two rooms—one double bed in each room—call (417) 847–2330 or (800) 334–6946; www.roaringriver.com. Lodge rooms are $84.50 per night and up.

The park is located on the southwestern edge of the Ozark Mountains and has more than 3,000 acres of rugged, scenic terrain. There are caves, springs, glades, and forested areas in the park, most of which is preserved in a natural state. You can see where more than twenty million gallons of water per day gush from a spring to form the headwaters of Roaring River. The stream is stocked daily from March through October and provides excellent fishing for rainbow trout. The park has a swimming pool, hiking trails, a stable where horses can be rented, 200 campsites, twenty-six cabins, and the Roaring River Inn, a twenty-five-room lodge with a restaurant.

Mark Twain National Forest Cassville District

This district has camping and picnic areas directly on Table Rock Lake. The **Big Bay** area offers thirty-eight campsites, drinking water, restrooms, and trailer space. Take Highway 76 south to Highway 39 south, then east on Highway YY. The **Piney Creek Wilderness,** more than 8,000 acres of hickory, oak, and pine forest with steep side slopes and deep hollows, has five isolated hiking and horseback-riding trails that total 13½ miles. To reach the trailhead, take Highway 76 east to Lake Road 76-6. For information call the Cassville district office at (417) 847–2144; www.fs.fed.us/r9/marktwain.

For More Information

Cassville Chamber of Commerce.
504 Main Street, Cassville 65625; (417)
847–2814; www.cassville.com.

Noel

Traveling to the southwestern corner of the state yields this tiny town flanked by three excellent canoeing streams: Elk River, Indian Creek, and Big Sugar Creek. You can arrange a float trip by canoe, boat, or tube on any one of these beautiful small streams, which are all rated for safe, family floats. Visit www.4noel.com to learn more about the area.

River Ranch Resort (ages 5 and up)
Highway 59 at the Elk River Bridge, Route 1, Box 126A, Noel 64854; (417) 475–6121 or (800) 951–6121; www.riverranchresort.com. Tent campsites are $7.00 per person, $25.00 a night for electrical hookups. Cabins are $60.00 to $225.00 per night, depending on capacity.

Tons of campsites and forty cabins on a full mile of riverfront make this an excellent place to set up camp for a float. You can rent a canoe, raft, or kayak, and resort employees will launch you 4 to 8 miles upstream and you can float back to your car, cabin, or campsite. Floating season is April through September, weather permitting. For availability and prices call (800) 951–6121.

Sycamore Landing (all ages)

Highway 59 north on the Elk River, P.O. Box 550, Noel 64854; (417) 475–6460 or (800) 475–6460; www.noelrafting.com. Rentals are $15.00 per person. Camping is $6.00 per person.

This is a great place to camp, thanks to the hot showers and a fifty-acre site on the Elk River that's fantastic for swimming and fishing. It's centrally located for easy access to several good floating streams. If you don't want to float or camp, you can swim and fish for a daily fee of $3.00 per person; children ages five and under **free.**

Bluff Dwellers' Cave (all ages)

State Highway 59 south of Noel; Route 2, Box 230, Noel 64854; (417) 475–3666; www.4noel.com/bluffd. Open daily 8:00 A.M. to 6:00 P.M. $–$$; children ages 4 and under free.

This living cave, which once sheltered an indigenous civilization, also has a museum of rocks, fossils, arrowheads, and minerals from all over the United States.

Pineville

Nestled in the Ozark foothills in prime float country, this little town of slightly more than 500 residents is the McDonald County seat. Each August it's also the site of **Jesse James Days,** a five-day festival commemorating the fact that actors Tyrone Power, Henry Fonda, Randolph Scott, and Nancy Kelly came to town with a crew from Hollywood to shoot the film *Jesse James* in 1938. The festival features a carnival, contests for kids, bingo, raffles, arts, crafts, food, and music nightly. Memorabilia from the film is on display at the McDonald County Library in Pineville. Call (417) 223–4368 for information.

Dube's Three River Campground, Inc. (all ages)

Highway 71 south to Junction W; drive 75 feet and turn right at King Street, go around bend, and follow signs to Dube's, 112 Rhine, P.O. Box 697, Pineville 64856; (417) 223–4746 or (800) 496–3261. Rental ranges from $19.00 to $35.00 per aluminum canoe. Camping is $4.00 per person. Children ages 5 and under free.

Three- and six-hour floats on Big Sugar Creek and the Elk River are popular here, and the campground, with tent and RV sites, has clean rest rooms, hot showers, and a dumping station.

Diamond

George Washington Carver National Monument (all ages)
West from Diamond of County Road V then south on Carver to 5646 Carver Road, Diamond 64840; (417) 325–4151; www.nps.gov/gwca. Open daily 9:00 A.M. to 5:00 P.M. No admission charge; donations requested.

The national park covers 210 acres of land that belonged to Moses and Susan Carver, the family who owned George's mother at the time of his birth and who raised him after the Civil War. Stop at the visitor center to hear the inspirational story of the slave child who grew up to become one of the greatest scientists of his day. Then you can walk along the short trails through beautiful wooded and prairie areas to see the Carver family cemetery, the 1881 Carver home, and the site of George's birth. It's also an excellent place for bird-watching and wildlife sightings. **Carver Day** in July celebrates the significance of the site with educational programs and music performances. **Prairie Day** is held every September at the park and features activities that celebrate early pioneer life, including plant identification walks, living-history demonstrations, musical performances, wagon rides, and hayrides. Only picnicking is permitted in the park.

Joplin

The city of Joplin is the hub of the four-state region where Missouri borders Kansas, Oklahoma, and Arkansas. Thanks to films, it is known to many as one of the places where populist gangsters roared through in the 1930s when being chased by G-men from Herbert Hoover's fledgling FBI.

Amazing
Missouri Facts

Where was George Washington Carver born?

Diamond

Joplin Museum Complex (all ages)
Located in Schifferdecker Park, Seventh Street and Schifferdecker Avenue, Joplin 64802; (417) 623–1180. Open 10:00 A.M. to 5:00 P.M. Tuesday through Saturday, 1:00 to 5:00 P.M. Sunday; closed Monday. $

The complex, comprised of the Dorothea B. Hoover Historical Museum and the Everett J. Richie Tri-State Mineral Museum, is located in a park that also has a swimming pool, playgrounds, picnic tables, tennis and basketball courts and a full-blown golf course. The purpose of the museums is to chronicle Joplin's history and its role in the tristate mining district.

The Hoover museum offers an in-depth look at family life in the Victorian era, 1840 to 1910. You can see a typical kitchen, dining room, office, parlor, and bedroom, and a miniature room equipped with the kinds of toys children of this era used. The museum also features more than sixty antique dolls dating from 1890 and an animated miniature circus.

The mineral museum explains the importance of lead and zinc mining to the economies of Missouri and adjacent Oklahoma and Kansas. There are many specimens of the minerals and interesting pictorial and photographic displays and exhibits showing how a working mine looked.

A Cosby Family **Adventure**

If your family has an interest in the strange and unusual, and isn't afraid of the dark, you can go looking for the Spooklight while you're in the Joplin area. According to local legend, an eerie light appears in the middle of a lonely road almost every night. It is often described as a giant ball of light bouncing over the hills and across the fields. It has been rumored to come right up to cars and land on the hood, then bounce off or disappear and reappear behind the car. As the legend has it, the light has been spooking people since 1886.

We waited for nearly a half hour and thought at one time that just maybe we saw something in the distance. But we decided the whole thing was getting too spooky (it's very dark out there!), so we went into for an ice cream before turning in.

To go looking for the light, take Highway 44 west from Joplin to Highway 43. Turn south on Highway 43 and drive approximately 6 miles. When you see Highway BB is on your left, turn right onto Iris Road. Drive approximately 3 miles to the end of the road, and turn right. Drive 1 mile to the second dirt road on the left. Turn left here and drive ¼ mile. You are now on Spook Light Road. Park anywhere along the side of the road and wait. There are several roads off this one that you can turn onto and possibly see the "Light." Find a dark spot to wait—the darker the better.

Captain John's Sports and Scuba (all ages)

North of Joplin at 302 MM Highway, P.O. Box E, Oronogo 64855; (417) 673–2724; www.oronogo.com. Open 4:00 P.M. to 8:00 P.M. Friday, 9:00 A.M. to 6:00 P.M. Saturday March through December. $$$$.

Captain John's is on Blue Water Lake, which once was one of the largest open-pit mines in the world. The fourteen-acre flooded mine now is a great place to swim or scuba dive without being bothered by people fishing or boating. There is also a safe swimming area, as well as camping areas with RV hookups. Or, you can learn rappelling skills on a 36-foot tower.

Frisco Greenway Trail (all ages)

The 4 miles between Joplin and Webb City; (417) 781–1664. Open year-round. Free.

The trail, a section of the old St. Louis and San Francisco Railroad roadbed, has been cleared and smoothed into a hard-packed surface for biking, hiking, and walking and is accessible for wheelchairs and baby strollers. The beautiful stretch is lined with trees, bushes, and wildflowers. Bicycle Specialists, 300 Hodgdon (across from North Park Mall; 417–781–1664), rents mountain bikes and sponsors trail events.

Tilt (all ages)

101 Rangeline Road, Joplin 64801; (417) 623–7448; www.tilt.com. Open 10:00 A.M. to 9:00 P.M. Monday through Saturday, 10:00 A.M. to 6:00 P.M. Sunday. Games are individually priced. $–$$.

This full-blown arcade has dozens of games and is located in a mall, which, when game time is over, should give parents time to pick up other items that might be needed on the trip. Tickets are awarded for prize redemption.

For More Information

Joplin Convention and Visitors Bureau.
222 West Third Street, Joplin 64801; (800) 657–2534 or (417) 625–4789; www.joplincvb.com.

Missouri Tourist Information Center.
Highway 44 rest area, P.O. Box 2275, Joplin 64803; (417) 629–3030; www.visitmo.com. Open 8:00 A.M. to 5:00 P.M. daily. Great place to fill up with travel info from throughout the state.

Redings Mill

Paintball Ridge (ages 10 and up)

3483 Coyote Drive (2 blocks north of Highway 44), Joplin 64801; (417) 781–7703. Open 10:00 A.M. to 5:30 P.M. Tuesday through Sunday. Players must be ages 10 and older; parents must sign consent forms for children. Prices depend on amount of equipment and paintballs needed. $$–$$$$

This is a great place to do battle with paintballs, those little pellets that splatter you with paint when properly aimed by an opponent. There are ten wooded "fields" to play in, including a lighted night field and a pro shop loaded with equipment. You can bring your own equipment or rent what you need here. And of course, you'll have to sign a waiver if you want your kid to play.

Carthage

Immediately to the east of Joplin, Carthage offers an unusual variety of attractions for such a small place. This city was the site of a major battle during the Civil War and by 1864 was completely destroyed by guerrilla warfare in the area. Today a magnificent obsession of widely popular artist Sam Butcher, creator of the Precious Moments line of collectibles, attracts thousands of tourists annually. Don't miss the town square. It's ringed with friendly businesses and is fun to simply walk around. For more information, call the visitors bureau (417) 358–2373.

Precious Moments Inspiration Park (all ages)
Alternate Highway 71 south of Carthage, then west on Highway WW and follow the signs; send mail to P.O. Box 802, Carthage 64836; (800) 543–7975; www.preciousmoments.com. Open daily; call for hours. Day pass is available for all attractions; call for admission prices. $–$$.

You'll find several gardens, a Christian chapel, an art museum, a restored Victorian house, and an inspirational show that can all best be described in one word: cute. The site was built by Precious Moments artist Sam Butcher, and everything is decorated with murals and statues of the doe-eyed children that continue to make him rich and famous.

It doesn't cost anything to roam the grounds and visit the chapel, which has fifty biblical murals, exquisite stained-glass windows, wood and bronze carvings, and intricate wrought-iron gates. The gardens are beautifully landscaped and feature several unique settings. Several gift shops offer Precious Moments items of every size, shape, and material. Royal Delights, a small restaurant, offers sandwiches, drinks, and side items, and Souper Sam's Homestyle Buffet offers a wider spread.

You'll have to pay a fee if you want to see the newest attraction—the Art Museum—or the Fountain of Angels or Wedding Island. The Fountain of Angels is a laser light and water show accompanied by outstanding inspirational music and vocals. Referred to by some locals as "the Jewel of the Ozarks," the show was located in an outdoor amphitheater but was brought under roof. The Art Museum is a renovated and enlarged farmhouse on the property that Butcher once used but now is filled with artworks he has collected from around the world.

Wedding Island contains an old church and Victorian home—moved to the site from the city—both of which have been lovingly and beautifully restored. It's open to public tours for a fee when it isn't being used for weddings.

There's also the Studio Tour, featuring a world-class collection of miniature art donated by Mary Fisher, curator of the collection.

This isn't the place for family members who can't tolerate an overdose of sweetness. But those who like that sort of thing are in for a precious and spiritual time.

Civil War Museum (all ages)

205 North Grant Street, Carthage 64836; (417) 237–7060. Open Monday through Saturday 8:30 A.M. to 5:00 P.M., Sunday 1:00 to 5:00 P.M. Free admission; donations accepted.

This small museum provides artifacts and detailed information about the battle that was waged in this small town and the guerrilla activity from both sides that forced most towns-people to flee their homes. It's a great small museum that gives a powerful picture of a terrible time. Kids enjoy the battle diorama outlining the sequence of the fighting with miniature figures.

The Old Cabin Shop (all ages)

155 North Black Powder Lane, Carthage 64836; inside Missouri (417) 358–6720; outside Missouri (800) 799–6720. Call for hours. Free admission.

Visitors to this unusual and quaint combination of museum and business will find an old log cabin built in the 1830s and used as the county courthouse in 1841. A newer building next door sells guns, muzzle-loading equipment, archery equipment, Boy Scout items, and beekeeping supplies. In the back of the store is a marvelously quaint small "museum" of the owner's private collections of Native American artifacts, toys, and old guns. It's a great rough-and-ready place and well worth a visit if you or your children are interested in these subjects.

Royal Oaks Arena (all ages)

9895 Cork Lane, Carthage 64836; (417) 548–7722. Call for schedule of events.

This indoor/outdoor 2,000-seat arena is where you can see bull riding, horse and mule shows, concerts, and rodeos.

Immaculate Heart of Mary Shrine (all ages)

1900 Grand Avenue, Carthage 64836; (417) 358–8580. Call for hours. Free admission; donations accepted.

The shrine was built and is maintained by Catholic Vietnamese immigrants to the area and puts on a drive-through lighting exhibit from Thanksgiving through January 1 called the Way of Salvation Lighting Ceremony. It features biblical scenes illuminated with more than 700,000 lights.

Powers Museum (all ages)

1617 West Oak Street, Carthage 64836; (417) 358–2667. Open March through December Tuesday through Saturday 11:00 A.M. to 4:00 P.M., Sunday 1:30 to 5:00 P.M. Free admission.

Getting **Squirrelly** in Marionville

This small town of 2,000 people east of Carthage on Highway 60 draws tourists from all over the world, even though there is only one attraction: hundreds of albino, snow-white squirrels. It's one of only a few places in the country where you can find these beautiful scampering creatures. Townspeople feed them, provide nesting boxes, and watch for predators that may threaten their special residents. Anyone wishing to see the squirrels in person and not just imprinted on the souvenirs available everywhere in town is advised to come on a cloudy fall day when the critters are busy collecting acorns and walnuts throughout the area. For more information, call City Hall at (417) 258–2466.

The history of Carthage from the late nineteenth and early twentieth centuries is told through artifacts collected by a notable local family and rotating local exhibits, and the history of Missouri is explained through traveling exhibits.

Festivals

MARCH

Branson Fest. Held during late March or early April at one of the city's larger theaters, this festival is a five-day sampler of everything Branson offers. There are indoor and outdoor music events, a parade, art show, celebrity autograph sessions, plenty of food booths, and gaily decorated information booths sponsored by most of the local theaters. Call (800) 214–3661, or visit www.explorebranson.com. $$$–$$$$, many events **free.**

JUNE

AirFest. Held in late June at Joplin Regional Airport, this festival features a variety of air entertainment, ranging from traditional professional flying acts to military aircraft. You'll also find a small carnival, food booths, displays, and other activities for kids and adults. Call (417) 626–0483. $–$$.

JULY–AUGUST

Ozark Empire Fair, the second largest fair in Missouri, is held at the Ozark Empire Fairgrounds on Norton Avenue in Springfield. It runs approximately ten days in late July and early August. Live entertainment, livestock competitions, exhibits, food, and a glittering midway featuring carnival attractions of all types bring families in from all over the state. Other events throughout the year at the fairgrounds include horse, dog, and car shows; agricultural fairs; and rodeos. Call (417) 833–2660. $$; children ages twelve and under **free.**

SEPTEMBER–OCTOBER

Festival of American Music and Craftsmanship. Held during September and October in Silver Dollar City near Branson, this is the largest gathering of craftspeople in the United States and offers more than a dozen musical acts daily. This festival brings people from all over the country to join in this harvest festival to provide country music, craft demonstrations, and autumn food. Call (800) 952–6626, or visit www.silverdollarcity.com. $$$$; family rates available.

NOVEMBER–DECEMBER

Festival of Lights, beginning in early November and running through the end of the year, sets Springfield aglow for the holidays. There is a Christmas parade to kick off the festival, and you can get a map of the Festival of Lights Trail so you can drive by buildings ablaze with lights, decorated in Christmas finery and sporting Christmas displays and scenes. The fairgrounds are aglow with more than one million lights and 400 displays. A train decorated with lights and designated the Santa Express transports Santa around the Springfield area so he can visit with children of all ages. Call (800) 678–8767. **Free.**

Old Time Country Christmas. During this festival at Silver Dollar City, near Branson, more than four million lights decorate the park, and Christmas music and holiday food are provided in theaters and restaurants. The atmosphere is alive with the spirit of the season, and the park provides a fairy-tale Christmas experience with carolers wandering about, a nightly tree-lighting ceremony, and holiday music filling the air. Open 1:00 to 10:00 P.M. daily November through December. $$$$; children ages three and under **free.** Call (800) 952–6626, or visit www.silverdollar city.com.

Carthage at Christmastime. The city lights up for Christmas in November and December with lighting displays in the downtown Carthage area, at the Precious Moments Inspiration Park, and at the Immaculate Heart of Mary Shrine. **Free**; donations accepted. Call (417) 359–8181, or visit www.visit-carthage.com.

Where to Eat

SPRINGFIELD

Country Kitchen Family Restaurants. 3405 East Battlefield Road at Highway 65, Springfield 65802; (417) 887–4545. Open Sunday through Thursday 6:00 A.M. to 11:00 P.M., Friday and Saturday 24 hours a day. This is the place to get substantial sandwiches, french fries, dinners, and breakfast all day long. $$

Cracker Barrel Old Country Store. 2858 North Glenstone Avenue, Springfield 65803; (417) 831–4600. Open every day at 6:00 A.M.; closes Sunday through Thursday at 10:00 P.M., Friday and Saturday at 11:00 P.M. A family-style restaurant with good food, healthy portions, and plenty of side dishes, as well as an

interesting store that is a great place for kids to wait if there is a line. $$

McGuffey's Restaurant. 2101 Chesterfield Boulevard, Springfield 65806; (417) 882–2484. Open every day at 11:00 A.M.; closes 10:00 P.M. Sunday through Thursday, 11:00 P.M. Friday and Saturday. They serve everything from burgers to steaks. $$

Pizza House. 1349 South Glenstone Avenue, Springfield 65802; (417) 881–4073. Open Tuesday through Saturday 5:00 to 8:45 P.M. Nothing fancy here, just great pizza and salads. If you're going to get pizza anywhere, make this your stop. $$

Schlotzsky's Deli. There are four in Springfield: 1316 North Glenstone Avenue, (417)

868–8188; 4116 South Campbell Avenue, (417) 889–2445; 3120 East Sunshine Street, (417) 888–0822; 3825 South Glenstone Avenue, (417) 890–0595. Open daily 10:30 A.M. to 9:00 P.M. House specialties are a variety of scrumptious grilled meat and cheese sandwiches on a round sourdough bun, fantastic soups, and salads. The kids won't find french fries, but there are plenty of chips. $

OZARK

Lambert's Cafe: Home of Throwed Rolls. Highway 65 South, 1800 West Highway J, Ozark 65721; (417) 581–6755; www.throwedrolls.com. Open daily 10:30 A.M. to 9:00 P.M. A tasty and entertaining refueling stop the kids will love. During your meal, fresh-baked rolls will be thrown your way, and you will be offered "pass arounds," side dishes that change daily and are provided **free** of charge. Huge portions, reasonable prices, a menu with enough choices to satisfy the pickiest of eaters, and a roll of paper towels provided on every table in lieu of napkins make this a family restaurant that can't be beat. $$

BRANSON

There are more restaurants than you can shake a stick at in this town, but here are a few that should please the kids and offer a full meal.

Branson Cafe Bakery and Pie Shop. 120 South Main Street, Branson 65616; (417) 334–3021. Open Monday through Saturday 5:30 A.M. to 8:00 P.M. year-round. Branson's oldest restaurant, a popular stop for locals, serves fantastic food family style as well as burgers and fries for the children—and, as the name implies, incredible pies and cobblers. $

McFarlain's Restaurant. 3562 Shepherd of the Hills Expressway, Branson 65616; (417) 336–4680. Open daily 7:30 A.M. to 9:00 P.M.

March through December; shorter hours in winter. Down-home Ozark cooking includes homemade pot roast, pot pies, and dessert pies as well as pasta, shrimp, and steak. Children's menu. $$

Mr. G's Chicago Style Pizza. 202½ North Commercial Street, Branson 65616; (417) 335–8156. Open daily 11:00 A.M. to 9:00 P.M. Salads and sandwiches are available but Chicago-style pizza is, of course, the house specialty. Order a cheese or pepperoni pie for the kids and treat yourself to a supreme. $

POINT LOOKOUT

Friendship House. College of the Ozarks campus, P.O. Box 17, Point Lookout 65726; (417) 334–6411, extension 13341. Open Monday through Saturday 7:00 A.M. to 7:30 P.M., Sunday 7:00 A.M. to 3:00 P.M. Prepared and served by students, the food here ranges from hamburgers, sandwiches, french fries, and dinners to a complete buffet on Sunday. $

JOPLIN

Geppetto's Pizzeria, Inc. 3222 South Rangeline Road, Joplin 64804; (417) 624–8129. Open 11:00 A.M. daily, close 10:00 P.M. Monday through Saturday, 9:00 P.M. Sunday. Pizzas are the fare, even a chicken Alfredo pizza. $–$$

Richardson's Candy House. Located 2 miles south of I–44 off Highway 86 at 454 Reddings Mill Road, Joplin 64804; (417) 624–1515 or (800) 624–1615; www.candyhouse.net. Open 9:30 A.M. to 5:30 P.M. Monday through Saturday, 12:30 to 5:30 P.M. Sunday. Try the free samples of magnificent English toffee, hand-dipped chocolates, peanut brittle, and peanut butter fudge (from $4.50 to $6.50 a half pound). The kids will flip over a wide assortment of hand-pressed lollipops ($1.49 each and up).

Stogey's Coney Island. 2629 East Seventh Street, Joplin 64801; (417) 623–2020. Open 10:30 A.M. to 8:30 P.M. Monday through Thursday; 10:30 A.M. to 9:00 P.M. Friday and Saturday; closed Sunday. Chili is the specialty here, over hotdogs or with spaghetti and cheese; burgers, too. $

Under Cliff Grill. 6385 Old Highway 71, Joplin 64804; (417) 623–8382. Open 11:00 A.M. to 9:00 P.M. Wednesday through Friday, 9:00 A.M. to 9:00 P.M. Saturday, 9:00 A.M. to 3:00 P.M. Sunday. Great burgers, sandwiches, salads, ribs, and chicken breasts, and breakfast on Saturday and Sunday. $$

MARIONVILLE

Grant's Restaurant. 310 South Highway 60 (across from Dairy Queen), Marionville 65705; (417) 258–2288. Open daily 6:00 A.M. to 8:00 P.M. Great meat loaf and chicken, and hamburgers and fries for the kids. $

Where to Stay

SPRINGFIELD

There are plenty of motels in town, especially along Glenstone. Here is a sampling.

Days Inn–Bass Pro. 621 West Sunshine Street, Springfield 65807; (417) 862–0153. Checkout time is 11:00 A.M.; check-in time is when available. Sixty-nine rooms, indoor pool. Children ages 13 and under **free.** $$$

Holiday Inn North. 2720 North Glenstone Avenue, Springfield 65803; (417) 865–8600 or (800) HOLIDAY. Checkout time is noon; check-in time is 3:00 P.M.; 188 rooms, indoor pool, sauna, Jacuzzi, exercise room. Children ages 18 and under **free.** $$$

Merigold Inn. 2006 South Glenstone Avenue, Springfield 65804; (417) 881–2833. Check-in and checkout times are noon. Seventy-one rooms, outdoor pool. $$

Red Roof Inn. 2655 North Glenstone Avenue, Springfield 65803; (417) 831–2100. Checkout time is noon; check-in time is 2:00 P.M.; 112 rooms. Children ages 18 and under **free.** $$

Sheraton Hawthorn Park Hotel. 2431 North Glenstone Avenue, Springfield 65803; (417) 831–3131 for reservations (800) 223–0092. Checkout time is noon; check-in time is 2:00 P.M.; 201 rooms, indoor-outdoor pool, Jacuzzi, exercise room. Children ages 17 and under **free.** $$$–$$$$

FORSYTH

Shadow Rock Park and Campground. Highway 160 in Forsyth; (417) 546–2876, if no answer, call (417) 546–4763. A municipal facility with trailer and tent sites, restrooms, and showers. Boating, canoeing, and fishing are available on-site or close by. Camping is $9.00 per day; electrical hookups are $12.00 per day. $

BRANSON

Motels and hotels are plentiful here and rates vary widely. Here's a sampling.

City of Branson Campground. 300 South Boxcar Willie Drive (on Lake Taneycomo), Branson 65616; (417) 334–2915; 325 full-hookup sites, fishing docks, boat ramps, and picnic shelters are all available in downtown Branson year-round. $

Compton Ridge Campgrounds and Lodge. Highway 265, ¾ mile south of intersection with Highway 76; (417) 338–2911 for information, (800) 233–8648 for reservations; www.comptonridge.com. Open March 15 through November. There are 234 campsites on eighty-five wooded acres offering tent camping and full RV hookups, twenty-five lodge rooms (some with kitchens), five motel rooms, two outdoor swimming pools, one indoor heated pool, one kiddie pool, video game room, playground, three laundry facilities, a store selling groceries and supplies, and planned children's activities June through August. Campsites range from $21.00 to $30.00 for two adults, plus $2.00 each additional person ages 6 and up; children ages 5 and under free. Lodge and motel rooms range from $43.95 to $119.00 for two adults, plus $5.00 each additional person ages 6 and up; children ages 5 and under free.

Ramada Inn. 1700 Highway 76, Branson 65616; (417) 334–1000; 297 rooms, outdoor pool. In the shoulder-to-shoulder Branson sprawl, the motel offers twenty-seven wooded acres of green space for families who need some breathing, running, and playing room where they stay. Children ages 17 and under free. $$

Settle Inn. 3050 Green Mountain Drive, Branson 65616; (800) 677–6906; 295 rooms, two indoor pools, video arcade, deluxe continental breakfast, laundry facilities. There also are thirty-five rooms with whirlpools that are decorated in exotic or fantasy themes ranging from Sherwood Forest to the Circus Big Top that were decorated by local artist Bill Holden. The Mystery Comedy Dinner Theatre, located in the inn, also has a murder mystery every week. Children ages 17 and under free. $$$

JOPLIN

Joplin is loaded with hotels, especially along Rangeline. Here are a few.

Baymont Inn & Suites. 3510 Rangeline Road, Joplin 64804; (866) 627–9876. Checkout time is noon; check-in time is 3:00 P.M. 104 rooms, indoor and outdoor pools, fitness center, continental breakfast with waffles. $$$

Comfort Inn & Suites. 3500 Rangeline Road, Joplin 64804; (800) 228–5150. Checkout time is noon; check-in time is 3:00 P.M. 82 rooms, indoor heated pool, exercise room, continental breakfast. $$

Days Inn. 3500 Rangeline Road, Joplin 64804; (800) 329–7466. Checkout time is noon; check-in time is 2:00 P.M. 106 rooms, outdoor pool, continental breakfast. $$

Hallmark Inn. 3600 Rangeline Road, Joplin 64802; (417) 624–8400 or (800) 825–2378 . Checkout time is noon; check-in time is 4:00 P.M. Ninety-five rooms, outdoor pool, health club, continental breakfast. Children ages 12 and under free. $$

Hampton Inn. 3107 East 38th Street, Joplin 64802; (417) 659–9900 or (800) 426–7866. Checkout time is noon; check-in time is 3:00 P.M. Eighty-nine rooms, outdoor pool, health club, continental breakfast. Children ages 18 and under free. $$$

Motel 6. 3031 Rangeline Road, Joplin 64802; (417) 781–6400 or (800) 466–8356. Checkout time is noon; check-in time is after noon. 122 rooms, outdoor pool. Children ages 17 and under free. $$

Central
Missouri

The middle region of Missouri is a land of artificial lakes. In the southern part of the region are two small lakes, Stockton Lake and Pomme de Terre Lake, both unspoiled and rugged. North of these are two large lakes: Truman Lake, surrounded by natural countryside and open spaces and, east of that, Lake of the Ozarks, with widespread development and tourist attractions of every type and description. But besides water sports and recreation, this region has the capital city; the Missouri wine country meandering alongside the Missouri River; the city of Columbia, home of the main campus of the state university system and the popular Missouri Tiger athletic teams; and Sedalia, the small city that hosts the state fair each year, so there's plenty to do and see here.

Access to both sides of the Lake of the Ozarks was greatly improved with the opening of the Community Bridge at Horseshoe Bend. Previously visitors had to drive an extra hour or more to the north or the south to get around the lake. The ½-mile-long, two-lane toll bridge runs between the intersection of Business Route 54 (Bagnell Dam Boulevard) and County Road HH in Lake Ozark, south to the tip of Shawnee Bend and connects to Highway 5. The bridge is open twenty-four hours a day, year-round. The toll for passenger cars is $2.50 in season and $1.50 out of season.

Nevada

Schell-Osage Conservation Area (all ages)
Highway 54 to County Road AA, north to County Road RA, east to area headquarters; P.O. Box 123, Shell City 64783; (417) 432–3414; www.mdc.state.mo.us.

This is one of the best places in the state for viewing wildlife. You can see waterfowl, pelicans, shorebirds, herons, turtles, wild turkeys, river otters, and—in the wintertime—bald eagles. In the fall, the goose population swells to several thousand, and eagles follow the annual duck migration.

CENTRAL MISSOURI

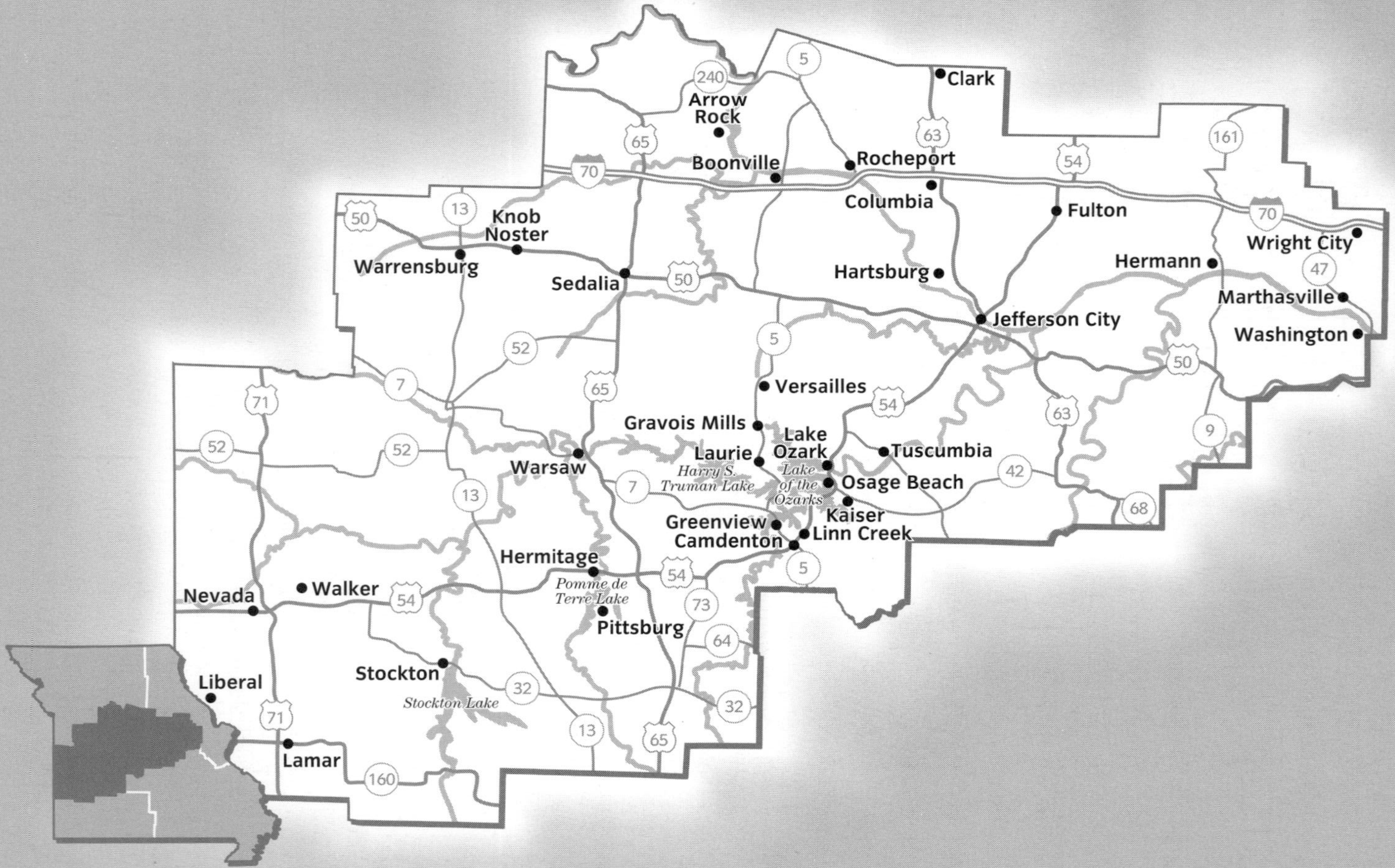

Bushwhacker Historical Museum & Old Jail Historic Site (all ages)
231 North Main Street, Nevada 64772; (417) 667–9602; www.bushwhacker.org. Open Monday through Saturday 10:00 A.M. to 4:00 P.M. May 1 through end of October. $

Nevada was named the "Bushwhacker Capital" in 1863 by Union troops after Southern loyalists killed two federal troops in the town square. Two days later, the soldiers came back and politely invited residents to leave their homes before burning down everything in town but the 1860s jail. The jail and adjacent 1870s sheriff's office and home once housed the museum but now are undergoing renovation—although still open—and exhibits have been moved into the new museum, a restored 1920s Ford motor car dealership and garage. The museum has an authentic turn-of-the-twentieth-century doctor's office and waiting room once used by Dr. J. T. Hornback. A kitchen, dining room, parlor, bedroom, and a boarder's room have been restored to the 1930s period. A twelve-minute video gives an overview of Nevada and surrounding Vernon County, and displays highlight activities relating to the border war, the Civil War, and other military history relating to nearby Camp Clark.

Walker

Osage Village State Historic Site (all ages)
Highway C, 9 miles north of Highway 54; c/o Harry S Truman Birthplace State Historic Site, 1009 Truman, Lamar 64759; (417) 682–2279 or (800) 334–6946; www.mostateparks.com. Site open daily year-round, sunrise to sunset. Free.

Here you'll see a mound used to support a structure and rocks where tools were sharpened by the Osage Indians who lived at the site from 1673 to 1780. The village is believed to have had at least 2,000 residents at its height. There are no facilities at the park. But if you enjoy hiking, there is a self-guided tour of the area that gives an inkling of what the Osage who lived here might have felt when walking at this site. An informational kiosk at the site has literature about the area and village.

Lamar

Harry S Truman Birthplace State Historic Site (all ages)
1009 Truman Street, one block north of Highway 160, Lamar 64759; (417) 682–2279 or (800) 334–6946; www.mostateparks.com. Site open year-round. Visitor center open Monday through Saturday 10:00 A.M. to 4:00 P.M., Sunday noon to 4:00 P.M. Free admission.

You can take a guided tour of the birthplace of the only Missourian to be elected president. The house where Truman was born on May 8, 1884, and lived the first eleven months of his life has been furnished to fit the period. The Austrian pine planted the day he was born by his father, a livestock dealer, still stands in the front yard.

Randy and Jane's
TopPicks in Central Missouri

1. Harry S Truman Dam And Reservoir Visitor Center, Warsaw

2. Ha Ha Tonka State Park, Camdenton

3. Big Surf Water Park and Big Shot Raceways and Fun Park, Linn Creek

4. Miner Mike's Adventure Town and Buster's, Osage Beach

5. Runge Conservation Nature Center, Jefferson City

6. Katy Trail State Park, Missouri River Corridor

7. Missouri Wine Country, Missouri River Corridor

8. Arrow Rock State Historic Site, Arrow Rock

Liberal

Prairie State Park (all ages)

Highway 160 west, turn north (right) on Highway NN, turn west (left) onto Central Road, then north (right) to 128 NW 150th Lane, Liberal 64762; (417) 843–6711 or (800) 334–6946; www.mostateparks.com. Park is open year-round. Visitor center is open year-round Tuesday through Saturday 8:30 A.M. to 5:00 P.M., Sunday 1:00 to 5:00 P.M. April through October; closed Monday. During winter closed Monday and Tuesday. **Free** admission. Two primitive campsites available; must call park for reservation.

Prairie State Park has the state's largest remaining section of the vast tallgrass prairie that once covered hundreds of miles of the Midwest. There are bison, prairie chickens, elk, white-tailed deer, and coyotes in this 3,700-acre park. More than 10 miles of trails will take you past prairie streams, hundreds of species of wildflowers, and numerous wildlife habitats. Stop at the visitor center for maps, information, and a slide show that has images of the prairie environment throughout the year. There also are displays, a prairie diorama, hands-on exhibits, and frequently a naturalist who can answer questions or give the kids an idea for a project while in the park. Nature programs are offered year-round.

Park **Call**

Missouri's excellent state park system is operated by the Department of Natural Resources. Call (800) 334–6946 or (800) 379–2419 (TDD) around the clock for recorded information, or during daily office hours to reach an attendant, or visit online at www.mostateparks.com. Call (877) 422–6766 at least forty-eight hours in advance for camping reservations. There is an $8.50 registration fee.

Stockton

Great sailing and fishing and miles of natural, undeveloped shoreline can be found about 1½ miles east of Stockton at **Stockton Lake.** If you and your family like the great outdoors, you'll enjoy the remoteness of this 25,000-acre lake that the U.S. Army Corps of Engineers built by damming the Sac River. Twelve public-use areas around the lake offer boat ramps, picnic areas, fishing docks, beaches, eight campgrounds with hundreds of sites, and many trails.

Make sure you visit the corps information center on Highway 32 at the dam to get information about the lake and surrounding area and to take in the magnificent view from the overlook atop the dam. Fishing and sailboating are big here. Orleans Trail Marina (417–276–5161) rents fishing and pontoon boats.

For more information about Stockton Lake and its facilities, call the corps office; (417) 276–3113. Camping is about $12 for basic sites and $16 to $18 for RV electrical hookups. The campgrounds often are full on weekends in the summer; for reservations contact the National Reservation Service, (877) 444–6777; www.reserveusa.com.

Stockton State Park (all ages) Ⓐ ⊖ ⚠

Highway 215; send mail to P.O. Box 218, Stockton 65785; (417) 276–4259 or (800) 334–6946; www.mostateparks.com. Open year-round. Campsites are $8.00 per day for basic site, $14.00 per day for RV electrical hookups. State Park Marina and Inn; (417) 276–5329. Motel rooms $; cabins with kitchens $$. Open April through October 31. Houseboat rental ranges from $750.00 to $1,240.00, depending on number of nights.

This park covers more than 2,000 acres along the shore of the lake and has forty-five campsites, a motel, cabins, a restaurant, and a large marina where fishing boats and houseboats can be rented. A store at the marina also sells bait, supplies, and some canned goods. The restaurant is open daily from 7:00 A.M. to 9:00 P.M. April through October and serves breakfast, lunch, and full dinners.

Hammons Products Pantry and Visitors Center (all ages)

414 North Street, Stockton 65785; (417) 276–5121; www.hammonspantry.com. Open Monday through Friday 10:00 A.M. to 3:00 P.M. January through July, 10:00 A.M. to 5:00 P.M. August through December. Thirty-minute tours of the processing plant are given during most days in September; call for schedule.

Stop in and see the largest black walnut processor in the world. The visitors center has many hands-on exhibits and the gift shop has nuts of all kinds, candy, and plenty of affordable gifts.

For More Information

Stockton Chamber of Commerce. P.O. Box 410, Stockton 65785; (417) 276–5213; www.stockton-mo.com/scofc/.

Hermitage and Pittsburg

These small towns to the east of Stockton are right next to **Pomme de Terre Lake,** a small 7,800-acre lake where fishing and swimming are the main attractions. You can visit the **1872 Jail–Visitors Center** in the Hermitage town square to find out about the area. It's primarily rural, but there are four marinas and several motels, resorts, and parks with campsites and picnic areas. In addition to enjoying lake sports, you can rent a canoe and float along the Pomme de Terre River, which shows few signs of civilization and promises a true get-away-from-it-all trip. For information about the area call the Pomme de Terre Lake Area Chamber of Commerce; (800) 235–9519.

Pomme de Terre State Park (all ages)

Highway 64B to Pittsburg area, Highway 64 to RD Road to Hermitage area; send mail to HC 77, Box 890, Pittsburg 65724; (417) 852–4291 or (800) 334–6946; www.mostateparks.com. Free admission. Campsites are $8.00 per day for basic site, $14.00 per day for RV electrical hookups. State Park Marina; (417) 852–4567.

You'll find 700 acres along the lakeshore in two separate areas: The Pittsburg area is on the south shore, the Hermitage area is on the east shore. Each area has 128 campsites, a public beach, picnic sites, and hiking trails. The Indian Point Trail in the Pittsburg area ends at a rock platform overlooking the lake that has a magnificent view. You can rent a boat at State Park Marina in the Pittsburg area and fish for crappie, catfish, bass, muskie, and numerous sunfish. A naturalist oversees programs in both areas from June through August.

Warsaw

If you get a chance to stop in Warsaw, make sure you walk across the old **Swinging Bridge,** Highway 7 and Main Street. This relic is one of many bridges that used to provide area residents with a way to cross the river. There are several other sites of interest in this small town, but the big draw in this area is Harry S Truman Reservoir, known as Truman Lake.

Although the lake covers 56,000 acres, it is remarkably free of commercialization. Since the area isn't as built up as the Lake of the Ozarks to the east, boating is the primary diversion. The highways aren't lined with tourist attractions, but there are plenty of motels, resorts, and campsites to accommodate those who want a natural, quiet vacation on the water.

Harry S Truman Dam and Reservoir Visitor Center (all ages)

Highway 65; send mail to R.R. 2, Box 29A, Warsaw 65355; (660) 438–2216. Open daily 9:00 A.M. to 5:00 P.M. March through October. Free admission.

You shouldn't miss the visitor center's spectacular viewing room with two spotting scopes for visitors to observe the lake and wildlife. There is a reproduction of an archaeological dig of a Pleistocene spring located in the area as well as other exhibits on local history. A theater provides films and slide presentations about the natural features of the region. You can also tour the powerhouse exhibit area to view colorful displays explaining how the dam works to control flooding in the area.

Harry S Truman State Park (all ages)

Highway 7, HCR66, Box 14, Warsaw 65355; (660) 438–7711 or (800) 334–6946; www.mostateparks.com. Free admission to park. Campsites are $8.00 per day for basic site, $14.00 per day for RV electrical hookups. Truman State Park Marina; (660) 438–2423.

Surrounded by Truman Lake on three sides, the park offers plenty of opportunities for water recreation. The 1,400-acre park has 201 campsites in the forest and on the lakeshore, and a boat ramp, a sand swimming beach, and several hiking trails. Nature pro-grams, presentations, and films are offered Friday and Saturday during the summer months. A full-service marina rents fishing, pontoon, and ski boats and has a small store that sells fishing supplies and some groceries.

Benton County Museum (all ages)

700 Benton Street, Warsaw 65355; (660) 438–6707. Open Tuesday through Sunday 1:00 to 5:00 P.M. Memorial Day through Labor Day. Open weekends in September and October. $; children ages 6 and under free.

Benton County Museum is located in the former twelve-room school sitting atop "school-house hill." The building, which opened as a school in 1886 and closed in the 1960s, is filled with unique historical items, many donated by local residents. Several of the rooms are furnished according to a theme, including a one-room rural schoolhouse, bedroom, living room, and an old post office.

Lost Valley Hatchery and Visitor Center (all ages)

Country Road 620, east of Highway 65, R.R. 5 Box 3CA, Warsaw 65355; (660) 438–4465; www.mdc.state.mo.us. Open 9:00 A.M. to 4:00 P.M. daily March 15 through October, Tuesday through Saturday only November through March 15. Admission is free; children ages 15 and under are allowed to fish and even provided with poles and bait if needed.

One of the largest hatcheries of its kind in the country, this 971-acre Missouri Department of Conservation site has seventy-eight rearing ponds filled with walleye, muskellunge, channel catfish, largemouth bass, striped and hybrid striped bass, bluegill, and hybrid sunfish bound for the state's public waterways. Don't miss the visitor center's 12,700-gallon aquarium stocked with several native species.

For More Information

Warsaw Area Chamber of Commerce.
P.O. Box 264, Warsaw 65355; (800)
927–7294; www.warsawmo.org.

Versailles

This town (pronounced "Ver-sales") celebrates the **Old Tyme Apple Festival** the first weekend of October. It features several categories of walks and runs, a fiddlers' contest, food booths, arts-and-crafts booths, and activities for the whole family. Call (573) 378–4401. The **Royal Arts Council** provides musical productions and performances, several for children, at the Royal Theater from September through August. Call (573) 378–6226.

Morgan County Historical Museum (all ages)

120 North Monroe, Versailles 65084; (573) 378–4401. Open Monday through Saturday 12:30 to 4:30 P.M. Memorial Day through Labor Day. $.

This museum is located in the Martin Hotel, an area landmark for more than a century and now listed on the National Register of Historic Places. The lobby contains the eight-day

Amazing
Missouri Facts

What president is the namesake of the state capital?

Thomas Jefferson (Jefferson City)

Seth Thomas wall clock, the keyboard and room keys, and the desk that were in the hotel when it opened. Twenty-eight rooms of the hotel are uniquely decorated in different themes, including a chapel room, weaving room, barbershop room, schoolroom, and the Miss Lucy Room, named for the last surviving member of the Martin Thomas family.

For More Information

Versailles Chamber of Commerce. 118 North Monroe, Versailles 65084; (573) 378–4401; www.vchamber@thelake.net.

Gravois Mills

The Lake of the Ozarks is a popular vacation destination with more than 1,000 miles of shoreline on a 58,000-acre artificial lake, one of the largest in the country. The area offers hundreds of resorts of every type from world-class luxury accommodations to small family-owned operations where guests stay in old-fashioned cabins and are treated like family. Powerboating is big at this lake, as are waterskiing, fishing, golfing, and tennis. This is the place to come if your family likes plenty of activity.

The western side of the lake is less built up and in a more natural state than the crowded, highly developed eastern side. This is gradually changing as more visitors coming from the east decide to take the new Community Bridge across the lake in search of more pristine areas. Before the bridge, visitors from both directions had to drive around the lake to get to the other side, a trek of an hour or more that simply didn't make sense for weekend trips from either St. Louis or Kansas City.

There are, however, many small resort communities on the western side where you can find a family resort to your liking. Many of the tourist attractions that bring people to the area still are located on the busy eastern side. Numerous family resorts, motels, and condominiums are available there. For information about resorts and attractions in the area call (800) 386–5253.

Jacob's Cave (ages 5 and up)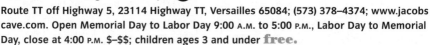

Route TT off Highway 5, 23114 Highway TT, Versailles 65084; (573) 378–4374; www.jacobs cave.com. Open Memorial Day to Labor Day 9:00 A.M. to 5:00 P.M., Labor Day to Memorial Day, close at 4:00 P.M. $–$$; children ages 3 and under free.

Jacob's Cave, the largest cave in the lake area, offers a mile-long tour during which you'll see prehistoric bones and mastodon teeth, fractured columns and other evidence of three earthquakes, and every type of cave formation imaginable, including reflective pools that create an optical illusion of great depth while being no more than a few inches deep. The cave temperature is fifty-two degrees Fahrenheit year-round, so visitors are asked to bring a jacket.

Greenview

Lake of the Ozarks Marina (all ages)
Highway 5 north at Niangua Bridge, 8 miles north of Camdenton; (800) 255–5561. House-boat rental starts at $1,495 for a three-day weekend cruise for ten people.

The marina rents 56-foot Forever 10 houseboats, which sleep ten people, for three-through seven-day cruises. Rental of the boats, which have full kitchens and one full and one-half bath, starts at $1,495 for a three-day cruise. The marina also rents fishing boats and a 26-foot deck cruiser.

Camdenton

Until the Community Bridge was completed, this town was the hub between the west and east shores of the lake. It's a small rural community that is home to many year-round lake residents, unlike some areas on the eastern side of the lake that have large numbers of summer-only residents. Every April this town celebrates the beautiful wild dogwoods blooming on the hills with the **Dogwood Music Festival,** held at various locations throughout town. Festivities include a parade, carnival rides, a petting zoo, a fine art exhibit and crafts show, a variety of musical entertainment throughout the weekend, and Ozark food for your enjoyment. Call the Camdenton Area Chamber of Commerce; (573) 346–2227 or (800) 769–1004.

Ha Ha Tonka State Park (all ages)
State Highway D, R.R.1, Box 113M, Camdenton 65020; (573) 346–2986 or (800) 334–6946; www.mostateparks.com. Open daily 8:00 A.M. to sunset. Permit required to enter caves.

You can see both natural and man-made wonders. The hulk of a magnificent castle built by prominent Kansas City businessman Robert McClure Snyder and his family and destroyed by fire in 1942 is a popular attraction. But the 3,000-acre park, which overlooks the lake from towering limestone bluffs, also offers impressive natural scenery, described in displays and exhibits outside the park office. There are picnic sites and trails for the handicapped.

The area is characterized by sinkholes, caves, underground streams, large springs, and natural bridges. Scenic trails lead through deep ravines and bowls caused by collapsed caves, past a 100-foot natural bridge and a theaterlike pit called the Colosseum. According to legend, the Colosseum was used for Native American tribal meetings.

Bridal Cave (all ages)
2 miles north of Camdenton on Highway 5, Box 255, Camdenton 65020; (573) 346–2676; www.bridalcave.com. Open daily 9:00 A.M. to 4:00 P.M. Extended hours during spring, summer, and fall months. $$; children ages 4 and under free.

Thanks to a legend about a Native American wedding ceremony, this romantic cave has become a popular site for weddings: There have been more than 1,850 and that number is growing. Considered one of the most scenic caves in the country, it has several rooms that have doubled the size of the area open to the public. Guided tours are approximately one hour long.

Linn Creek

Camden County Museum (all ages)
V Road off Highway 54, Linn Creek 65052; (573) 346–0375. Open Monday through Friday 10:00 A.M. to 4:00 P.M. May through October. Free admission; donations accepted.

This tiny town just to the north of Camdenton preserves memories of the past in the old Linn Creek School. The museum has many photographs and antique household furnishings, tools, and memorabilia from area schools, doctors' and dentists' offices, and churches.

Big Surf Water Park (all ages)
Route 2, Box 355, Linn Creek 65052; (573) 346–6111; www.bigsurfwaterpark.com. Open 10:00 A.M. to 7:00 P.M. June through August, slightly shorter hours remainder of Memorial Day through Labor Day period. $$$–$$$$; children ages 3 and under free.

Big Surf's twenty-two acres of landscaped water attractions include Zambesi Falls, a tube slide in a huge bowl; Tropical Splash Island for toddlers and babies; a wave pool; a whirlpool spa; body flumes; a lazy river; and a "Bubble Beach" kiddie area specifically for children ages seven and younger. In addition to the water rides, you can play sand volleyball, Ping-Pong, shuffleboard, or horseshoes. Lifeguards are always on duty.

Big Shot Raceways and Fun Park (all ages)
Highway 54 and State Road Y, Route 2, Box 355, Linn Creek 65052; (573) 346–6111; www.bigsurfwaterpark.com. Open daily 10:00 A.M. to 5:00 P.M. March through October. Open until midnight during summer months. No admission charge; pay per ride. Limited rides included in some Big Surf packages. $–$$

Here are go-karts on a quarter-mile track, a slick track for drivers ages sixteen and older, bumper boats, and an eighteen-hole miniature golf course. Rides range from two to six tickets each; tickets cost $1.25 each.

Osage Beach

This area is the heart of summer activity at the lake and offers more diversions than your family will ever be able to handle. It's difficult to believe there is anyplace on earth with more T-shirts for sale per square mile. Everything any member of your family will need to enjoy water sports is available somewhere around here.

Miner Mike's Adventure Town (ages 12 and under) and Buster's (ages 13 and older)

4515 Highway 54 (east of the Grand Glaize Bridge), Osage Beach 65065; (573) 348–2126 or (800) 317–2126; www.minermikes.com. Memorial Day to Labor Day, open at 11:00 A.M., Miner Mike's closes 9:00 P.M. Sunday through Thursday, 10:00 P.M. Friday and Saturday; Buster's closes at 11:00 P.M. daily. Shorter hours April, May, and October through December. Miner Mike's admission is $10.00 for the maze, $8.00 for rides, $14.00 for entry to both. There is no admission fee to Miner Mike's arcade or Buster's. Games at both arcades take 25-cent tokens.

These two connected indoor fun centers target distinctly different audiences. Miner Mike's aims at younger children, with more than 25,000 square feet of space filled with mazes and climbing tunnels, a miniature-train roller coaster, Ferris wheel, a gyrocopter, triple slide, blaster tower, and an arcade of electronic games, some of which are even educational.

Buster's, featuring a Wild West theme, is an arcade aimed at teenagers and adults, offering a range of games that include powerboat, fishing, and NASCAR simulators; skee ball; and numerous other electronic and virtual reality games. Sandwiches, french fries, soft drinks, and snacks are available.

Pirates Cove Adventure Golf (all ages)

Highway 54 just east of Route KK, Osage Beach 65065; (573) 348–4599; www.piratescove.net. Open daily April 1 through November 1, 10:00 A.M. to 10:00 P.M. Memorial Day through Labor Day, and shorter hours other times. $$

Two beautiful eighteen-hole golf courses with decorations steeped in swashbuckling chic lead golfers through caves, over a foot bridge, and right into the midst of pirate lore. Snacks and soft drinks are available.

Amazing Missouri Facts

Amazing Missouri Facts

How many counties are in the state?

114 counties plus one independent city: the City of St. Louis

Putt'N Stuff Family Fun Center (all ages)

Highway 54 west of Grand Glaize Bridge; (573) 348–2127. Open daily 10:00 A.M. to midnight weather permitting, mid-March through mid-October. $$

In addition to two eighteen-hole golf courses, you'll find go-karts, bumper cars, and a special track for little ones.

Factory Outlet Village (all ages)

Highway 54 east of Grand Glaize Bridge; (573) 348–2065; www.lakelinks.com/shopping/factory_outlet_village. Open 9:00 A.M. daily, closed 9:00 P.M. Monday through Saturday, 6:00 P.M. Sunday.

Shop at 110 top-name manufacturers' outlet stores offering men's, women's, and children's clothing and shoes as well as housewares and consumer goods. This is outlet store heaven and it's growing all the time.

Celebration Cruises (all ages)

Kirkwood Lodge, Osage Beach Road, Osage Beach 65065; (573) 302–0023. *Celebration* cruises March through December 31; call for schedule of public and dinner cruises. Scenic cruise tickets are $14.00 per person. Dinner cruises are $39.95 per person, with children ages 12 and under half price.

The *Celebration* holds 149 passengers during its ninety-minute scenic cruises that kids will like. The leisurely trip is punctuated with occasional comments by the captain and made more enjoyable by a cold drink and snack from the full bar. Casual dress is allowed on dinner cruises, where the dining is fine and meals are served on china. Call for a schedule.

Tan-Tar-A Resort and Golf Club (all ages)

State Road KK, 2 miles west of Highway 54, P.O. Box 188–T, Osage Beach 65065; (573) 348–3131, reservations (800) 826–8272. Open year-round.

This is truly a self-contained resort. This 400-acre complex has more than 900 rooms in luxury suites and condominiums and five restaurants, plus a Burger King and Sbarro. There is a complete range of recreational opportunities including bowling, fishing, golf, horseback riding, jogging, racquetball, parasailing, and tennis. You'll also find a marina, a health spa, a playground, a video game room, and supervised children's activities. You can rent boats of every type, motorbikes, mountain bikes, wave runners, and touring carts. Rooms with two double beds accommodating four people range from $127 a day and up during the summer. There also are two golf courses.

Ozark Princess (all ages)

Tan-Tar-A Resort; (573) 348–3131. Cruises April through October; call for times and availability. $–$$; children ages 2 and under free.

This ninety-passenger paddle wheeler offers a one-hour narrated cruise that covers about 2½ miles of the lake and a good bit of local lore.

Lee Mace's Ozark Opry (all ages)

Highway 54; P.O. Box 242, Osage Beach 65065; (573) 348–2270. $$–$$$; children ages 4 and under **free.** Performances Monday through Saturday at 8:00 P.M. April through October.

This is the oldest country-music show at the lake, dating from 1953. The traditional Ozark-style family show offers country, bluegrass, and gospel music with big dollops of humor, provided in large part by Bubba, who leaves much to be desired when it comes to drumming and musicianship.

Main Street Music Hall (ages 4 and up)

Highway 54; 1048 Main Street, Osage Beach 65065; (573) 348–9500; www.mainstreet musichall.com. Performances are Monday through Saturday at 8:00 P.M. May through October. A special Christmas show is presented during November and December. $$–$$$

This show is heavy on the country, blending new music with older standards, including a 1950s medley.

Gran Rally Karts (ages 5 and older)

Highway 54, west of Grand Glaize, 1/4 mile east of Highway KK; send mail to P.O. Box 576, Linn Creek 65052; (573) 348–2012. Open daily, weather permitting, April through October.

A hilly, winding European-style course provides fun for adults and kids, who also can ride in a double kart with mom or dad. Soda and snack machines available.

Lapointe Racing (all ages)

Highway 54 at Lake Road 54-22; (573) 348–6011. Open daily, weather permitting, April through October. $$

You'll find your basic oval track here, but the karts are fast and it's on the main drag.

Kaiser

Lake of the Ozarks State Park (all ages)

Highway 42; send mail to P.O. Box 170, Kaiser 65047; (573) 348–2694 or (800) 334–6946; www.mostateparks.com. Campsites are $8.00 per day for basic site, $14.00 per day for RV electrical hookups. Two-night minimum on primitive cabins (no water or electricity); $61.00 for four people.

This magnificent park's 17,300 acres make it the largest in the state park system. There are 230 campsites available, half with hookups, and eight primitive (no water or electricity) log cabins are available year-round for those without an RV who don't want to pitch a tent. The park has two **free** sand swimming beaches, numerous picnic sites and shelters, boat-launching facilities, lake-view trails, and horseback riding. Naturalists present nature programs in an open-air amphitheater throughout the summer months. Nine hiking and horseback-riding trails cover more than 20 miles through the park. Guided hikes are

A Cosby Family **Adventure**

Our family has headed to the Lake of the Ozarks for several days every June for the past twenty years. We used to stay farther to the south, away from Bagnell Dam, at resorts along Highway 5 between Camdenton and Laurie. It's definitely quieter there, with fewer powerboats and more fishermen per square mile. But the past several years we have cut more than thirty minutes off our commute time to the lake by staying at resorts farther north in Lake Ozark, where fishing is allowed but powerboating and water sports reign.

The proliferation of resorts at the lake requires a bit of research to get just what you need. A swimming pool is a necessity; a kiddie pool and playground were required when our children were very young. Swimming in the lake is a big thing now—with life jackets, of course—but a pool still remains the most refreshing way to top off the day. It's easier to scout for other resorts when you're already at the lake, so keep your eyes open from one year to the next. But if you find a place that has everything you want, hang on to it and book for next year.

Another reason we moved up the lake was to be near other attractions, such as those along U.S. Highway 54. Stops at Sugar Creek, a beautifully land-scaped place with two eighteen-hole miniature golf courses, and Gran Rally, with its twisting go-kart course, now are required components of our trip. A half-day rental of a pontoon boat also has become an annual ritual.

While we change our resort from time to time, there always is one constant about these lake adventures. When we pull away from the resort to head home, the kids already are talking about next June.

also available. A marina rents boats and other water-sports accessories; call the park for availability.

Ozark Caverns (ages 5 and up)

Off Highway A in Lake of the Ozarks State Park; send mail to P.O. Box 170, Kaiser 65047; (573) 346–2500. Open daily 9:00 A.M. to 6:00 P.M. June 1 through August 15, Saturday and Sunday 9:00 A.M. to 5:00 P.M. August 16 through the end of May. $; children ages 5 and under free.

The cave is located in the park and can be explored with the help of handheld lanterns. The guided tour takes approximately one hour. You'll enjoy the visitor center's exhibits about the natural features of the cave and the area. During the summer months, specialty tours are available; call for a schedule.

Lake Ozark

This area by **Bagnell Dam** is where everything started in 1931, when the Osage River was dammed to control flooding, provide electricity, and form what would become the most popular recreational lake in the state. The original 1930s strip area here is lined with all kinds of arcades, souvenir shops, and food shops designed to entice you to break your travel budget. A short **free** tour of the dam shows how electricity is generated and how the dam was built. Tours offered Wednesday through Sunday. Call (573) 365–9330.

At Casino Pier, a half block west of the dam, *Captain Larry Don* and *Commander,* 130-passenger excursion boats, offer one- or two-hour sightseeing cruises from Memorial Day through Labor Day. Breakfast and dinner buffet cruises are also available. Cruises leave at 10:00 A.M., noon, and 2:00, and 4:00 P.M. Labor Day through October, weather permitting. The dock has a cafe and a small trolley that brings you down the steep hill to the waterfront. Call (573) 365–2020. $$–$$$; children ages three and under **free.**

Willmore Lodge (all ages)

Business Highway 54, northeast of Bagnell Dam; (573) 964–1008 or (800) 451–4117. Open Monday through Friday 8:00 A.M. to 5:00 P.M., Saturday and Sunday 10:00 A.M. to 3:00 P.M. Free admission.

With its great big view, the lodge now serves as offices for the Lake Area Chamber of Commerce and as a museum housing exhibits that tell about the area before Bagnell Dam was built and the construction of the dam. Designed in the Adirondack style, the lodge was completed in 1930 by the Union Electric Company, the utility that built Bagnell Dam. It was used as an entertainment and administrative center for the dam project, and several of its more than two dozen rooms were named after towns displaced or destroyed by the project. The western pine logs used to construct the lodge were cut and assembled into a lodge in Oregon before being shipped to Missouri.

Tom Sawyer (all ages)

West end of the dam; (573) 365–3300. Open Friday and Saturday Memorial Day through Labor Day. $–$$; children ages 6 and under free. Call for cruise schedules.

This paddle wheeler offers narrated one- and two-hour cruises with a captain who was born and raised in the area. Your kids can feed giant fish from the dock. Huckleberry's Restaurant, a Cajun-style bar and grill, is located on the dock.

Lodge of the Four Seasons (all ages)

Horseshoe Bend Parkway (State Road HH), P.O. Box 215, Lake Ozark 65049; (573) 365–3000 or (800) 843–5253. Call for comprehensive brochures. Open year-round. Rates for lodge rooms or condominiums: $$$$.

It's a full-service resort with luxury rooms and condominiums along 72 miles of shoreline. The lodge has a complete fitness center and spa, three outdoor pools, one indoor-outdoor pool, golf and tennis facilities, seven restaurants, a food court, a full-service marina, a movie theater, and an extensive variety of sports activities from biking and cross-country skiing (weather permitting) to trapshooting and "walleyball."

Tropic Island Cruises (all ages)
Lodge of the Four Seasons, State Road HH; mail to P.O. Box 734, Osage Beach 65065; (573) 348–0083; www.tropicislandcruises.com. Cruises offered April through October. Call for schedule of public cruises. $$–$$$; children ages 3 and under **free.**

You'll ride the *Tropic II,* an 80-foot luxury motor yacht carrying 149 passengers. Music by Jimmy Buffett, reggae groups, and other musical performers from the tropics sets the mood for the ninety-minute cruise, and the captain provides informative narration when needed.

Mike Fink's Marina (all ages)
Two blocks south of the dam on Highway 54, P.O. Box 1081, Lake Ozark 65049; (573) 365–6557. Open April through end of September.

This is a good place for you to rent just about any gas-powered device designed to create fun in the water.

Sugar Creek Miniature Golf (all ages)
Business Highway 54, Lake Ozark 65020; (573) 365–2226. Open daily April through October. Call for hours. $$

You and the kids will love either of the two eighteen-hole golf courses here. They are in a hollow that is beautifully landscaped, with a creek running through the site. Both courses have holes that are attractive and, at times, challenging. Your kids will want to come back every year.

Leman's Karts (all ages)
Business Highway 54, Lake Ozark; send mail to P.O. Box 172, Brumley 65017; (573) 365–5551. Open daily April through October. Call for hours. No admission fee; pay per ride. $$

Your kids will enjoy steering a go-kart over the twisting and turning Grand Prix–style raceway. They have single and double karts and even a few kiddie cars for the wee ones in a separate enclosed area. You purchase individual ride tickets.

Castle Rock Family Fun Park (all ages)
Business Highway 54, P.O. Box 1359, Lake Ozark 65049; (573) 365–6559. Open daily 10:00 A.M. to 1:00 A.M. March through November. No admission fee; pay per ride. $–$$

You'll find two go-kart tracks for big folks who are at least 54 inches tall, and another for kiddies who are at least age four. There also is an eighteen-hole miniature golf course.

For More Information

Lake of the Ozarks Convention & Visitor Bureau. P.O. Box 1498, Osage Beach 65065; (800) 386–5253; www.funlake.com.

Lake Area Chamber of Commerce. (800) 451–4117; www.lakeareachamber.com.

Tuscumbia

Miller County Historical Society Museum (all ages)
Highway 52 west, Tuscumbia 65082; (573) 793–2750. Open Monday, Wednesday, and Friday 10:00 A.M. to 4:00 P.M. mid-May through mid-September. Free admission.

This museum is a wonderful example of a free rural museum organized and operated by dedicated volunteers who simply want to preserve their past. The museum's two floors of exhibits examine life in this region before the lake was created. Antique items highlighting Native American heritage and early pioneer home accessories, machines, and crafts are displayed in the old Anchor Mill building.

Jefferson City

Jefferson City's most impressive building is the state capitol, which sits high atop a bluff overlooking the Missouri River. The seat of state government was moved to Jefferson City from St. Charles in 1826, just five years after Missouri became a state. Completed in 1924, the Renaissance-style building is the third capitol: The others burned down in 1837 and 1911. Don't forget to stop at the Missouri Veterans Memorial on the capitol grounds. Many of the other buildings you also will want to visit while here are in the historic downtown area near the capitol.

State Capitol (all ages)
201 West Capitol (overlooking the Missouri River), Jefferson City 65201; (573) 751–2854; www.mostateparks.com. Guided tours Monday through Saturday on the hour from 8:00 A.M. through 4:00 P.M. Free admission.

Don't miss the Missouri Museum on the first floor; you'll learn as much as you'll ever need to know about Missouri. Make sure you also see the magnificent Thomas Hart Benton mural in the House lounge, and many more works by Benton, Sir Frank Brangwyn, N. C. Wyeth, and other artists. You can see these on your own or on a tour. If you visit when the legislature is in session from January through mid-May, you can show your children how laws are enacted by watching from the visitor's gallery Tuesday, Wednesday, or Thursday mornings.

Governor's Mansion (all ages)
100 Madison Street, Jefferson City 65201; (573) 751–7929; www.missourimansion.org. Guided tours on the half hour Tuesday and Thursday 10:00 to 11:00 A.M. and 1:00 to 2:30 P.M. Closed August and December, except for Christmas candlelight tours. Due to security concerns, tours require a twenty-four hour advance reservation.

Costumed docents provide guided tours of the first floor of the mansion, which has been authentically restored in the Renaissance revival style popular when the building was constructed in 1871. The building is perched on a bluff overlooking the Missouri River and the well-traveled route of the Lewis and Clark expedition. The tour includes a great hall, library, double parlor, dining room, and porch. Portraits of Missouri's first ladies are displayed in the rooms. Traditional candlelight tours are held on two days in December. You also might want to visit the Governor's Garden, adjacent to the mansion grounds. For information about the garden, which is not part of the mansion tour, call (573) 751–7929.

Cole County Historical Museum (all ages)

109 Madison Street, Jefferson City 65101; (573) 635–1850. Open Tuesday through Saturday 1:00 to 3:30 P.M. Closed December 15 through January 31. $; children ages 4 and under free.

The top floor of the museum, which recently doubled its size through a renovation project, houses Grandma's Attic, with toys and artifacts of particular interest to children. The state memorabilia in the rest of the museum includes displays with the inaugural ball gowns of former first ladies of the state and a collection of historic furniture donated by former governors and prominent families in the area.

Missouri State Museum and Jefferson Landing State Historic Site (all ages)

Room B2, State Capitol Building, Jefferson City 65101; (573) 751–2854 or (800) 334–6946; www.mostateparks.com. Open Tuesday through Saturday 10:00 A.M. to 4:00 P.M. Free admission.

The site on the north end of Jefferson Street, has three separate buildings, two of which offer tours. Start at the Lohman Building visitor center, a limestone structure dating from the 1830s, where you can take a short self-guided tour of the exhibits and see a fifteen-minute slide presentation on the history of the city. The Union Hotel next door has art and cultural exhibits and houses the Amtrak station on the first floor.

Museum of Missouri Military History (all ages)

2007 Retention Drive, Jefferson City 65101; (573) 638-9603; www.moguard.com /museum/MONG.museum.htm. Open Monday through Friday 8:00 A.M. to 3:00 P.M. Free admission.

The exploits and history of the Missouri National Guard are the principal focus here, but exhibits range all the way back to 1808, before Missouri was a state. Exhibits also cover other famous Missourians, or folks whose actions have inextricably linked them to the state, such as aviator Charles Lindbergh, President Harry S Truman, and explorers Lewis and Clark.

State Archives and Records Division at the Missouri State Information Center (all ages)

600 West Main Street, Jefferson City 65101; (573) 751–3280; www.sos.state.mo.us/archives. Open Monday through Friday 8:00 A.M. to 5:00 P.M., Thursday until 9:00 P.M., Saturday 8:30 A.M. to 3:30 P.M. Free admission.

This place is loaded with genealogical data. Let your kids look up information about your ancestors. Who knows what you might

Missouri **Wine** Country (all ages)

As you head east from Jefferson City, follow Highway 94 and the Missouri River for a winding, dipping ride and scenic views of the bluffs and the wildlife that live along the river corridor. You are now in the heart of the Missouri Wine Country and you will begin to notice vineyards alongside the roads. This is approximately the same route followed by the Katy Trail.

uncover? The Missouri archives, county courthouse records, census records, military records, land purchase records, birth, death, and marriage certificates and more can be viewed on microfilm for **free.**

Missouri Highway Patrol Safety Education Center (all ages)

1510 East Elm Street, Jefferson City 65101; (573) 526–6149; www.mshp.state.mo.us. Open Monday through Friday 8:00 A.M. to 5:00 P.M. **Free** admission.

Your kids can test their emergency reaction time, see the wreckage of a car crash in which passengers' lives were saved by seat belts, look at illegal drugs, and learn about the effects of drug abuse. They also can see a 1931 Model A Ford Roadster like the ones driven by the first highway patrolmen and view antique and homemade weapons and many other law enforcement items.

Go Carts at 63 Speedway (ages 5 and up)

Old highway 63, 12575 Renz Farm Road, Jefferson City 65101; (573) 636–0063. Season is late March through early December. Open noon to midnight Tuesday through Sunday from Memorial Day through Labor Day, shorter hours other days. $$

This is a good place to stop when the kids feel the need for speed because the figure-eight track is "slick," meaning carts slide around quite a bit, thereby adding a high level of excitement to the eight-minute ride. There also are double carts for kids who want to ride with dad or mom. A great concession stand offering hot dogs, sandwiches, and much more makes lunch here a possibility.

Runge Conservation Nature Center (all ages)

Highway 50 west to Jamestown exit, then ¼ mile on Highway 179 to center, Jefferson City 65109; (573) 526–5544; www.mdc.state.mo.us. Open Monday through Saturday 8:00 A.M. to 5:00 P.M., Sunday noon to 5:00 P.M. **Free** admission.

This is a beautiful interactive center operated by the Missouri Conservation Department that features hands-on exhibits about the wildlife and vegetation of this area. Your kids will love "Bubba," an enormous model of a bullfrog; the 2,500-gallon aquarium; the walk-through cave; and the wildlife viewing area. Five short nature trails surround the center, which offers a complete schedule of nature programs and films year-round.

Missouri Veterinary Medical Foundation Museum (ages 4 and up)

2500 Country Club Drive, Jefferson City 65109; (573) 636–8737. Open Wednesday through Friday noon to 4:00 P.M. **Free** admission.

You'll find all kinds of artifacts from the history of veterinary medicine—everything from tables, tools, lighting devices—and a selection of specimens that the kids will either love or hate. Among these exhibits are a huge hair ball and Siamese piglets. Be sure to ask for a guided tour; it's **free** and informative.

Turkey Creek Golf Center (all ages) ●

1616 Oil Well Road, Jefferson City 65101; (573) 636–7833. Open 8:00 A.M. to midnight April 1 through Labor Day, 8:00 A.M. to dusk rest of year. $–$$.

Here you'll find a miniature golf course for the kids and a driving range with putting and bunker greens, and a lighted, nine-hole, par 3 course for Mom and Dad.

Marvic Skate Center (all ages) ●

301 Flora Drive, Jefferson City 65101; (573) 635–5000. Open 7:00 to 11:00 P.M. Friday, 7:00 to 9:00 P.M. Saturday. $–$$

This is where roller skaters show their form . . . or lack of it. Operated by the same family since 1961, this rink is targeted to families, with skating sessions accompanied by popular music and rooms available for birthday parties. Rental skates are available.

For More Information

Jefferson City Convention & Visitors Bureau. 213 Adams Street, Jefferson City 65101; (800) 769–4183; www.visitjefferson city.com.

The **Katy** Trail

Katy Trail State Park, the longest hiking and biking trail in Missouri, cuts across the northern part of this region of the state. It starts in St. Charles in the eastern part of the state and follows the Missouri River all the way to Boonville, then turns south and west to Clinton. Trail parking is available at many of the small towns that border it: Augusta, Dutzow, Marthasville, Treloar, Jefferson City, Columbia, Rocheport, and Boonville. The easy grade of this trail makes it perfect for family cycling or hiking. All sections of the trail may not be open; call (800) 334–6946 for trail information and maps before you set out; www.katytrailstatepark.com.

Hermann

This proud community was inundated with German immigrants in the mid-1800s because it resembled their Rhine Valley homeland. The current residents maintain both their German heritage and its winemaking tradition with pride and enthusiasm. The Hermann Welcome Center, located at 312 Market Street, is open 9:00 A.M. to 5:00 P.M. Monday through Saturday, 11:00 A.M. to 4:00 P.M. Sunday. Call (800) 932–8687; www.hermannmo.com.

German School Building (all ages)

312 Schiller Street, Hermann 65401; (573) 486–2017 (800–932–8687 out of season). Open daily 10:00 A.M. to 4:00 P.M. April 1 through November 1 except Sunday, open at noon. $; children ages 6 and under free.

You can learn a lot about the area in this museum on the upper floor of the schoolhouse. There's a mock-up of a pilot house, a bell from an old steamboat, models of boats, and a children's room with displays of toys, games, and dolls. The first floor has a gift shop with German imports.

Stone Hill Winery (all ages)

Route 1, 1110 Stone Hill Highway, Hermann 65041; (800) 909–9463; www.stonehill winery.com. Tours and tasting Monday through Saturday 8:30 A.M. to dusk; Sunday 11:00 A.M. to 6:00 P.M.

A twenty-minute tour of this winery is fascinating even if you're not a wine drinker. This winery dates from 1847, and the tour takes you through the enormous brick main house and the vaulted catacomb wine cellars before ending with a free sample of wine or grape juice. The winery's hilltop grounds are steeped in history and charm and provide a perfect place for a picnic. A gift shop sells wine, cheese, sausage, and souvenirs. A full-service vintage restaurant is next door.

Deutschheim State Historic Site and Museum (all ages)

109 West Second Street, Hermann 65041; (573) 486–2200 or, from Missouri (800) 334–6946. Open daily 9:00 A.M. to 4:00 P.M.; guided tours at 9:30 and 11:15 A.M. and 1:00 and 2:30 P.M. $; children ages 5 and under free.

German-American artifacts and folk art are used to examine the customs, traditions, culture, and heritage of nineteenth-century German immigrants and their impact on the area.

Wilding Museum (all ages)

523 West Ninth Street, Hermann 65041; (573) 486-5544. Open year-round; call for hours. $

This museum features a collection of tools and wooden birds hand-carved by Clem Wilding, a noted folk artist.

A Cosby Family **Adventure**

One of the best ways to enjoy Missouri's scenery while traveling with the kids is to hop aboard an Amtrak train. There are two trains each way daily, stopping in St. Louis, Kirkwood, Hermann, Jefferson City, Sedalia, Warrensburg, Lee's Summit, Independence, and Kansas City.

Our family has taken the trip on several occasions, most recently to Sedalia to visit relatives and to Jefferson City, where we linked up with a relative driving to the Lake of the Ozarks.

We find the train ride gives us a chance as a family to discuss the sights we are passing without worrying about keeping a car on the road. The kids love going back to the snack car for a soda and sandwich. There's also something oddly enjoyable about walking on a moving train; it's a sensation not unlike that of an amusement park ride.

We have learned that train travel is best done by daylight if young children are along for the ride. Boredom sets in quickly when kids no longer can see the passing scenery or find cows to count, and the trip's excitement seems to wane once boredom has taken hold.

At 7:50 each morning a train leaves the St. Louis Amtrak station, 550 South Sixteenth Street, and arrives at the Kansas City station, 2200 Main Street, at 1:30 P.M. A train leaves Kansas City at 7:55 A.M. and arrives in St. Louis at 1:35 P.M. Trains also leave both cities at 3:30 each afternoon and arrive at the other city at 9:00 P.M.

The cost of an adult one-way ticket between Kansas City and St. Louis ranges from $27 to $58; ticket prices vary depending on demand. The fare is less if you're getting off somewhere in between the two cities, and children ages two through fifteen ride for half price. There also are periodic promotions that further reduce fares. Call (800) 872–7245 or go online at www.amtrak.com for more information or to make reservations.

Washington

This tiny river town is home to the only manufacturer of corncob pipes in the world. **Missouri Meerschaum,** 400 West Front Street, has an old display room where you can peruse an extensive and interesting collection of pipes. There is no admission fee. The display room is open Monday through Friday 8:00 A.M. to 3:30 P.M. Call (636) 239–2109.

Washington Town and Country Fair (all ages) Ⓜ
Washington Fairgrounds, 323 West Fifth, Washington 63090; (636) 239–2715. Starts first Wednesday in August. $$

This is the perfect fair for families on a budget since the one-price admission charge is good for all fair activities. The Main Stage provides big-name entertainers each evening of the fair, and the Motor Sports Area has events such as truck and tractor pulls, motocross racing, and professional bull riding. Carnival rides, livestock shows, and food booths provide all the ingredients needed for a great time.

Marthasville

Dozens of authentic old German farm skills are demonstrated during **Deutsch Country Days,** held from 9:00 A.M. to 5:00 P.M. Saturday and Sunday on the third weekend in October at Luxenhaus Farm, Highway O. This extraordinary living-history event takes place on a farm that is home to nineteen restored historic buildings. This event is the only time during the year that the farm is open to the public. Among the sixty crafts and skills demonstrated are braided rugs, crosscut sawing, sheep shearing, natural dyeing, paper marbling, primitive folk-art gourds and *kloppelei,* also known as bobbin lace. Call (636) 433–5669. $–$$$

Fulton

In this small college town in central Missouri, you can show your children a piece of the Iron Curtain. A twelfth-century church, **St. Mary Aldermanbury Church,** was rebuilt here to serve as the Winston Churchill Memorial and Library at Westminster College. This

BIG Eats

If you're passing the small town of Wright City at the 200-mile marker on I–70 during mealtime, you'll want to stop in and eat at Big Boy's Restaurant, located on the South Service Road. This family restaurant specializing in fried chicken and home cooking has been satisfying big appetites since 1924. Big Boy's is open Monday through Thursday 11:00 A.M. to 9:00 P.M., Friday and Saturday 7:00 A.M. to 9:00 P.M., and Sunday 8:00 A.M. to 9:00 P.M. Call (636) 745–2200. $$

is where Churchill coined the term *Iron Curtain* in a speech after World War II. After the 1989 fall of the Berlin Wall, a 30-foot graffiti-covered section of it was used as the basis for a massive sculpture that now stands in front of the church. Concerts, special activities, and services are held in the church, which is now part of a larger memorial.

Winston Churchill Memorial (ages 5 and up)

Westminster Avenue and Seventh Street, Fulton 65251; (573) 592–5369. Open daily 10:00 A.M. to 4:30 P.M. Admission includes the church. $; children ages 5 and under free.

If you want to see the church, you've got to pay to get into the memorial. But be sure to take the self-guided tour of the museum. It is filled with exhibits about and artwork by a British statesman who surely was one of the most interesting and influential figures in the twentieth century. *The Living Memorial,* a thirteen-minute film, explains how the church and memorial landed in Fulton. Kids will enjoy the weapons and the interactive aspects of the museum, including pushing buttons to call up many of the statesman's famous speeches.

For More Information

Kingdom of Calloway Chamber of Commerce. 409 Court Street, Fulton 65251; (800) 257–3554; www.callowaychamber.com.

Columbia

Sitting halfway between St. Louis and Kansas City, this city looks like a typical college town, but in fact it's a *three*-college town. The largest campus is part of the University of Missouri system, and two smaller, private colleges are located here. Consequently, when school is in session, there are college-age students everywhere.

Founded in 1839, the **University of Missouri** is the oldest land-grant university west of the Mississippi, and some of the older, hallowed halls of learning here seem steeped in tradition. Don't miss walking around historic Francis Quadrangle, the heart of the campus and also the site of President Thomas Jefferson's original grave marker and a bronze sculpture of him. You'll see six Ionic columns, all that remains of Academic Hall since a fire destroyed it in 1892. The eighteen surrounding buildings are on the National Register of Historic Places. Teens will enjoy touring the large campus and checking out the various colleges and programs. You can pick up information at the Donald W. Reynolds Alumni and Visitor Center, Conley Avenue, across from the quadrangle. You may be able to join up with a scheduled group to get a free tour of the campus, open daily 8:00 A.M. to 5:00 P.M. Call (573) 882–6333 or (573) 882–2121 for campus-wide information.

To really feel at home here, you must attend a **Mizzou Tigers** game. During home football games everything seems focused on **Faurot Field,** Providence Road and Stadium

Boulevard. The team competes in the Big Twelve Confer-
ence, and residents all over the state, alumni or not, follow
the games. The excitement has risen over the past few years
under the guidance of head coach Gary Pinkel.

Basketball also is big news, with head coach Quin Snyder
leading the way. You can watch the men's and women's teams
play at the new 15,000-seat Paige Sports Arena, Stadium Boulevard and Mick Deaver Drive beginning in the 2004-2005 season. MU
teams include baseball, track and field, wrestling, and gymnastics.
Pick up a complete semester schedule at the arena or call (800)
228–7297.

The university has a theater department that performs in several locations. Dramas, comedies, musicals, and experimental shows are directed
and performed by students September through April. Some productions
may not be suitable for children, but you can call (573) 882–7529 for a
schedule, description, and ticket prices.

There also are several, **free** on-campus museums and displays
worth seeing. Drop in if you're not on a schedule, but it never hurts to call ahead to make
sure someone is there. They include:

- **Museum of Art and Archeology.** *Pickard Hall; (573) 882–3591. Open Tuesday
  through Friday 9:00 A.M. to 5:00 P.M., Thursday also 6:00 to 9:00 P.M., Saturday and
  Sunday noon to 5:00 P.M.* This museum has one of the largest art collections in the
  state, displaying only about one-tenth of its collection at a time. The first level of the
  museum is a casts gallery, with reproductions of noted pieces of sculpture. The second floor contains several galleries housing American and European paintings by
  modern and past artists. There also are archaeological artifacts from several digs,
  including pottery, coins, lamps, tools, a mummy shroud, and Greco-Roman and
  Mesopotamian items.

- **Museum of Anthropology.** *100 Swallow Hall; (573) 882–3764. Open Monday through
  Friday 9:00 A.M. to 4:00 P.M.* This pocket museum has items representing Native American cultures and state history. The Native American collection includes Navajo weav-
  ings and artifacts from the Arctic that include ivory tools and a raincoat made from seal
  gut. Stone tools and other artifacts also are on display.

- **Entomology Museum.** *Agricultural Building; (573) 882–2410. Open Monday through
  Friday 9:00 A.M. to 4:00 P.M.* If you like creepy crawlies, this is the place to find them.
  This research center has six million exotic and common insect specimens, making it the
  largest university collection of preserved insects in the world. But the museum's display
  covers only one wall and focuses on beetles, butterflies, and other insects found primarily in Missouri.

- **Anheuser-Busch Natural Resources Center.** *(573) 882–6446.* Building open daily.
  Two excellent collections of mounted wildlife are displayed **free** in the first-floor hall-
  ways of this building. The Yuckel collection of large wildlife, straight in the front door in
  the hall near the auditorium, is a magnificent collection of mounted mammals, some

full-body mounts but mostly heads, with information about the animals. The Smart Collection of waterfowl life, located in the student teachers' wing to the right as you enter the front door, has a large number of mounted birds.

Rock Bridge Memorial State Park (all ages)

5901 State Highway 163, Columbia 65203; (573) 449–7402 or (800) 334–6946; www.mostateparks.com. Open daily dawn to dusk. **Free** admission.

Located about 7 miles south of I–70, this 2,273-acre day park has several interesting features to explore, including a natural rock bridge, a spring-fed creek, and numerous sinkholes. A boardwalk and trails lead visitors to the geologic formations and through prairie and wooded areas. A small playground and picnic areas also are available. Another natural feature of the park, Devil's Icebox Cave, is only open to the public on a few scheduled guided tours limited to people ages fourteen and older for a fee of $25 per person.

Finger Lakes State Park (all ages)

Highway 63 North, 1505 East Peabody, Columbia 65202; (573) 443–5315 or (800) 334–6946; www.mostateparks.com. Park is open year-round. Office is open daily 8:00 A.M. to 4:30 P.M., until 5:00 P.M. in the summer. Campsites are $8.00 per day for basic site, $14.00 per day for RV electrical hookups. If you call (877) 427–6766 at least forty-eight hours in advance for reservations, an $8.50 registration fee applies.

Don't expect sylvan vistas and beautiful hiking trails in this 1,132-acre park. But at the same time, don't be surprised if it turns out to be one of your kids' favorite spots. This old strip-mining area is now used for swimming, fishing, and canoeing. The holes left from the strip mining have resulted in excellent swimming lakes, and one has a sand beach. But be warned that the swimming holes are extremely deep, and there are no shallow areas. Make sure all children wear life jackets. This park permits the use of off-road motorcycles and all-terrain vehicles. Picnic areas and campgrounds are also available, although water is turned off at campsites from November through April.

Columbia City **Parks**

This growing city has a fabulous parks system, overseeing more than 2,000 acres at 51 sites, and offering visitors just about any outdoor activity imaginable. There are swimming pools at Oakland Park and Lake of the Woods Recreation Area; a sandy beach and lake swimming with a deck and diving platform, as well as paddleboat and fishing boat rentals at Twin Lakes Recreation Area; a skate park, tennis courts, horseshoe pits, and ball fields at Cosmopolitan Recreation area; and numerous hiking trails, including the 8.9-mile MKT Trail, which links Columbia to the cross-state Katy Trail. For further information contact Columbia Parks and Recreation Department, 1 South Seventh Street, Columbia 65201; (573) 874–7460; www.gocolumbiamo.com.

Walters Boone County Historical Museum and Visitors Center
(all ages)

3801 Ponderosa Street, Columbia 65201; (573) 443–8936. Open Tuesday through Saturday 1:00 to 4:00 P.M. April through October. Open Wednesday, Friday, Saturday, and Sunday 1:00 to 4:00 P.M. November to March. Free admission.

You'll find numerous exhibits highlighting westward expansion along the Booneslick Trace and on the heritage of Boone County, as well as information on Native Americans. A broadax, a weaving loom, and a collection of antique toys, such as an airplane pedal car, are among the artifacts that will interest the kids. There also is a gallery displaying the work of local artists. And make sure you stop next door to walk the grounds of Maplewood, a nineteenth-century farmstead with a beautiful two-story home and outbuildings. House tours sometimes are available; check with the museum.

Cool Stuff (all ages but teens for sure)

808 East Broadway, Columbia 65201; (573) 875-7912. Open 10:00 A.M. to 9:00 P.M. Monday through Saturday, 11:00 A.M. to 6:00 P.M. Sunday.

Self-dubbed "the store to explore," Cool Stuff has a cool collection of sunglasses, jewelry, clothing, other accessories, and even beads and other items for one who wants to make his or her own jewelry.

Candy Factory (all ages)

Seventh and Cherry streets, Columbia 65201; (573) 443–8222. Open 9:30 A.M. to 5:30 P.M. Monday through Friday, 10:00 A.M. to 5:00 P.M. Saturday; closed Sunday.

Fresh chocolates are made daily in this old-fashioned candy store and gift shop. Better yet, visitors can go upstairs to watch a chocolate enrober do its deed or to view the goings-on in candy-cooking kitchens and a chocolate-molding room.

Mid-Missouri Mavericks (all ages) ⬤

810 Walnut Street, Columbia 65201; (573) 256–4004 or (866) 812–4004; www.mid momavs.com. $–$$

This new minor-league baseball team joined the Frontier League in 2003, hiring former St. Louis Cardinals player Jack Clark to manage the team. The Mavs have a ninety-game schedule, with home games played on the University of Missouri campus in 3,000-seat Taylor Field, which is the home field for MU's baseball Tigers. Your kids will never have a better chance to get up close and personal with professional players than they will at this level, and they'll get a chance to run the bases before special games, and meet team mascot Marshall Maverick during most games.

For More Information

Columbia Convention & Visitors Bureau. (573) 875–1231; (800) 652–0987; www.visitcolumbiamo.com.

Boonville

This little town on the river has a proud history and approximately 400 homes on the National Register of Historic Places, making it a picturesque place to visit. Thespian Hall, Main and Vine Streets, is the oldest theater west of the Allegheny Mountains and hosts the annual Big Muddy Folk Festival, a traditional-arts festival held in early April. In August there is a special children's performance at the hall. For information about this and other attractions in town, call the Boonville Chamber of Commerce, (660) 882–2721.

Old Cooper County Jail and Hanging Barn (all ages)

614 East Morgan Street, Boonville 65233; (660) 882–7977. Open year-round Monday through Friday 9:00 A.M. to 5:00 P.M. From Memorial Day through Labor Day also open Saturday 10:00 A.M. to 5:00 P.M., Sunday 1:00 to 4:00 P.M. $: pre–elementary-school children free.

This site has a marshal's office and what was the longest continuously used jail in the state, having been open for business from 1844 through 1979. The hanging barn out back also was the site of the last public execution in Missouri, the hanging in 1930 of a juvenile convicted of murder. There also is plenty of information about the history of Boonville and the surrounding area.

Boone's Lick State Historic Site (all ages)

Highway 87 north from Boonville about 11 miles to Highway 187; then follow signs to site; send mail c/o Arrow Rock State Historic Site, Arrow Rock 65320; (660) 837–3330 or (800) 334–6946; www.mostateparks.com. Open daylight hours. Free admission.

This is a small park with a self-guided trail that leads down a hillside to the salt springs where Daniel Boone's sons started a salt-manufacturing business in 1805. There are no facilities in the 51-acre historic site except picnic areas.

Arrow Rock

Settlers heading west in the past century founded this town that sits on a bluff of the Missouri River where Osage Indians once gathered flint to make arrowheads. During the twentieth century progress bypassed this tiny town, but the residents have turned that to their advantage. They have done a remarkable job of preserving the past while inviting modern tourists to visit and enjoy a unique experience.

There are nine historic buildings in town open to the public, including the Old Stone Jail, the home of artist George Caleb Bingham, and the Old Tavern, where you can eat in an 1800s atmosphere. Gun buffs and small boys may enjoy the extensive gun collection at the John P. Sites Jr. Pioneer Gunshop.

Enjoy a wonderful family production at the state's oldest professional regional theater. The Lyceum Theater provides a full schedule of productions in a beautiful old Baptist church, Wednesday through Sunday from June through August. Reservations are recommended. For times and ticket prices call (660) 837–3311.

Arrow Rock State Historic Site (all ages)

Highway 41, Arrow Rock 65320; (660) 837–3330 or (800) 334–6946; www.mostateparks.com. Visitor center open daily 9:00 A.M. to 4:00 P.M. March through November, weekends only December through February. Tour is $5.00 for adults, $1.50 for children up to eighth grade. Campsites are $8.00 for tent sites, $14.00 for RV hookups. Call (877) 427–6766 at least forty-eight hours in advance for reservations. There is an $8.50 registration fee.

You'll find a Free visitor center with exhibits and dioramas about the famous people who lived here and the events that took place in this area. For a small fee you can sign up for a walking tour of the town. The 167-acre historic site has hiking trails and a campground with forty-three sites.

Sedalia

This once-rugged frontier prairie city served as a terminal point for cattle drives. Today it plays host each August to the eleven-day **Missouri State Fair.** In addition to the state fair, the fairgrounds hosts numerous activities and events throughout the year, ranging from car races and sports tournaments to carnivals and concerts. Call (800) 422–3247 in-state or (660) 530–5600 out of state for a schedule.

Sedalia also is near the western end of the **Katy Trail State Park.** To reach the Sedalia trailhead go north on Engineer Avenue, then turn east onto Boonville Road to the park. For trail information and maps call (800) 334–6946.

Katy Depot Historic Site (all ages)

600 East Third Street, Sedalia 65301; (800) 827–5295; www.sedaliakatydepot.com. Open 9:00 A.M. to 5:00 P.M. Monday through Friday, 10:00 A.M. to 3:00 P.M. Saturday. Free admission.

This recently renovated depot houses not only a fine collection of exhibits touting Sedalia's long railroad heritage but also its chamber of commerce and convention and visitors bureau. The depot is an official Welcome Center for travelers on the Katy Trail and has a wide range of tourism information. A rest area also is on the grounds. The railroad heritage exhibits include a working telegraph, an audiovisual presentation, a youth activity room, and several other informational displays outlining the importance of the historic site.

Missouri State Fair (all ages)

State Fairgrounds, Highway 65, 2503 West Sixteenth Street, Sedalia 65301; (800) 422–3247 in-state or (660) 530–5600 out of state. Fair runs eleven days in August. Admission to the fairgrounds is $6.00 for adults; children ages 12 and under free. Parking is free. Performances, events, and activities are individually priced.

This fair always has a gigantic midway of carnival rides. But the event also includes agricultural exhibits and shows presenting the state's finest in crops and livestock; big-name entertainers performing nightly; displays and contests of traditional homemaking skills such as canning, baking, and quilting; rodeo performances; tractor pulls; animal shows, motorcycle stunt shows, auto races, and demolition derbies; and other contests and shows of all kinds. It's the perfect place to take kids, because there are always several petting zoos and other varieties of family entertainment throughout the fairgrounds. Special prices and ride passes are available on certain days.

More than 2,000 campsites are available on the fairgrounds. Call for campsite rental fees.

Tip to fair-goers: The first weekend is way too crowded. Try going through the week or on the next weekend.

Bothwell Lodge State Historic Site (all ages)

Off Highway 65 at 19349 Bothwell State Park Road, Sedalia 65301; (660) 827–0510 or (800) 334–6946; www.mostateparks.com. Tours of lodge are available 10:00 A.M. to 4:00 P.M. Monday through Saturday, noon to 5:00 P.M. Sunday. $; children ages 5 and under free. The park surrounding the lodge is open daily from 8:00 A.M. to sunset.

Local lawyer and philanthropist John Bothwell built this massive stone house between 1897 and 1928 on the side of a cliff. A guide takes you through the three-story house, pointing out the unusual design elements of the owner, who was influenced by the Arts

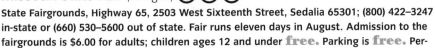

Amazing
Missouri Facts

Where did Scott Joplin live when he published his now famous "Maple Leaf Rag"?

Sedalia (John Stark published the music in 1899 in Sedalia.)

and Crafts movement. The site has picnic facilities and a self-guided hiking trail that provides information about the property when it was the country getaway of Bothwell.

Daum Contemporary Art Museum (all ages)

3201 West Sixteenth Street, Sedalia 65301; (660) 530-5888; www.daummuseum.org. Open 11:00 A.M. to 5:00 P.M. Tuesday through Friday, 1:00 to 5:00 P.M. Saturday and Sunday. **Free** admission.

This museum is on the campus of State Fair Community College. Its nine galleries contain art collected over the past three decades by Dr. Harold F. Daum, a local collector who compiled an amazing collection of art produced since the mid-twentieth century. Young children likely will be interested in many of the photos and some of the sculptures, particularly "Reflection of the Flame," a row of semicircular structures standing 5 feet tall and stretching 60 feet across.

Liberty Center (ages 4 and up)

111 West Fifth Street, Sedalia 65301; (660) 827–3228. Call for schedule.

The renovated Liberty Theater hosts a year-round schedule of shows, including productions staged or booked by Liberty Center's board, and performances by the Sedalia Community Theater group.

For More Information

Sedalia Area Convention & Visitors Bureau. 600 East Third Street, Sedalia 65301; (660) 826–2222 or (800) 827–5295; www.visitsedalia.com.

Knob Noster

Knob Noster State Park (all ages)

Highway 23, 1 mile south of Highway 50, Knob Noster 65336; (660) 563–2463 or (800) 334–6946; www.mostateparks.com. Open year-round. Visitor center open daily 8:00 A.M. to 4:30 P.M. Campsites are $8.00 per day for basic site, $14.00 per day for RV electrical hookups. Call (877) 427–6766 at least forty-eight hours in advance for camping reservations. There is an $8.50 registration fee.

This park has a savanna landscape of prairie grasses and widely spaced trees. There is a visitor center with photographic displays and a naturalist on hand to answer your questions. The park has hiking and equestrian trails, several small lakes and a stream for fishing, and a wooded campground with seventy-three sites. Stop at the park office to find out about nature programs offered year-round. A map of an orienteering trail is also available.

Whiteman Air Force Base (all ages)
Highway 23 off Highway 50; (660) 687–6133. Open house usually is in summer; call for date.

Once a year you can visit the home base of the Stealth bomber. During an annual open house you can climb into older planes, view displays about aircraft and the air force, and see guard dogs, a mobile command station, and other military items. An air show and aerial demonstrations take place throughout the day.

Warrensburg

Powell Gardens (all ages)
Highway 50, 20 miles east of Lee's Summit, 20 miles west of Warrensburg; (816) 566–2600. Open daily 9:00 A.M. to 6:00 P.M. April through October, open until 5:00 P.M. November through March. Chapel open Monday through Friday 10:00 A.M. to 5:00 P.M., Saturday and Sunday 11:00 A.M. to 4:00 P.M. Cafe open daily 11:00 A.M. to 2:00 P.M. Gift shop open Monday through Friday 10:00 A.M. to 2:00 P.M., Friday and Saturday 10:00 A.M. to 5:00 P.M. $–$$; children ages 4 and under free.

This beautiful 800-acre botanical garden has two structures by famed architects Fay Jones and Maurice Jennings, demonstration gardens, native-plant landscapes, a twelve-acre lake, and several types of specialty gardens. The Visitor Education Center, a limestone-and-glass structure designed by Jones and Jennings, gives the illusion of being outdoors while indoors. The building includes a conservatory with spectacular indoor displays of seasonal plants, the Gifted Gardener gift shop, Cafe Thyme, and a large, roomy entrance-way for welcoming visitors. The pair of architects also designed the Marjorie Powell Allen Chapel, where they have designed a wood-and-glass structure to fit perfectly into its location beside the lake and in front of a wood. Your children will enjoy walking along the lakeshore and through a wonderful wooded area that has wooden bridges spanning a babbling brook. The garden sponsors a full schedule of educational programs, many designed especially for children.

Amazing
Missouri Facts

What does the Native American word Missouri mean?

"Town of large canoes."

Festivals

MARCH

Wurstfest, Hermanhoff Festhalle and other locations throughout historic Hermann; (800) 932–8687. Last Saturday and Sunday in March. This citywide celebration of the art of German sausage making is a festive display of German culture with plenty of samples and demonstrations.

MAY

Maifest. Throughout Hermann; (800) 932–8687. Third weekend of May. This fun and popular festival has two parades, children's activities in the park, beer and wine gardens, German music and dancing, carnival rides, and activities throughout the town.

JUNE

Downtown Twilight Festivals. Downtown Columbia, (573) 442–6816; www.downtown columbia.org. From 6:00 to 10:00 P.M. on Thursday nights in June and September, kids and adults are treated to a low-key schedule of events that includes a kids' camp, horse-drawn carriage rides, a variety of musical performances, local artists demonstrating their craft, and more.

Jubilee Days. Drake Harbor, downtown Warsaw; (660) 438–5922 or (800) 927–7294. Held in mid-June, this celebration has carnival rides, a street dance, kids' games, contests, a parade, and food and crafts booths.

Scott Joplin Ragtime Festival. Historic downtown Sedalia and fairgrounds; (660) 826–2271; www.scottjoplin.org. First week in June. Since 1974, people have been coming from all over the world to listen to ragtime in concerts and open-air performances, to dance to it, and to attend symposia about Joplin and swap sheet music. Joplin, who came to Sedalia in 1893 to attend the now-defunct George R. Smith College, left in 1904 to take the new form of music he was defining to the St. Louis World's Fair.

SEPTEMBER

Annual Heritage Festival. Historic Maplewood Farm in Nifong Park, Columbia; (573) 874–7460; www.gocolumbiamo.com. On the third weekend in September, this festival celebrates the history of mid-Missouri with a variety of demonstrations and displays, including a Lewis and Clark encampment, cowboys and a chuck wagon, native American tepees, and artisans and trades-people exhibiting their talent and skills. This wonderful event also offers hayrides, storytelling, children's activities, four entertainment stages for music, and lots of kettle corn.

Walnut Festival. Stockton City Park; (417) 276–5213. Held during the last weekend in September, this festival has carnival rides, **free** nightly entertainment, arts and crafts for sale, craft demonstrations, a parade, and various competitions you or your children can enter.

OCTOBER

Octoberfest, citywide in historic downtown Hermann; (573) 486–2744 or (800) 932–8687. First four weekends in October. This traditional German celebration offers authentic German food, music, arts, and a bunch of crafts. Just about every business in historic downtown gets into this salute to Hermann's German heritage.

Hartsburg Pumpkin Festival. Hartsburg, (573) 657–4556. In mid-October, this quaint river town south of Columbia brings in more than 150 crafts vendors during a family-friendly festival that offers a petting zoo, pony rides, food booths, and an unparalleled variety of pumpkins and pumpkin-related activities.

NOVEMBER

Festival of Lights. Long Shoal Campground, Highway 7, Warsaw; (660) 438–5922 or (800) 927–7294. Friday, Saturday, and Sunday 5:30 to 10:00 P.M. Thanksgiving through January, Long Shoal Campground is transformed into a **free** drive-through lighting display more than a mile long.

Lake of Light Festival. Osage Beach and Lake Ozark area; (573) 365–3002 or (800) 451–4117. November and December. Everything seems to light up for the holidays.

Activities include a parade and Christmas shows. Tan-Tar-A Resort is also lit up and offers **free** holiday activities.

DECEMBER

Christmas Park of Dreams. Hermann City Park; (800) 932–8687. Open 6:00 to 10:00 P.M. Friday, Saturday, and Sunday in December. The city sets up a drive-through trail of animated lighting displays in the park. **Free** admission. Other holiday activities, including a Kris Kringle Fair, take place throughout the town.

Where to Eat

NEVADA

Echo's. 1819 West Austin Boulevard, Nevada 64772; (417) 667–5100. Open Tuesday through Saturday 7:00 A.M. to 9:00 P.M. Great Reuben sandwiches are among the daily luncheon specials; prime rib and chicken are excellent for dinner. Kids' menu available. $$

J.T. Maloney. 2117 East Austin Boulevard, Nevada 64772; (417) 667–7719. Open Monday through Saturday 11:00 A.M. to 2:00 P.M. and 4:00 to 10:00 P.M., Sunday 11:00 A.M. to 2:00 P.M. Daily luncheon sandwich specials and great prime rib, steaks, chicken, shrimp, crab, and fish. Kids' menu available. $$

VERSAILLES

Pioneer Restaurant. Junction of Highway 52 and Highway 5, Versailles 65084; (573) 378–5886. Open daily 6:00 A.M. to 9:00 P.M., close at 8:00 P.M. during the winter. Great family food at good prices. They bake their own bread, the chicken and ribs are fantastic, and they have several buffets. $$

GREENVIEW

Burt's Place. Highway 5 North and Highway 7, 8779-1 North State Highway 5, Camdenton

65020; (573) 873–5266. Open Wednesday through Saturday 8:00 A.M. to 8:00 P.M., Friday and Saturday 8:00 A.M. to 9:00 P.M., Sunday 8:00 A.M. to 2:00 P.M. The fried chicken and tenderloin are tasty, but desserts definitely reign here; the cream puffs are incredible. There's also a wide variety of cream pies; try the coconut or lemon meringue. $$

CAMDENTON

Captain's Galley. Lake Road 589 (31-mile marker), Box 1104, Camdenton 65020; (573) 873–5227 in season, (573) 873–5058 in winter. Open daily 8:00 A.M. to 10:00 P.M. April through October. Biscuits and gravy is a house specialty, but they have great sandwiches, salads, tasty fajitas, and Caribbean-flair dishes from Jamaica. $$

LINN CREEK

Tonka Hills Restaurant. Highway 54, east of Camdenton, Linn Creek 65052; (573) 346–5759. Open Tuesday through Friday 7:00 A.M. to 7:30 P.M., Saturday and Sunday 7:00 A.M. to 2:00 P.M. This is an excellent stop for home-style cooked meals. The fried chicken and catfish are excellent, but they also have delicious soups and sandwiches. $

OSAGE BEACH

Country Kitchen Family Restaurants.
5256 Highway 54, Osage Beach 65065; (573)
348–4554. Open daily 6:00 A.M. to midnight.
This is the place to get substantial sandwiches, french fries, dinners, and breakfast all
day long. $$

Cozy Coney 3754. Highway 54, across from
Stonecrest Mall, Osage Beach 65065; (573)
348–3324. Open daily 6:30 A.M. to 2:30 P.M.
You can get breakfast and plenty of hot dogs
and sandwiches. The kids will like it. $

Pasta House Company. 4204 Highway
54, Osage Beach 65065; in front of Wal-
Mart; (573) 348–2207. Open Sunday
through Thursday 11:00 A.M. to 10:00 P.M.,
Friday and Saturday 11:00 A.M. to 11:00 P.M.
The house salad is a staple, and it's supple-
mented with plenty of great pastas, veal,
steak, and chicken. The kids will like the
toasted or boiled ravioli. $$$

Tres Hombres: A Mexican Cantina. On
Highway 54, 939 Ches Street, Osage Beach
65065; behind the outlet mall; (573)
348–6789. Open Sunday through Thursday
11:00 A.M. to 10:00 P.M., Friday and Saturday
11:00 A.M. to 11:00 P.M. Look for the children's
entrees on the menu, which has great fajitas,
chimichangas, burritos, and flautas for the
big folks. $$

LAKE OZARK

Bayou Bill's. Business Highway 54 to HH to
Bittersweet Road; send mail to P.O. Box 793,
Lake Ozark 65049; (573) 365–6464 in season,
(573) 348–3201 in winter. Open 11:00 A.M. to
midnight May through October. Gumbo, jam-
balaya, and Cajun cooking is the specialty,
but they've also got a kids' menu and burg-
ers. $$

Randy's Frozen Custard. Highway 54, in
King's Mall near Consumers', Lake Ozark

65049; (573) 348–0711. Open daily April
through October or so. Great frozen custard. $

JEFFERSON CITY

Arris' Pizza Palace. 117 West High Street,
Jefferson City 65101; (573) 635–9225. Open
11:00 A.M. to 10:00 P.M. Monday through
Thursday, 11:00 A.M. to 11:00 P.M. Friday and
Saturday, 4:00 to 10:00 P.M. Sunday. Great
pizza and Greek food are served in a kid-
friendly atmosphere. $–$$

Central Dairy. 610 Madison Street, Jefferson City 65101; (573) 635–6148. Open Monday through Saturday 8:00 A.M. to 6:00 P.M.,
Sunday 10:00 A.M. to 6:00 P.M. A wonderful
place for an ice-cream treat with a selection
of more than forty flavors. Owned by the
same family since the 1920s, this dairy has
been making and serving delicious ice cream
for decades. $

Paddy Malone's. 700 West Main Street, Jefferson City 65101; (573) 761–5900. Open
11:00 A.M. to 1:30 A.M. Monday through Friday, 3:00 P.M. to 1:30 A.M. Saturday. This place
has delicious homemade chili and soups,
pasta, and sandwiches, including a great
bratwurst. It's an excellent lunch stop for families but less so at night, when it becomes
more of a pub and its kitchen shifts gears to
concentrate on catering jobs. $$

Viet's Diamond Restaurant. 2001 Mis-
souri Boulevard, Jefferson City 65109; (573)
635–1213. Open Tuesday through Saturday
5:00 to 10:00 P.M. Full menu with fried
chicken, daily specials, lots of sandwiches,
and french fries, too. $$$

Zesto's Drive-In. Two locations in Jefferson
City: 1730 Jefferson, (573) 659–7117; and
501 Broadway, (573) 635–0712. Open 9:00
A.M. to 10:00 P.M. year-round. Here you get
old-fashioned ice cream with great shakes
and sandwiches, including a foot-long hot dog.

HERMANN

Downtown Deli and Custard Shop Shoppe. 215 East First Street, Hermann 65401; (573) 486–5002. Open daily 10:00 A.M. to 10:00 P.M. Sandwiches served on fresh-baked bread, salads, homemade pies, and hand-dipped and soft-serve ice cream make this a great stop for everyone. $

Simms on the Waterfront. 4 Schiller Street, Hermann 65041; (573) 486-2030. Open 11:00 A.M. to 8:00 P.M. Wednesday through Sunday; closed Monday and Tuesday. There are plenty of options on a menu offering steak, seafood, barbecue, and a soup and salad bar. On Sunday there's a fried chicken special.

Vintage 1847 Restaurant at Stone Hill Winery. 1110 Stone Hill Highway; Hermann 65401; (573) 486–3479. In summer open daily 11:00 A.M., closed Sunday through Thursday at 8:30 P.M., Friday at 9:00 P.M., Saturday at 10:00 P.M. Delicious breaded pork cutlets, prepared Jaeger style with red wine and mushrooms or German style with sour cream and dill, served with potato pancakes and red cabbage. All kinds of German food plus soups, salads, hamburgers, and pasta. $$$

COLUMBIA

G&D Pizza-Steak. 2101 West Broadway, Columbia 65203; (573) 445–8336. Open 11:00 A.M. to 11:00 P.M. Monday through Saturday; closed Sunday. This place offers a wide variety of sandwiches and kid-pleasing pizza, along with several Greek specialties. $-$$

Peggy Jean's Pies. 1605 Chapel Hill Road, Suite B, Columbia 65203; (573) 447–1119; www.peggyjeanspies.com. Open 7:00 A.M. to 7:00 P.M. Monday through Saturday; closed Sunday. Decorated like Grandma's kitchen, these incredible pie makers create thirty-one types of handmade pies and nearly a dozen daily special "baby" pies. They also offer fresh soups, salads, quiche of the day, and sandwiches. You can take a pie or two for the road or order them on-line after you get back home. $$

Shakespeare's Pizza & Wine Bar. Two locations in Columbia: 225 South Ninth Street, (573) 449–2454 and 3304 Broadway, (573) 447–1202. Open Monday through Thursday 11:00 A.M. to midnight, Friday and Saturday 11:00 A.M. to 1:00 A.M., Sunday 11:00 A.M. to 11:00 P.M. Your kids will love watching their own pizza being made. Go early in the evening to avoid the crowd. $$

63 Diner. Highway 63, 3 miles north of Columbia, 5801 Highway 763 North, Columbia 65202; (573) 443–2331. Open Tuesday through Friday 11:00 A.M. to 9:00 P.M., Saturday 6:30 A.M. to 9:00 P.M., closed Sunday and Monday. You'll know you are there when you see the red Cadillac jutting from the front of the building. They serve great diner-type food that your children will love. $$

SEDALIA

El Tapatio. 1705 West Broadway, Sedalia 65301; (660) 827–5553. Open Monday through Thursday 11:00 A.M. to 9:00 P.M., Friday and Saturday 11:00 A.M. to 10:00 P.M., Sunday 11:00 A.M. to 9:00 P.M. Authentic Mexican food, with great tacos, burritos, and the like. $$

Kehde's Barbecue. Twentieth Street and Limit (South Highway 65), Sedalia 65301; (660) 826–2267. Open daily 10:30 A.M. to 9:00 P.M. Great barbecue—all kinds—stuffed potatoes, and even a few Mexican dishes. $

LeMaire's. 3312 South Highway 65, Sedalia 65301; (660) 827–3563. Open Sunday through Wednesday 11:00 A.M. to 9:00 P.M., Thursday through Saturday 11:00 A.M. to 3:00 A.M. This is as rustic and casual as a restaurant gets, but the fried catfish, hush puppies, and "dirty" rice are delicious—the kids love them—and there's oysters, shrimp, and crawfish for bigger folks. $$

Mighty Melt. 2402 West Broadway, Sedalia 65301; (660) 827–2290. Open Monday through Friday 10:00 A.M. to 8:00 P.M., Saturday 10:00 A.M. to 4:00 P.M., closed Sunday. Deli sandwiches with homemade bread, soups, and salads. $

Where to Stay

We have visited the Lake of the Ozarks regularly since 1985 and during that time have stayed in at least nine different resorts. The reasons we picked these particular resorts varied from referrals from friends to having stumbled upon them when randomly looking for a new place to stay. The point is, there are hundreds of resorts at the lake, not to mention thousands of condominiums for rent and thousands more campsites.

There's really no way to adequately check out more than a few resorts before making a decision. But one way to narrow the field is by visiting the Lake of the Ozarks Convention & Visitor Bureau Web site at www.funlake.com. The site doesn't have all the resorts and campgrounds in the area, but there's a long list and several have comprehensive sites of their own. If you have other questions, call the bureau at (800) 386–5253.

NEVADA

Country Inn & Suites. 2520 East Austin, Nevada 64772; (417) 667–9292. Checkout time is noon; check-in time is 2:00 P.M. Forty-five rooms, indoor pool, hot tub, Jacuzzi in some rooms, continental breakfast, and fitness center. Children seventeen and under **free.** $$$

WARRENSBURG

Teresa's Ristorante. 717 South Maguire Street, Warrensburg 64093; (660) 747–6296. Open 11:00 A.M. to 9:00 P.M. Sunday through Friday, 4:00 to 10:00 P.M. Saturday. This wonderful little restaurant is a great surprise and worth a slight detour. Specializing in Italian food, it has wonderful salads, sandwiches, desserts, and, for those St. Louisans who can't eat an Italian meal without them, toasted ravioli.

Ramsey's Nevada Hotel. 1514 East Austin Boulevard, Nevada 64772; (417) 667–5273. Checkout time is 11:00 A.M.; check-in time is when available. Thirty rooms and outdoor pool. Children twelve and under **free.** $$

Super 8. 2301 East Austin, Nevada 64772; (417) 667–8888. Checkout time is 11:00 A.M.; check-in time is 3:00 P.M. Fifty-nine rooms, indoor pool, hot tub, continental breakfast. Children ages twelve and under **free.** $$

LAKE OZARK

Alhonna Resort and Marina. 1237 Outer Drive, Lake Ozark 65049; (573) 365–2634. Open year-round. Located on the lake, the resort has indoor and outdoor heated pools, a sauna, a fishing and swimming dock, a boat launch, boat slips, a small restaurant, and a small bar; also a pool table and a few video machines. The marina rents ski, fishing, and pontoon boats and deckboats. $$$

Majestic Oaks Park. Paved State Route W, 4½ miles northwest of Bagnell Dam, P.O. Box 525, Lake Ozark 65049; (573) 365–1890 or (800) 616–1890; www.majesticoakspark.com. Open April 1 to October 31. The campground has seventy-eight spaces, sixty with hookups, and a swimming pool, playground, laundromat, game room, wooded trails, picnic tables, sand volleyball court, horseshoes, shuffleboard, basketball, and more. The daily fee for one space with four adults is $13.00 for tents, $18.50 for 30 amp RV hookups, $22.50 for 50 amp hookups (also includes cable television), with an extra-person fee of $3.00 per person for visitors ages 10 or older. $

Point Randall. Highway HH, at 400 Susan Road, Lake Ozark 65049; (573) 365–2081. Open year-round. All units are near the water's edge and have a full kitchen and a deck or patio that overlooks the water. Resort has a heated swimming pool, hot tub and deck, boat rental, recreation room with Ping-Pong and video games, padded covered docks, and excellent fishing with 1,000 feet of shoreline. Availability is limited between mid-June and mid-August; call ahead. $$$

JEFFERSON CITY

Econo Lodge. 1926 Jefferson Street, Jefferson City 65109; (573) 636–2797. Checkout time is 11:00 A.M.; check-in time is 2:00 P.M. Fifty-two rooms, continental breakfast, outdoor pool. Children ages 18 and under free. $$

Super 8 Motel. 1710 Jefferson Street, Jefferson City 65101; (573) 636–5456. Checkout time is 11:00 A.M.; check-in time is 2:00 P.M. Seventy-seven rooms, continental breakfast, exercise room. Children ages 12 and under free. $$$

HERMANN

Harbor Haus Inn & Suites. 113 North Market Street, Hermann 65041; (888) 942-7529. Twelve rooms, four minutes from Amtrak station. Check-in time is 3:00 P.M.; checkout time is 11:00 A.M. Full Dutch breakfast; pet friendly. Children ages 17 and under stay free. $$$

Hermann Motel. 112 East Tenth Street, Hermann 65041; (573) 486–3131. Checkout

time is 11:00 A.M.; check-in time is 4:00 P.M. Twenty-four rooms, no frills. Children twelve and under free. $$

COLUMBIA

Days Inn. 1900 I–70 Drive SW, Columbia 65203; (573) 445–8511. Checkout time is 11:00 A.M.; check-in time is 3:00 P.M.; 160 rooms, outdoor pool, exercise room, full breakfast at adjacent restaurant. Children ages 13 and under free. $$$

Hampton Inn. 3410 Clark Lane, Columbia 65202; (573) 886–9392; www.hampton inn.com. 122 rooms, continental breakfast bar, indoor pool, whirlpool, exercise facility. $$$

Regency Premier Hotel Downtown. 1111 Broadway, Columbia 65201; (573) 443–2090; www.regencydowntown.com; 102 rooms, quick-start breakfast center, pool, whirlpool, free access to Gold's Gym. $$$

Stoney Creek Inn. 2601 South Providence Road, Columbia 65203; (800) 659–2220; www.stoneycreekinn.com; 142 rooms, indoor-outdoor pool, whirlpool spa, dry sauna, video game room, continental breakfast. $$$

SEDALIA

Best Western. 3120 South Limit, Sedalia 65301 (South Highway 65); (660) 826–6100. Checkout time is noon; check-in time is 3:00 P.M. 119 rooms, indoor pool, sauna. Children ages 18 and under free. Call early; many rooms are booked for the Missouri State Fair. $$$

Comfort Inn. 3600 West Broadway, Sedalia 65301; (660) 829–5050 or (800) 228–5150. Checkout time is 11:00 a.m.; check-in time is 3:00 p.m. Seventy-six rooms, indoor pool and spa, deluxe continental breakfast. Children ages 18 and under free. $$$

Hotel Bothwell. 103 East Fourth Street, Sedalia 65301; (660) 826–5588; www.hotel bothwell.com. Checkout time is 11:00 A.M.; check-in time is 3:00 P.M. Dating from 1927, this elegant hotel in downtown Sedalia might seem a bit much for the kids, but it's just the type of treat parents on the road need once in a while. It has a gourmet coffee shop, delectable pastries—a continental breakfast comes with the room—and del Amici's ($$$), a restaurant offering Italian specialties. And it's just a short walk from the Amtrak station and the Katy Trail. $$$$

Super 8. 3402 West Broadway, Sedalia 65301; (660) 827–5890 or (800) 800–8000. Checkout time is 11:00 A.M.; check-in time is 2:00 P.M. Eighty-seven rooms, continental breakfast, use of nearby athletic club. Children ages 12 and under **free.** $$

Northwest Missouri

Although the northwestern region of the state is primarily rural, you'll find that Kansas City and the surrounding suburbs offer big-city fun with numerous first-class tourist attractions, big-league sports teams, and museums and historic sites of national importance. North of Kansas City the Missouri River Valley is a major flyway for waterfowl, bald eagles, and songbirds, providing ample opportunities for bird-watching and wildlife viewing. As you travel northeast in the region you'll find farms and small towns dotting the countryside, with abundant locations for outdoor recreation.

Randy and Jane's
TopPicks in Northwest Missouri

1. Kansas City Zoological Park, Kansas City

2. Science City at Union Station, Kansas City

3. Pony Express Museum, St. Joseph

4. Kaleidoscope and Hallmark Visitors Center, Kansas City

5. Worlds of Fun, Oceans of Fun, Kansas City

6. *Arabia* Steamboat Museum, Kansas City

7. Squaw Creek National Wildlife Refuge, Mound City

8. American Royal Museum and Visitor Center, Kansas City

9. Patee House Museum, St. Joseph

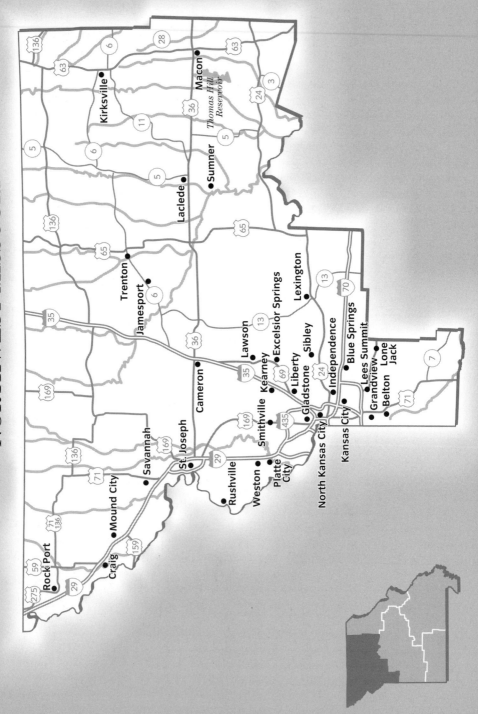

NORTHWEST MISSOURI

Kansas City

This city, where East meets West, is known for great barbecue, jazz, and having more fountains than any city in the world except Rome. Although it shares the name of the neighboring state to the west, most of the city is in the state of Missouri. But any family looking for adventure shouldn't leave town without checking out what Kansas City has to offer on both sides of the state line. In addition to what you will find listed here, the city has many great things to see and do in the state of Kansas. For information about all attractions in the area, call (800) 767–7700 or see www.visitkc.com.

KC Trolley Grand Tour (all ages)

Crown Center, Twenty-fifth and Grand, or any one of nineteen other locations; (816) 690–6100; www.koolnites-limousine.com. The trolleys run Monday through Saturday 10:00 A.M. to 6:00 P.M. Tickets for all-day passes, available from the drivers, are $8.00 for adults, $5.00 for children ages 2 through 11; children ages 1 and under free.

This is a great way to get an all-in-fun narrated tour of the city where you'll get jokes and silly stories along with the historical facts. You can stay on the trolley for a ninety-minute tour or get off anywhere along the route. Your tickets are good all day. The tour covers almost all the tourist attractions from the city market to the Plaza.

Airline History Museum (all ages)

201 Lou Holland Drive (southernmost hangar at Downtown Airport), Kansas City 64116; (816) 421–3401 or (800) 513–9484; www.airlinehistorymuseum.com. Open Monday through Saturday 10:00 A.M. to 4:00 P.M., Sunday noon to 4:00 P.M. $

If propeller-driven commercial transport craft are of interest to you, you'll like this small, esoteric museum. It tells the story of early aircraft with photos, artifacts, and two restored aircraft: a Lockheed Constellation and a Martin 404. Volunteers also are rebuilding a Douglas DC-3.

Fiesta Cruise (all ages)

100 Ward Parkway, Brush Creek at Wyandotte, Kansas City 64190; (816) 756–1331. Tour departs at the top of the hour. Open 6:00 to 10:00 P.M. Thursday and Friday, 1:00 to 10:00 P.M. Saturday. $$; children ages 2 and under free.

Hear a narrated history of Country Club Plaza, the nation's oldest shopping center, and see the waterfalls and fountains in the plaza as this forty-eight-passenger boat cruises for thirty minutes along the winding Brush Creek from Wyandotte to Jefferson, Grand, and back.

Crown Center (all ages)

Next door to the world headquarters of Hallmark Cards, 2450 Grand Boulevard, Kansas City 64108; (816) 274–8444; www.crowncenter.com. Open Monday through Wednesday and Saturday 10:00 A.M. to 6:00 P.M., Thursday and Friday 10:00 A.M. to 9:00 P.M., Sunday noon to 5:00 P.M.

Your visit to Kansas City wouldn't be complete without a stroll around Crown Center, with its shops, restaurants, theaters, and hotels in a splendid luxury setting. Entertainment is regularly provided on the lower level, and throughout the Christmas season musicians, puppeteers, and other seasonal entertainers perform.

- **The Coterie Theater:** *Level One; (816) 474–6552; www.thecoterie.com. Open October through the end of July. Tickets are $6.00.* The theater offers a full season of delightful family theater productions designed to be enjoyed by children and adults. Call ahead for age recommendation on each show.
- **American Heartland Theater:** *Third Level; (816) 842–9999; www.ahtkc.com. Open year-round.* A beautiful 420-seat theater presents everything from mysteries to Broadway musicals.
- **Ice Terrace:** *Crown Center Square; (816) 274–8411. Open daily 10:00 A.M. to 9:00 P.M. November through March. $–$$.* This is a great outdoor rink where you can rent skates or bring your own.

Hallmark Visitors Center (all ages)

2450 Grand Boulevard, (adjacent to Crown Center), Kansas City 64108; (816) 274–3613; www.crowncenter.com. Open 10:00 A.M. to 6:00 P.M. Monday through Wednesday and Saturday, 10:00 A.M. to 9:00 P.M. Thursday and Friday, noon to 5:00 P.M. Sunday. Free admission to center. Parking is free at the Crown Center Garage with a three-hour validation. Enter the garage on the east side of Grand where the HALLMARK VISITORS CENTER sign is visible.

You'll have a lot more fun than you've ever imagined learning about the world's largest greeting-card company. There are fourteen exhibits ranging from memorabilia collected during eighty years in business to clips of *Hallmark Hall of Fame* television dramas and an automatic bow-making machine that turns out bows on demand. Your kids will love the room with 6-foot pencils, markers, brushes, paint tubes, and jars, where they can view a video illustrating how artists create greeting-card designs.

Kaleidoscope (ages 5 through 12)

2501 McGee in Crown Center, Kansas City 64108; (816) 274–8300 or (816) 274–8301; www.hallmarkkaleidoscope.com. Open year-round, but more public sessions are held in summer months. Call for hours of public sessions. Tickets are distributed free on a first-come, first-served basis, so get there early.

This is a part of the Hallmark Card facility that provides creative experiences for kids ages five through twelve. The sessions are primarily for children, although a few parents are allowed to stay and help with the activities. Factories that make cards, ribbon, wrapping paper, and party supplies have great stuff left over. It's bright, colorful, attractive, and fod-

A Cosby Family **Adventure**

If you have a budding artist in the family and a soft spot for "cornography"—those commercials aimed dead center at your heart—you'll love the Hallmark Visitors Center and Kaleidoscope in Crown Center. We were able to put trips to both together on a Saturday and had a thoroughly enjoyable adventure.

Hallmark, which never fails to tug at the heartstrings with its commercials, has put them all together here, along with clips of its stellar *Hallmark Hall of Fame* television dramas. Having seen most of the dramas on video or television, the kids loved the clips. They also were fascinated by an automatic bow-making machine that they can activate and a room full of enormous art supplies. Our daughter the artist was captivated by a video that showed how artists create designs for greeting cards and by a printing and folding machine and its operator, who works behind glass in the visitor center.

The center primed us for the trip next door to Kaleidoscope, a Hallmark-sponsored hands-on adventure in art for children ages five through twelve. The sessions are primarily for children, but we and a few other parents were allowed to stay and help out. The idea here is to give the kids activities to create art from the bright, colorful ribbon, wrapping paper, and other supplies left over from Hallmark's factories.

The result was a frenzy of creative effort that not only consumed our resident artist but also our son, who until this experience had never claimed an affinity for anything artistic. After much cutting, pasting, coloring, and taping, each of them carried home a bag filled with creations and an ego filled with the warm feeling of satisfaction brought on by a job well done. But you wouldn't expect anything less from Hallmark, would you?

der for fun. That's how this creative art experience center works. Kids are exposed to activities intended to stimulate their creative juices and then set loose with all those Hallmark factory leftovers. They cut, paste, tie, twist, color, draw—anything their creative little hearts desire. They get to keep what they make. Don't let your kids miss this experience.

American Royal Museum and Visitor Center (all ages)

1701 American Royal Court, Kansas City 64102; (816) 221–9800; www.americanroyal.com. Open Tuesday through Friday 10:00 A.M. to 4:00 P.M., Saturday and Sunday by appointment only. $; children ages 2 and under free.

In this museum your children can sit on an English or Western saddle, weigh themselves on a livestock scale, play with farm items, see a film about the annual rodeo, and learn about the people who make the event so successful. The interactive exhibits are excellent ways of explaining the role agribusiness plays in our lives. The museum is a great stop at any time, but it's especially fun during November, when the rodeo and livestock competitions are in full swing.

American Royal Livestock, Horse Show and Rodeo (all ages)

For ticket prices and a schedule, call (816) 221–7979 or (800) 821–5857; www.american royal.com.

This is one of the top twenty professional rodeos in the nation and draws contestants and spectators from all over. During the two-month season from early October to mid-November, the complex has a commercial trade show, a petting area with a variety of animals, and a full schedule of livestock shows, competitions, rodeos, and big-name entertainers. The event begins with the city's largest parade. Throughout the rest of the year, a wide variety of events and performers are scheduled at the complex.

Kemper Arena (all ages)

1800 Genessee, Kansas City 64102; (816) 513–4000; www.kcconvention.com.

The arena hosts a full range of events, with automated information about upcoming events and ticket prices. Sports buffs also can watch soccer action from October through April. The Kansas City Comets professional indoor soccer team's tickets range from $5.00 to $50.00. Call (816) 474–2255; www.kccomets.com.

City Market (all ages)

20 East Fifth Street, Suite 201, Kansas City 64106; (816) 842–1271; www.kc-citymarket.com. Open Monday through Friday 10:00 A.M. to 5:00 P.M., Saturday 7:00 A.M. to 4:00 P.M., Sunday 9:00 A.M. to 4:00 P.M.

Show the kids what shopping centers used to look like. Here by the river in the area where the city began, and where the market started in 1857, more than thirty vendors offer everything from fresh produce to art and entertainment. On Saturday and Sunday farmers come in from rural areas to sell their wares.

Amazing
Missouri Facts

What momentous baseball event took place in Missouri in 1985?

The I-70 World Series, in which Kansas City beat St. Louis four games to three

Arabia **Steamboat Museum** (all ages)

400 Grand Boulevard, Kansas City 64106; (816) 471–4030; www.1856.com.
Open Monday through Saturday 10:00 A.M. to 6:00 P.M., Sunday noon
to 5:00 P.M. Free parking. $–$$; children ages 3 and under free.

Finding buried treasure is a common childhood fantasy, and at this
museum your children can learn the fascinating details of a real-
life treasure hunt. You can meet the treasure hunters and see
their spoils displayed in 30,000 square feet of exhibit space in
the City Market.

In 1856 the steamboat *Arabia* hit a log snag while steaming up
the Missouri River and sank in 15 feet of water, taking her 200-ton frontier cargo with her. But the river changed course and that sunken
steamboat ended up buried in a farmer's field. From 1988 to 1989,
five families excavated the steamboat from underneath 45 feet of
mud. The recovered treasure comprises the largest collection of
pre–Civil War artifacts in existence. You can study the contents of this
time capsule from the American frontier and talk to one of the hard-
working and determined people who performed the salvage operation
and preserved the artifacts.

Penn Valley Park (all ages)

Pershing Road between Main Street and Southwest Boulevard; (816) 513–7500;
www.kcmo.org/parks. Open daily year-round. Free admission.

This city park has several overlooks where you can get a great view of the city skyline and
use the picnic facilities. A dog park also is being planned.

City Hall Observation Deck (all ages)

Thirtieth floor of City Hall, 414 East Twelfth Street, Kansas City 64106; (816) 513–1313;
www.kcmo.org. Open Monday through Friday 8:30 A.M. to 4:30 P.M.; closed during high
winds. Free admission.

Here's the place to go for free, breathtaking view of the city. Take the elevator to the
twenty-eighth floor and walk up two flights of stairs to the observation deck.

Federal Reserve Bank of Kansas City (ages 5 and up)

925 Grand Boulevard, Kansas City 64198; (816) 881–2683; www.kc.frb.org. Open Monday
through Friday 8:00 A.M. to 3:30 P.M. Free admission.

Don't get the idea that this is too complex and will bore your children; give it a try. The display in the mezzanine of the bank is great for school-age children. Kids can compare real
and counterfeit money, see a twenty-seven-pound gold bar in the Money Museum, examine money from other countries, and learn how much a Happy Meal costs in seven other
countries. A multimedia computer program lets you test your skill as chairman of the Federal Reserve Board, and an automated teller machine spits out real receipts and lets little

ones play with something usually reserved for grown-ups. The best part comes at the end of your visit when you receive a small bag of money, unfortunately shredded beyond any hope of ever using it.

Kansas City Board of Trade (ages 10 and up)

Third-floor observation deck at 4800 Main Street, Kansas City 64112; (816) 753–7500. Open Monday through Friday 8:15 A.M. to 3:30 P.M. The most active times generally are 9:30 A.M. or 1:15 P.M. Free admission.

Older kids might get a kick from watching the trading of Value Line stock index futures, as well as the world's largest winter-wheat futures market. This place gets pretty exciting sometimes.

Kansas City Museum (all ages)

3218 Gladstone Boulevard, Kansas City 64123; (816) 483–8300; www.kcmuseum.com. Open Tuesday through Saturday 9:30 A.M. to 4:30 P.M., Sunday noon to 4:30 P.M. $

This is a wonderful combination of history and science museum, housed in a luxury turn-of-the-century mansion and several buildings on the surrounding grounds. Your kids will have a great time as they explore interactive displays and hands-on exhibits that tell about the early history of the Kansas City area and explain about the weather, the forces of nature that affect us, and other scientific concepts. On the lower level you'll find a replica of a 1910 drugstore complete with a soda fountain selling ice-cream treats and old-fashioned phosphates. The museum has a yearlong schedule of special events and learning activities to promote history and science.

Kauffman Stadium (all ages)

Blue Ridge Cutoff on I–70; One Royal Way, Kansas City 64129; (800) 676–9257; www.kc royals.com. Tickets range from $5.00 to $22.00. Toddlers 32 inches tall and under are admitted free. Call for dates.

This is the home of the Kansas City Royals baseball team, the field of dreams for Hall of Famer George Brett and a passel of other great American League players.

Arrowhead Stadium (all ages)

Blue Ridge cutoff on I–70, One Arrowhead Drive, Kansas City 64129; Chiefs (816) 920–9300 or (800) 676–5488; www.kcchiefs.com; tickets range from $51 to $70. Wizards (816) 920–9300; www.kcwizards.com; tickets range from $12 to $17.

This is the home of the Kansas City Chiefs football team—the reason everyone in this part of the state wears red-and-white, arrowhead-emblazoned jackets—and the Kansas City Wizards outdoor soccer team, which plays from April through October.

Science City at Union Station (all ages)

30 West Pershing Road, Kansas City 64108; (816) 460–2222; www.sciencecity.com. Open year-round 10:00 A.M. to 5:00 P.M. Monday through Saturday, noon to 5:00 P.M. Sunday, extended hours from Memorial Day to Labor Day. $–$$; children ages 3 and under free.

Also available are discounted combination tickets that include a show at the City Extreme Screen theater in Union Station.

This is one of the most fascinating and exciting attractions you or your kids will find in Missouri. Divided into six distinct "neighborhoods," Science City offers a range of interactive activities unmatched anywhere else. Downtown visitors can design a car or create a robot; in Old Town kids can pump gas at a 1950s Skelly station or produce a 1940s radio show. There's a dinosaur dig on the Southside, a crime lab Uptown where kids can help solve a crime. In all, the city has fifty interactive environments and a good collection of park benches for parents who are having a hard time keeping up with the kids. There also are a variety of excellent shows available at Union Station's City Extreme Screen, a five-story screen with 3-D capabilities.

Horace M. Peterson Visitors Center (all ages)

1616 East Eighteenth Street, Kansas City 64108; (816) 474–8463; www.american jazzmusuem.com. Open Tuesday through Thursday 9:00 A.M. to 6:00 P.M., Friday and Saturday 9:00 A.M. to 9:00 P.M., Sunday noon to 6:00 P.M. Free admission.

The story of the 18th and Vine Historic District is told by the people who were there in *18th and Vine, a People's Journey.* The fifteen-minute film explains how the neighborhood gave birth to the very distinctive sound that became known as Kansas City jazz. Visitors also can see several artifacts on display in the center and are allowed to view the rotating exhibit gallery in the adjacent American Jazz Museum.

Negro Leagues Baseball Museum (all ages)

1616 East Eighteenth Street, Kansas City 64108; (816) 221–1920 or (800) 221–6526; www.nlbm.com. Open Tuesday through Saturday 9:00 A.M. to 6:00 P.M., Sunday noon to 6:00 P.M. Combination ticket with American Jazz Museum is available. $–$$

Located in the heart of the historic jazz district, the museum re-creates the look, sounds, and feel of Negro Leagues baseball. Video presentations, exhibits, and memorabilia are used to chronicle the history and heroes of the leagues from their origin after the Civil War to their demise in the 1960s. You can even compare your hitting against some of the greats in a batting cage that pitches at speeds similar to the pros.

American Jazz Museum (all ages)

1616 East Eighteenth Street, Kansas City 64108; (816) 474–8463; www.americanjazzmuseum.com. Open Tuesday through Thursday 9:00 A.M. to 6:00 P.M., Friday and Saturday 9:00 A.M. to 9:00 P.M., Sunday noon to 6:00 P.M. Combination ticket with Negro Leagues Baseball Museum is available. $–$$

The story of jazz and many of its greatest performers is told through dozens of interactive exhibits. *Jazz Is,* a sixteen-minute introductory film screened at the 1999 Sundance Film Festival, sets the tone for the museum visit by exposing you to the lingo and mind-set of the performers highlighted inside. Kids will love Jazz Discovery, a soundproof room with buckets, sticks, and other items where they can experiment at putting sounds together; and the mixing station, where you can put together your own "sound" by adding or subtracting prerecorded tracks of instruments.

The late Charlie Parker, one of the best musicians ever to come out of Kansas City, is among the legends honored in the Jazz Masters exhibit. The museum also hosts performances by local jazz artists in its Blue Room, a smoke-free environment. Call for hours and pricing.

Toy and Miniature Museum (all ages)

5235 Oak Street, Kansas City 64112 (on campus of University of Missouri–Kansas City); (816) 333–2055; www.umkc.edu/tmm. Open Wednesday through Saturday 10:00 A.M. to 4:00 P.M., Sunday 1:00 to 4:00 P.M. $; children ages 2 and under free.

You'll see incredible 1-inch scale miniatures, toys, dolls, and more than 100 dollhouses—one dating from 1810 and another 10 feet tall. A history of toys from years past is on display in this twenty-four-room Victorian mansion dating from the early twentieth century. A variety of traveling exhibits also rotate through the museum's Room 24.

Country Club Plaza (all ages)

450 Ward Parkway, Kansas City 64112; for map or information, call (816) 753–0100; www.countryclubplaza.com. Stores are open Monday through Saturday 10:00 A.M. to 7:00 P.M., Thursday until 9:00 P.M., Sunday noon to 5:00 P.M. Restaurants and some stores have extended hours.

Locals call it simply "the Plaza." This is a great place for serious shoppers and those who just want to window-shop or take a walk. This elegant 14-square-block area, located off Ward Parkway, is filled with specialty stores and restaurants. The area also sports so much great architecture and art that it brings to mind an Old World European city and could be considered an outdoor public art gallery. Get a brochure with a map of the fountains, sculptures, and murals, many portraying children, and go on a walking treasure hunt to find your favorites. Or you can catch a ride in a horse-drawn carriage for a thoroughly delightful experience. A visitor center is open daily at 4709 Central, just south of FAO Schwartz.

Don't miss the plaza during the Christmas season. At 7:00 P.M. on Thanksgiving, a lighting ceremony marks the beginning of the season, and the lights are turned on at 7:30 P.M. Until mid-January the entire area is lit by miles and miles of multicolored lights. During this time the shops are open later in the evening, and the atmosphere is enchanting.

Nelson-Atkins Museum of Art (all ages)

4525 Oak Street, Kansas City 64111; (816) 751–1278; www.nelson-atkins.org. Open Tuesday through Thursday 10:00 A.M. to 4:00 P.M., Friday 10:00 A.M. to 9:00 P.M., Saturday 10:00 A.M. to 5:00 P.M., Sunday noon to 5:00 P.M. Free admission.

The Nelson-Atkins Museum is considered one of the finest general art museums in the country. Children will be most interested in the cloister from a medieval French church, the knight in full parade dress, the modern sculpture room, authentic Chinese temple, and the rooms furnished with Oriental furniture. The museum also has reorganized its Egyptian collection to focus on that culture's beliefs about the afterlife. Pick up a map and you can walk around the seventeen-acre sculpture garden on the museum grounds. Kids will enjoy seeing the artwork, the most noticeable being the four giant badminton shuttlecocks on the lawn.

Kemper Museum of Contemporary Art (all ages)

4420 Warwick Avenue, Kansas City 64111; (816) 561–3737; www.kemper art.org. Open Tuesday through Thursday 10:00 A.M. to 4:00 P.M., Friday and Saturday 10:00 A.M. to 9:00 P.M., Sunday 11:00 A.M. to 5:00 P.M. Free admission. Free parking. Cafe Sebastienne serves lunch Tuesday through Sunday 11:00 A.M. to 2:30 P.M. and dinner Friday and Saturday 5:30 to 9:30 P.M.

Kids will be awed by this free museum's 1,600-pound bronze *Spider* sculpture on the front lawn, the "baby" spider crawling up the outside of the museum, the enormous Frank Stella sculpture careening off the atrium wall, and Deborah Butterfield's reclining horse, Ahulani, in the sculpture courtyard. The Kemper offers fun, free programming on weekends, and gallery games every day in each exhibition that kids and grown-ups can do together. Children also will love the colorful walls of Cafe Sebastienne, where 110 paintings called *The History of Art* fit together like a puzzle.

Westport (all ages)

Broadway Boulevard and Westport Road; send mail to 4123 Mill Street, Kansas City 64111; www.westporttoday.com.

This historic area was the jumping-off point for settlers leaving on the Santa Fe, California, and Oregon Trails. Today it's an entertainment area with unique small shops and restaurants where it's fun to stroll.

Historic Folly Theater (all ages)

300 West Twelfth Street, Kansas City 64105; (816) 474–4444; www.follytheater.com for show schedule. Open year-round. $–$$

Listed on the National Register of Historic Places, this beautifully renovated theater offers family and children's shows at various times from November through May. Call for schedule.

Swope Park (all ages)

6601 Swope Parkway, Kansas City 64130; (816) 513–7500; www.kcmo.org/parks. Open year-round. Free admission.

This is one of the largest municipal parks in the country, with 1,769 acres. You'll find picnic and athletic facilities, as well as the Blue River winding through the park. There also is Lake of the Woods, which is stocked with sun perch, bass, crappie, and catfish for fishing enthusiasts. During the holiday season the park features a display of lights.

Starlight Theater (all ages)

Swope Park at 6601 Swope Parkway, Kansas City 64132; (816) 363–7827 or (800) 776–1730; www.kcstarlight.com. Call for a schedule of events.

This 8,000-seat outdoor theater in the middle of Swope Park offers family entertainment including Broadway musicals and concerts by top national performers during the summer months.

Kansas City Zoological Park (all ages)

Swope Park at 6700 Zoo Drive, Kansas City 64132; (816) 513–5700; www.kansascityzoo.org. Open daily 9:00 A.M. to 5:00 P.M. Zoo closes at 4:00 P.M. October 15 to March 31. $–$$; children ages 2 and under free. Admission for all on Tuesday is $3.00. There is an additional fee to attend Sprint IMAX shows; call (816) 513–4629 for schedule and prices.

This 202-acre park is a zoo on the move. The newest residents are a pair of rare African hunting dogs. Other recent additions include a 95-acre Africa exhibit, an Australia area, and the Deramus Education Pavilion. The pavilion has interactive exhibits, films, and an IMAX theater with a wide range of films.

The Africa exhibit includes a seventeen-acre plains area, an eight-acre forest, and individual areas for chimpanzees, gorillas, cheetahs, lions, and rhinos. This large-scale re-creation of animal habitats in Kenya, Tanzania, Uganda, Botswana, and the Congolese forest makes you feel as if you have been transported to Africa. These exhibits attempt to be as realistic as possible and may require some patience and searching before you spot the animals. Authentic vegetation is incorporated into the exhibits, and the landscaping is an integral part of the immersion experience. An eleven-acre lake offers paddleboat and safari-boat rides.

The Australia area offers a five-minute film, a working sheep station, and opportunities to get close to kangaroos, dingos, emus, and kookaburras.

An exhibit called the Okavango Elephant Sanctuary, located in a section of the zoo called Botswana, provides a natural habitat without any bars separating you and the elephants. The International Festival and Farmland in the USA exhibits enable you to see exotic and domesticated animals up close. Train, camel, and pony rides are available in various locations. Presentations of birds, mammals, and reptiles take place throughout the zoo.

Sprint IMAX Theater (all ages)

Kansas City Zoo; Swope Park, 6800 Zoo Drive, Kansas City 64132; (816) 513–4629; www.kansascityzoo.org. Open year-round; call for shows and prices.

The six-and-one-half-story screen and 12,000 watts of digital sound make this—the first IMAX theater in a zoo—an incredible place in which to watch a film. The theater shows several films each day on a rotating basis, prefacing each performance with *Kansas City Presents,* a seven-minute film that highlights the fabulous zoo next door and other Kansas City attractions.

Lakeside Nature Center (all ages)

In Swope Park at 4701 East Gregory, Kansas City 64132; (816) 513–8960; www.kcmo.org/parks. Open Tuesday through Saturday 9:00 A.M. to 5:00 P.M., Sunday noon to 4:00 P.M. Free admission.

For a wonderfully intimate look at flora and fauna, don't miss the Lakeside Nature Center. Its workers rehabilitate injured wildlife, conduct environmental education programs, and maintain the exhibits focusing on native species and wildlife. The staff and volunteers offer hands-on activities for children and are always willing to seize a "teachable moment" with visitors. Trails near the center provide visitors with a view of natural areas in the park.

Harley Davidson Final Assembly Plant (ages 12 and up)

11401 North Congress Avenue, Kansas City 64153; (888) 875–2883 or (816) 270–8488. Museum and tour center open from 8:00 A.M. to 3:00 P.M. Monday through Friday; factory tours from 8:00 A.M. to noon. Free admission.

The free one-hour tour of a motorcycle-production plant is interesting even if you are not a biker, and there are plenty of souvenirs if you are one or know one whom you owe a gift. Children must be at least twelve years old and accompanied by an adult to take the factory tour. No open-toe shoes or cameras are allowed on the tour. Children under age 12 can visit the museum.

Piper Memorial Medical Museum St. Joseph Health Center (all ages)

1000 Carondelet Drive, Kansas City 64114; (816) 943–2183. Open 8:00 A.M. to 8:00 P.M. daily. Free admission.

This little lobby museum covers the history of medicine provided at St. Joseph Health Center from 1874 to the present. It has an early 1900s doctor's office, and features interesting rotating exhibits ranging from displays on new procedures and treatment to nineteenth-century medical practices.

Kansas City Jaycees ProRodeo (all ages)

Benjamin Ranch, 6401 East Eighty-seventh Street, Kansas City 64138; (816) 761–5055; www.benjaminranch.com. Fourth of July weekend. $$$

This rodeo, which lasts either three or four days, includes children's activities, a petting zoo, craft booths, pony rides, and fireworks. Professional rodeo performers compete in all areas, including bronc riding, calf roping, barrel racing, steer wrestling, and bull riding.

Cave Spring Interpretive Center (all ages)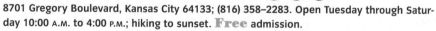

8701 Gregory Boulevard, Kansas City 64133; (816) 358–2283. Open Tuesday through Saturday 10:00 A.M. to 4:00 P.M.; hiking to sunset. Free admission.

Located on a thirty-six-acre site that was once a stopover on the Sante Fe Trail, the center features changing exhibits on the nature and history of the area and has several trails leading to a cave, a spring, and various wildlife habitats.

Museum Makes **Kids** the Stars

If you're visiting Kansas City with young children, you might want to step across the state line to the Children's Museum of Kansas City at 4601 State Street in Kansas City, Kansas.

Proclaiming itself a "magical learning journey where children are the stars," the museum has more than forty hands-on discovery-based learning activities, including role-play opportunities in a child-size grocery store, theater, city, and health-care setting.

But even if you don't have time to visit the museum, you might want to stop at the Recycled Materials Center next door. Crafters and teachers come from near and far to pay pennies for many items generously donated to the museum by companies that include Hallmark, Sprint, and Southwestern Bell.

The museum and center are open Tuesday through Saturday from 9:30 A.M. to 5:00 P.M. and Sunday from 1:00 to 5:00 P.M. Admission to the museum is $4.00 per person; children ages one and under are free. The recycling center is free.

For more information, call (913) 287–8888 or visit online at www.kid muzm.org.

Worlds of Fun (all ages)

Highway 435, exit 54 (Parvin Road); send mail to 4545 Worlds of Fun Avenue, Kansas City 64161; (816) 454–4545 or (816) 303–5220; www.worldsoffun.com. The park opens at 10:00 A.M. daily late May through late August; closing times vary. Open Saturday and Sunday only at 10:00 A.M. mid-April through late-May and September through mid-October. $$$–$$$$; children ages 3 and under free.

Two of the newest additions to the 175-acre park are ThunderHawk, a giant pendulum-like contraption that swings riders back and forth while soaking them, and Detonator, which shoots riders up 200-foot twin towers at 45 mph and then pulls them back to earth faster than a free fall. Camp Snoopy, featuring rides and attractions designed for families with young children, includes Woodstock's Airmail, a small-scale tower ride; Woodstock Express, a kiddie train; and Snoopy's Camp Bus, where children and parents ride with the Peanuts gang.

An impressive collection of roller coasters includes Boomerang, a twelve-story, corkscrew-shaped coaster that propels riders forward and then backward; Mamba, at 205 feet one of the tallest, longest, and fastest steel roller coasters in the world; Timber Wolf, a wooden coaster that remains one of the top-ranked roller coasters in the country; and the Orient Express, an immense steel roller coaster.

The park always offers several shows. Don't miss the Summer Spectacular, an extravaganza of laser light, music, and sounds held in the Forum Amphitheater in Americana; or

T-Bones Provide Some **Meaty Baseball**

The Kansas City T-Bones bring baseball a little closer to fans right across the state line in 4,500-seat CommunityAmerica Ballpark, 10800 State Avenue, in Kansas City, Kansas. Competing in the ten-team independent Northern League, the T-Bones, as do most minor-league teams, allow fans to get up close and personal with the players. That might not be Albert Pujols on the field, but it's still a lot of fun and a whole lot more afford-able. Tickets ranges from $4.50 to $9.50 and the parking is free. Call (913) 328–2255 for tickets and information, or go online at www.tbonesbaseball.com.

Stax of Trax, a tribute to music of the 1960s, 1970s, and 1980s held in the Moulin Rouge Theater in Europa. Kampground Karaoke for Kids is featured at the Snoopy Campground Theatre.

Oceans of Fun (all ages)

Highway 435, exit 54 (Parvin Road, adjacent to Worlds of Fun); send mail to 4545 Worlds of Fun Avenue, Kansas City 64161; (816) 454–4545 or (816) 303–5220; www.worldsoffun.com (click on rides and go to bottom of page). The park is open at 10:00 A.M. daily Memorial Day through late August; closing times vary. $$$–$$$$; children ages 3 and under free.

Paradise Falls is perfect for kids, featuring water cannons, sprays, tipping pails, net crawls, water slides, and bridges. Hurricane Falls, a 72-foot-tall superslide, is one of the park's most exciting rides. Described as "the roller coaster of the water park," the ride creates the excitement of a white-water rafting trip by carrying up to six sliders on a circular raft for nearly 680 feet down a fast-moving flume. This sixty-acre water park offers three dozen attractions, including Surf City, a million-gallon wave pool for body surfing and raft-ing; and Monsoon, where visitors riding in a twenty-passenger boat ascend a 50-foot lift into the eye of the monsoon and take a speedy and wet plunge into a lagoon. There also are giant water slides, such as Aruba Tuba; Buccaneer Bay, with kayaks and Bimini Bumper Boats; and Castaway Cove, an adults-only pool with a swim-up refreshment cabana.

Families with younger children also will enjoy Coconut Cove, a 20,000-square-foot area with a water-spraying mushroom and other play elements; Crocodile Isle, a "spray-ground" with water slides; and Captain Kidds, a pirate ship on Crocodile Isle that has slides, bursting water cannons, and other surprises.

And everyone will love the lazy, relaxing float provided by Caribbean Cooler.

Shoal Creek Living History Museum (all ages)

7000 NE Barry Road in Hodge Park, Kansas City 64156; (816) 792–2655. Open Tuesday through Friday 9:00 A.M. to 3:00 P.M. $

You can step into the past in Hodge Park at this living-history museum comprised of twenty period structures. You may see native Missouri elk, deer, foxes, or bison in the park. There is a self-guided tour of the park, or you can come during special events to get a more structured experience with costumed interpreters showing you the way things used to be.

Lee's Summit

Longview Park (all ages)

I–470 to Raytown Road or Viewhigh Drive, then south to park, Lee's Summit 64081; (816) 795–8200; www.jackson.gov.org. Tent campsites are $10 per day; RV hookups are $15 per day.

The centerpiece of Longview Park is 930-acre Longview Lake. It's great for powerboating, waterskiing, Jet-Skiing, or pontoon boating. Fishing is also popular here and includes bluegill, carp, channel cat, largemouth bass, walleye, and crappie. A full-service marina offers boat rental, marine supplies, and bait and tackle. The lake has a sand beach with volleyball facilities. You'll also find playground equipment, picnic facilities, a 7-mile asphalt lakeside bike path, and a campground with tent and RV sites that is open from mid-April through September 30. **Christmas in the Park,** at the park campgrounds from Thanksgiving through December, features an elaborate drive-through lighting display with more than 225,000 lights and 175 animated scenes. Donations are requested.

Paradise Park Family Entertainment Center (all ages)

1021 Northeast Colbern Road, Lee's Summit 64081; (816) 246–5224; www.paradise-park.com. Open daily, but hours vary depending on activity; call for current schedule. $–$$

This recently renovated entertainment center is a must-stop if you have the time. It has a lovely eighteen-hole miniature golf course, monopole baseball and softball batting cages, an arcade, and a snack bar. It also offers old-fashioned hayrides and campfires. But its crowning glory is a new 12,000-square-foot building providing what owners call "edutainment": learning-related offerings, such as art studios, a small-creature habitat, a pretend village, and a puppet-show performance. It also houses a cafe for parents and uses an armband security system to keep track of the small ones.

Blue Springs

Fleming Park (all ages)

Woods Chapel Road, south of Highway 70, Blue Springs 64015; (816) 795–8200; www.jack son.gov.org. Year-round campsites at Lake Jacomo are $10 for tents, $18 to $22 for RVs. Blue Springs Lake, available from mid-May to October 31, has RV sites ranging from $18 to $22.

Blue Springs's park has two lakes, each with its own campground. Several marked nature trails, a historic settlement, a paved airstrip for radio-controlled model airplanes, and a small lake for radio-controlled boats are also available. An archery range in the park has three scenic shooting trails and hosts several tournaments each year.

There also is a native hoofed-animal enclosure where bison and elk roam freely. An observation tower lets you watch the animals from on high. You can take a tour inside the enclosure on a hay-filled truck for a small fee on Saturday from April through October. Bring apples or pears to feed the animals. Tickets must be purchased the day of the tour.

Lake Jacomo has regulations limiting the horsepower of the boats, which makes the lake perfect for sailboat and pontoon-boat enthusiasts. A full-service marina provides boat rental, and marine and fishing supplies are available, as are tent and RV campsites.

Blue Springs Lake is great for powerboaters. It has a pleasant sand beach for sun-bathers and swimmers and RV campsites.

Missouri Town 1855 (all ages)

Fleming Park; send mail to 22807 Woods Chapel Road, Blue Springs 64015; (816) 795–8200, ext. 1260; www.jackson.gov.org. Open Wednesday through Sunday 9:30 A.M. to 4:30 P.M. April 15 to November 15. Open weekends during the rest of the year. $

More than thirty old houses and other authentic buildings have been moved to this location to re-create a typical 1850s farming community. Costumed craftsmen, guides, and musicians portray the lives of early settlers in the six-block community and provide information to anyone interested in learning about that time in history.

Kemper Outdoor Education Center (all ages)

Fleming Park; send mail to 8201 Jasper Bell Road, Blue Springs 64015; (816) 229–8980; www.jackson.gov.org. Open daily 9:00 A.M. to 4:00 P.M., except Saturday and Sunday only noon to 4:00 P.M. during the winter. Free admission.

You can observe white-tailed deer, wild turkeys, and songbirds attracted by wildlife feeding stations at the center. Inside, your kids will love seeing—and in some cases touching—displays of reptiles, amphibians, and native fish. The grounds offer nature trails and a beautiful water garden with Japanese koi.

Burr Oak Woods Conservation Nature Center (all ages)

1401 NW Park Road, Blue Springs 64015; (816) 228-3766; www.mdc.state.mo.us. Center open Monday through Saturday 8:00 A.M. to 5:00 P.M. Grounds open 8:00 A.M. to 8:00 P.M. daily. Call for a schedule of special events or for other information. Free admission.

This entertaining center offers hands-on interactive exhibits explaining the flora and fauna of the Kansas City area. Multimedia programs allow kids to make decisions about the environment and see the results immediately. The center regularly schedules special programs, concerts, and performances for children and adults. The facility is surrounded by more than 1,000 acres of state forest with several interpretive hiking trails and picnic facilities. No pets allowed.

Family Golf Park (all ages)

One mile east of I–470/State 291 at 1501 Northeast Highway 40, Blue Springs 64015; (816) 228–1550; www.familygolfpark.com. Open year-round, weather permitting. $; children shorter than 40 inches (3 feet, 4 inches) are free.

This complex has thirty-six holes of miniature golf, an arcade, bumper boats from May through October 1, and a complete golf practice facility, including lighted driving range with grass and carpet surfaces, putting and chipping greens, and a nine-hole, par-three golf course.

Independence

This frontier boomtown once served settlers heading west. This also is Harry S Truman country. The home Truman and his wife owned when he became president, his library and museum, and the farm where he grew up are either in Independence or nearby. You also can see the courtroom where he presided as a county judge at the Jackson County Courthouse. Take the Blue Ridge cutoff exit from Highway 70, and you can stop at the **Missouri Tourist Information Center** to collect information about attractions here and all over the state. Call (816) 889–3333; www.visitmo.com.

Park **Call**

Missouri's excellent state park system is operated by the Department of Natural Resources. Call (800) 334–6946 or (800) 379–2419 (TDD) around the clock for recorded information, or during daily office hours to reach an attendant, or visit online at www.mostateparks.com. Campsites can be reserved by calling (877) 422–6766 at least forty-eight hours in advance. There is an $8.50 registration fee, in addition to the rental fee, for this service.

National Frontier Trails Center (all ages)

318 West Pacific Avenue, Independence 64050; (816) 325–7575; www.frontiertrails center.com. Open Monday through Saturday 9:00 A.M. to 4:30 P.M., Sunday 12:30 to 4:30 P.M. $; children ages 5 and under free.

This town's important role in the history of westward expansion during the period between 1820 and 1855 is the focus of this center. You can see two authentic pioneer wagons, learn about the trades and businesses that prepared emigrants for the journey, examine artifacts found along the trails, and view *West,* a seventeen-minute film documenting this great exodus.

Truman Home Ticket and Information Center (all ages)

223 North Main Street, Independence 64050, on historic Independence Square; (816) 254–7199; www.nps.gov/hstr. Open daily 8:30 A.M. to 5:00 P.M.

This is the place to start your tour of Truman sites. Here you can view a free twelve-minute introductory slide program and buy tickets or join group tours of Truman's home and farm.

Truman Home (all ages)

219 Delaware Street, Independence 64050; (800) 254–9929; www.nps.gov/hstr. Tours start daily every fifteen minutes between 9:00 A.M. and 4:45 P.M. Closed Monday in winter months. $; children ages 16 and under free.

The house Truman and his wife, Bess, owned during his presidency is open for tours. All of the furnishings are authentic and were left there when the home was turned over to the government for use as a national historic site.

Harry S Truman Library and Museum (all ages)

Highway 24 and Delaware, Independence 64050; (800) 833–1225; www.trumanlibrary.org. Open Monday through Saturday 9:00 A.M. to 5:00 P.M., Thursday until 9:00 P.M., and Sunday noon to 5:00 P.M. $; children ages 5 and under free.

Children will enjoy this museum, especially the replica of the Oval Office as it looked during Truman's presidency. There also are many other interesting artifacts and photographs from that time.

1859 Jail, Marshal's Home and Museum (all ages)

217 North Main Street, Independence 64050; (816) 252–1892; www.jchs.org/jail. Open Monday through Saturday 10:00 A.M. to 5:00 P.M., Sunday 1:00 to 4:00 P.M. April through October. Open Monday through Saturday 10:00 A.M. to 4:00 P.M., Sunday 1:00 to 4:00 P.M. November, December, and March. Closed January and February. $; children ages 5 and under free.

The site has been authentically restored to provide a chilling look at frontier justice in the mid-1800s. Among the members of the James gang who were held here was Jesse's brother, Frank, who was incarcerated from October 1882 until he went to trial the following January. In August 1862, when the jail was used by the Union provost marshal, guerrilla William Quantrill led a Confederate assault that freed prisoners. The site has the house built for the jailer and the formidable limestone jail, both furnished with items from the period. There also is a modern museum focusing on the Civil War in Jackson County and the James gang's activities during the outlaw years in Missouri, roughly 1865 through 1883.

Cool Crest Family Fun Center (all ages)

10735 East Highway 40, Independence 64055, 1 mile east of the Sports Complex; (816) 358–0088; www.coolcrest.com. Open year-round, weather permitting; call for hours. Golf costs $5.00 per person; children ages 3 and under free.

Cool Crest has four eighteen-hole miniature golf courses, a 7,000-square-foot game room, a new go-kart track, and batting cages. The on-site concession area serves up pizza and ice cream.

Community of Christ Auditorium and Temple (all ages)

River Boulevard and West Walnut Street, Independence 64052; (816) 833–1000; www.cofchrist.org. Open 9:00 A.M. to 4:30 P.M. daily. Free admission.

The auditorium and temple are open to the public, and tours are available. Free organ recitals on one of the largest church organs in the country are performed in the auditorium daily at 3:00 P.M. from June through August and on Sunday during the rest of the year.

Children's Peace Pavilion (ages 5 though 12)

1001 West Walnut Street, Independence 64052; (816) 521–3033. Open Tuesday through Saturday 9:30 A.M. to 4:00 P.M. Free admission.

The Children's Peace Pavilion, inside the Community of Christ Auditorium, bills itself as the only museum in the world devoted to encouraging peace by teaching techniques of peace. Children can play games, listen to recorded stories of children's accomplishments, create arts-and-crafts projects, and make music by running through a series of colored lights.

Mormon Visitors' Center (ages 5 and up)

937 West Walnut Street, Independence 64052; (816) 836–3466. Open daily 9:00 A.M. to 9:00 P.M. Free admission.

When you arrive you'll be taken on a guided tour of the center, which presents the history of the Mormon religion with interactive video displays, paintings, and artifacts such as the facade of a log cabin and the mock-up of the interior of a cabin as it would have been furnished in the early nineteenth century.

For More Information

Independence Tourism Department.
(816) 325–7111 or (800) 748–7323;
www.indepmo.org/tourism.

Amazing
Missouri Facts

What is the state insect?

Honey Bee

Grandview

Truman Farm (all ages)

12301 Blue Ridge Boulevard, Grandview 64030; (816) 254–9929; www.nps.gov/hstr. Tours held Friday through Sunday 9:30 A.M. to 4:00 P.M. May through last weekend in August. Farm grounds open without tour. Free admission.

This farm 20 miles south of Independence is where Truman grew up and first learned you shouldn't pass the buck. There are regular tours of the house and outbuildings on the property.

Belton

Belton, Grandview & Kansas City Railroad Co. (all ages)

502 Walnut Street, Belton 64012; (816) 331–0630 or (816) 331–2632; www.orgsites.com/mo/beltonrailroad. Trains depart 11:00 A.M. and 2:00 P.M. Saturday and Sunday June through September; 2:00 P.M. only in May. $$; children ages 2 and under sitting on parents' laps free

Passengers on this great forty-five-minute round-trip train ride travel in a 1920s open window coach and a 1960s open-air flatcar with picnic tables. Two passengers also are allowed to ride in the 1957 diesel-electric locomotive for a $15 per person fee, and up to four people can ride in the red 1970s caboose for $10 per person. There also are special trips featuring evening runs, music, and themed events. A high point of this attraction is the enthusiasm of the workers, all of whom are volunteers.

Lone Jack

Lone Jack Civil War Battlefield and Museum (all ages)

301 South Bynum Road, Lone Jack 64070; (816) 697–8833. Open 10:00 A.M. to 4:00 P.M. Monday through Saturday. $

This small museum uses exhibits, dioramas, and special events to commemorate the Civil War battle that took place here in August 1862. There is a battlefield cemetery adjacent to the museum, which is located in a three-ace park site. About 200 men from both sides died in the battle, which locals believe may have taken place in a mile-wide area surrounding the park.

Sibley

Fort Osage National Historic Landmark (all ages)

U.S. 24 to north exit at Buckner, then 3 miles to 105 Osage, Sibley 64088; (816) 650–5737; www.historicfortosage.com. Open 9:00 A.M. to 4:30 P.M. Tuesday through Sunday March 15 through November 16, weekends only otherwise. $; children ages 4 and under free.

This reconstructed fort sits high on a bluff overlooking the Missouri River. The site first was noticed and deemed an excellent place for a fort by Meriwether Lewis and William Clark, who camped just across the river going and coming on their historic trip west in 1804-05. Clark came back in 1808 and built the fort. There now are several buildings, including a blockhouse, officers' quarters, and soldiers' barracks, that afford a magnificent view of the river.

A visitor center and costumed interpreters help you journey back to the time of 1812, when this fort was part of a federally controlled fur-trading system, and a nearby museum has many artifacts dating from the nineteenth century, including a keelboat.

Platte City

Platte City is north of Kansas City on I–29, about halfway between Kansas City International Airport and St. Joseph.

Ben Ferrel 1882 Platte County Museum and Library (all ages)

220 Ferrel Street, Platte City 64079; (816) 431–5121. Open Tuesday through Saturday noon to 4:00 P.M. April through October. $

The mansion housing the living museum, where docents offer tours, was built in 1882–83 and is furnished on three levels with artifacts from that period collected in and near Platte County. Similar to the Missouri governor's mansion in Jefferson City, the building has a German motif with a slate roof and wrought-iron decoration.

Lexington

This small historic town has more than 100 antebellum homes and buildings, which can be toured on foot or in your car. You can also visit the 1830s Log House on Main Street, a living-history museum restored to reflect family life during the early 1800s. For directions and information call (660) 259–3082.

East of town in the fertile Missouri River valley, take a scenic country drive along U.S. Highway 24, the route of the Santa Fe Trail. There are many small orchards and farms in this area, so watch for signs directing you to seasonal roadside markets and you-pick-it operations. During the spring you'll find asparagus, strawberries, and bedding plants. Summertime brings blueberries, blackberries, peaches, tomatoes, and sweet corn. In the fall you'll find apples, cider, pumpkins, gourds, peppers, and mums. The holiday offers Christmas trees, wreaths, greenery, and winter apples.

Battle of Lexington State Historic Site (all ages)

Tenth and Utah Streets, P.O. Box 6, Lexington 64067; (660) 259–4654 or (800) 334–6946; www.mostateparks.com. Visitor center is open Monday through Saturday 9:00 A.M. to 5:00 P.M., Sunday 11:00 A.M. to 5:00 P.M. March 1 through October 31. Closed Monday and Tuesday the rest of the year. $; children ages 6 and under free.

A visitor center explains the details of the early Civil War battle fought here, a Confederate victory that took place in 1861 and which also is called the Battle of the Hemp Bales. Pick up a map there and you can take a mile-long, self-guided walking tour of the battlefield, where the earthworks and trenches are still clearly visible, or fish in the Missouri River, which runs along the park. There also are guided tours of Anderson-Davis House, an antebellum home furnished to the period. The house is closed in January and February.

For More Information

Lexington Tourism Commission. 1029 Franklin Avenue, Lexington 64057; (660) 259–4711; www.historiclexington.com.

Excelsior Springs

At the end of the nineteenth century, this small town gained fame as a spa offering naturally occurring mineral water to visitors from all over the world. The Fishing River, a system of parks and trails that winds through the town following the creek and mineral springs, is a reminder of that past. This area includes hiking trails, playground equipment, picnic facilities, and the Superior Spring and Pagoda, the last of thirty-five wells that once supplied mineral water to visitors. If you wish, you can still get a mineral water massage at the

Hall of Waters, 201 East Broadway, or stay at the Elms Resort Hotel, Regent and Elms Boulevard. This luxury hotel has been serving visitors since 1888 and can boast famous and infamous guests from Harry S Truman to Al Capone. Call (816) 630–5500 or (800) 843–3567; www.elmsresort.com.

Liberty

The charming downtown square in this small suburb north of Kansas City is where you can start your explorations. Stop at the **Liberty Area Chamber of Commerce,** 9 South Leonard Street, to pick up tourist information and maps of local historic districts and attractions. Open Monday through Friday 8:30 A.M. to 5:30 P.M. Call (816) 781–5200. On Saturday from May through October you'll find the Liberty Farmers' Market, on the west side of the square, offering a variety of produce, flowers, and bedding plants for sale. Call (816) 781–2649.

Historic Liberty Jail (all ages)

216 North Main Street, Liberty 64068; (816) 781–3188. Open daily 9:00 A.M. to 9:00 P.M. Free admission.

Built in 1833, this tiny fourteen-square-foot jail is where Mormon president and prophet Joseph Smith was imprisoned from December 1838 to March 1839. Smith allegedly was jailed on trumped-up charges in the hope that his followers would grow tired of waiting for him to get out and disband. When that didn't happen and it became costly to continue feeding and housing him, Smith was released and charges were dropped. The two-story jail is open on one side to show the straw, blankets, and mannequins representing prisoners on the lower level, and the guards' area on the upper floor. There also are photographs of Smith and other people from the period.

Jesse James Bank Museum (all ages)

103 North Water Street on the Courthouse Square, Liberty 64068; (816) 781–4458. Open Monday through Saturday 10:00 A.M. to 4:00 P.M. Closed Sunday. $; children ages 7 and under free.

On Tuesday, February 13, 1866, this bank gained a degree of fame its depositors could have lived without: It was the first bank in peacetime in the United States to be robbed in daylight. Although no one ever was captured or convicted of the heist, which totaled $62,000, or the equivalent of about $6 million of modern currency, Jesse James and his gang are given credit for it. The bank and vault have been restored to their nineteenth-century condition, and guided tours explain what occurred as two of the robbers came into the bank and another eight to ten men stood watch outside. A small photo gallery has pictures of early Liberty and the James family.

Clay County Museum (all ages)

14 North Main Street, Liberty 64068; (816) 792–1849. Open Tuesday through Saturday 1:00 to 4:00 P.M. $

The museum is housed in an authentic nineteenth-century drugstore and includes artifacts and exhibits from the drugstore, the town newspaper, and a doctor's office as well as numerous items from everyday life in the 1800s.

For More Information

Clay County Visitors Bureau. Courthouse Square; 24-hour information line at (816) 792–7691.

North Kansas City

AMF Pro Bowl Lanes (all ages)

503 East Eighteenth Street, North Kansas City 64116; (816) 221–8844. Open year-round Tuesday through Thursday 9:00 A.M. to midnight, Friday and Saturday 9:00 A.M. to 2:00 A.M.; Sunday 9:00 A.M. to 11:00 P.M.

You'll find something for everyone in any family at this recreation complex that's only five minutes from downtown Kansas City. There's a forty-eight-lane bowling alley, a quarter-mile go-kart track, an eighteen-hole miniature golf course, batting cages, and even a complete pro shop for bowlers. The outside activities are open when the weather permits from about April onward.

Gladstone

Maple Woods Natural Area (all ages)

North of downtown; take Highway 169 north, turn east onto Barry Road, turn south onto North Oak, then turn east onto NE Seventy-sixth Street for 1½ miles; P.O. Box 10719, 7010 North Holmes, Gladstone 64188; (816) 436–2200; www.mdc.state.mo/areas. Open from 6:00 A.M. to 10:00 P.M. Free admission.

This is a magnificent eighteen-acre oasis of stately old-growth forest. The dense tree canopy offers tranquil hiking trails for observing songbirds, rabbits, squirrels, deer, foxes, and wildflowers.

Dolls 'n' Old Days Are Worth a Quick Trip to Kansas

If you've got a boy and a girl and find it difficult to please both on the same trip, take I–35 out of Kansas City to the Johnson Drive exit in Shawnee, Kansas. Go west (right turn) about 1 mile to Nieman, then turn right to the **Doll Cradle**, 5725 Nieman; (913) 631–1900.

This is one big and amazing doll store, with everything from antique to modern dolls and bears. A tour of the doll hospital is fascinating for kids and adults. The artists and doll restorers working here obviously love what they do and know how much their customers love their dolls.

Once you've pulled your daughter out of the Doll Cradle, go back to Johnson Drive and turn right; a couple blocks farther you'll find the re-created town of **Old Shawnee**. This collection of historic and reconstructed buildings is a museum and a tourist site all wrapped into one. Admission is $1.00 for adults, 50 cents for children ages six through twelve, and that price includes a map for a self-guided tour.

There are seventeen buildings here, including original log cabins and a territorial jail dating from 1843 that were moved here. A post office, general stores, fire station, and bank are among the replicas built here to complete the site. The place really comes alive in June for Old Shawnee Days, a festival that includes costumed reenactors, concerts, and a carnival.

Old Shawnee Town is open Tuesday through Saturday from noon to 5:00 p.m. Call (913) 248–2360.

If you want to give the kids one more thrill on the way back to Missouri, stop at **Fritz's Union Station Restaurant**, 1502 North Eighteenth Street in Kansas City, Kansas. The hamburgers and other sandwiches are excellent, but kids love the way they are delivered: An overhead steam engine carries a box with your food to your table and you use an "elevator" to bring it down to your level.

Take I–35 to the Eighteenth Street Expressway/Roe Avenue exit, head north about 5 or 6 miles until you go under the I–70 overpass; Fritz's is on the left at the third stoplight ahead. Fritz's is open Monday through Saturday 6:00 A.M. to 9:00 P.M., but train service doesn't start until 11:00 A.M. Call (913) 281–2777. A second Fritz's now is open seven days a week in Crown Center; (816) 474–4004.

Kearney

Jesse James Farm and Museum (all ages)

Highway 92 east, then north on Jesse James Road, Kearney 64060; (816) 628–6065; www.claycogov.com. Open daily 9:00 A.M. to 4:00 P.M., Sunday noon to 4:00 P.M. only from October to April. $–$$; children ages 7 and under **free.**

This is the log-and-clapboard cabin where Jesse James was born and where he and his brother, Frank, grew up during the mid-1800s. The cabin is furnished with items from the period. A visitor center shows a video about the James brothers, and three galleries display photographs and artifacts that help you learn about two of the nation's most notorious outlaws.

Lawson

Watkins Mill State Park (all ages)

Highway 92 to Highway RA, 26600 Park Road North, Lawson 64062; (816) 296–3357 or (800) 334–6946; www.mostateparks.com. Open daily from sunup to half-hour after sunset. Campsites are $8.00 per day for tents, $14.00 per day for RV electrical hookups. Call (877) 422–6766 at least forty-eight hours in advance for camping reservations. There is an $8.50 registration fee.

On the 1,442 acres of this park and adjacent historic site, you'll find recreational facilities and several historic buildings in the Bethany Plantation open for visitors. The park has more than 100 campsites for tents and recreational vehicles, modern rest-room facilities, picnic areas, a small lake for swimming and fishing, and hiking, biking, and horseback riding trails. **Harvest Weekend,** usually held the third weekend in October, features, crafts, and skills prevalent in the 1870s.

Watkins Woolen Mill State Historic Site (all ages)

Watkins Mill State Park, 26600 Park Road North, Lawson 64062; (816) 296–3357 or (800) 334–6946; www.mostateparks.com. During summer, tours run from 10:00 A.M. to 4:00 P.M. Monday through Saturday, 10:00 A.M. to 4:00 P.M. Sunday, shorter hours during winter. $; children ages 5 and under **free.**

You can visit the once bustling Bethany Plantation, which includes the Watkins Woolen Mill (with the original machinery), the Watkins home, a church, a school, and several smaller buildings. A large visitor center focuses on life in the region in the 1870s, the time period chosen to be reenacted at the site, which first was settled in 1839. Two one-hour tours focus on the house, which was occupied until the 1940s, and the mill, which closed in 1898. During the **Christmas Open House** in mid-December, the plantation is beautifully decorated, and costumed reenactors perform the music, crafts, and other activities, as well as serve refreshments, that were popular in the 1870s.

Smithville

Smithville Lake (all ages)

North of Kansas City take Highway 92 to Highway DD, P.O. Box 428, Smithville 64089; (816) 532–0174; www.mrk.usace.army.mil/smithville/smithville. Jerry L. Litton Visitor Center open daily 8:00 A.M. to 4:00 P.M. April through October. Campsites are $11 for basic, $15 for RV electrical hookups, $17 for electrical and water hookups.

At 7,000 acres, this is one of the newest large artificial lakes in the state. It has three recreation areas featuring more than 700 campsites, two swimming beaches with rest-room facilities, 200 picnic areas, and two full-service marinas where you can rent a boat or find services for your own boat. There is also a special launching area for the exclusive use of sailboaters. It's no wonder then that fishing tournaments and sailboat races are regularly scheduled here. You should stop at the Jerry L. Litton Visitor Center on Highway DD to find out all you need to know about this Army Corps of Engineers project and to get information on the area. Clay County manages the campgrounds, which do not have water, and therefore no showers, from November through April.

Weston

This small, quaint town north of Kansas City, at the juncture of Missouri Highways 45 and 273, has nearly a dozen antiques shops, two orchards, and several more specialty shops, including the Crimson Rose, a boutique featuring artistic designs on clothing.

Snow Creek Ski Area (ages 5 and up)

Highway 45, Snow Creek Drive, Weston 64098; (816) 640–2200; skisnowcreek.com. Open daily mid-December through mid-March. Open Monday through Thursday 1:00 to 9:30 P.M., Friday 1:00 to 10:30 P.M., Saturday 9:00 A.M. to 10:30 P.M., Sunday 9:00 A.M. to 8:00 P.M. Special weekend sessions from midnight to 6:00 A.M. Call for prices.

Wintertime outdoor fun is plentiful on the nine intermediate and two beginner ski runs served by two triple-chairlifts and three rope tows. Artificial snow is provided when Mother Nature doesn't oblige. Rental equipment and lessons at all levels are available.

Highway 45 offers a scenic drive along the river and many opportunities to enjoy nature. This road follows the Missouri River and passes several parks and natural areas where you can stop for outdoor recreation.

Weston Bend State Park (all ages)

Highways 45 and 273, 4 miles south of Weston, P.O. Box 115, 16600 Highway 45 North, Weston 64098; (816) 640–5443 or (800) 334–6946; www.mostateparks.com. Open year-round. Campsites are $8.00 per day for tents, $14.00 per day for RV electrical hookups. Call (877) 422–6766 at least forty-eight hours in advance for camping reservations. There is an $8.50 registration fee.

Weston Bend State Park, with thirty-seven campsites and 1,133 acres, is adjacent to the river and has picnic facilities, a campground, and hiking and biking trails. Access to the river for fishing is also provided.

Little Bean Marsh Conservation Area (all ages)

North of Weston off Highway 45; send mail to 701 North East College Drive, St. Joseph 64506; (816) 792–8662; www.mdc.state.mo.us.

This small marsh along the river was mentioned in the journals of Lewis and Clark for the abundance of wildlife here. You can still see various songbirds, bitterns, rails, and herons in the sloughs and backwaters. The spring migration draws several varieties of ducks, geese, and many other types of wetland birds. Blacktop roads take visitors to a handicapped-accessible viewing blind and a viewing tower. The tower provides a panoramic look at the 440 acres and is a great place to watch waterfowl, bald eagles, and marsh hawks during winter months.

Bluffwoods Conservation Area (all ages)

South of St. Joseph on Highway 59 to County Road 219, then follow the signs to the area; send mail to 701 North East College Drive, St. Joseph 64506; (816) 271–3100; www.mdc. state.mo.us.

These 2,000 acres are a remnant of the lush forests that once grew along the Missouri River. Watch for birds, raccoons, deer, foxes, rabbits, and opossum in the deep woods and open ridges. At the southwest end of the area you'll find Lone Pine Trail, which leads to a spectacular view of the river valley. Picnic areas and primitive campsites are available here.

Rushville

Lewis and Clark State Park (all ages)

Highway 138, 801 Lake Crest Boulevard, Rushville 64484; (816) 579–5564 or (800) 334–6946; www.mostateparks.com. Campsites are $8.00 per day for tents, $14.00 per day for RV electrical hookups. Call (877) 422–6766 at least forty-eight hours in advance for camping reservations. There is an $8.50 registration fee.

Thanks to 365-acre Sugar Lake, you'll find this is a great place to fish, swim, canoe, or waterski. There are twenty-six tent camping sites, forty-four more with RV electrical hookups, picnic sites, and bass, bluegill, and crappie in the lake.

St. Joseph

Joseph Robidoux already had proven himself as a fur trader and businessman when he was hired by the American Fur Company in 1826 to establish a trading post at the Black Snake Hills near the site of present-day St. Joseph. Over the next two decades he prospered and acquired land until July 26, 1843, when he filed plans for the city with the clerk of Common Pleas in St. Louis and began selling lots in St. Joseph.

Robidoux, who died at age eighty-five in 1868, was in his late seventies on April 3, 1860, when perhaps the most defining moment in the history of St. Joseph occurred. And like several other small cities in the state, St. Joe, as locals call it, has taken this small claim to fame and turned it into a great tourist experience for you. The event was the city's launching of the Pony Express. For the short span of eighteen months, riders took off from a small stable downtown and rode approximately 2,000 miles west to deliver the mail to Sacramento, California.

Pony Express Regional Tourist Information Center Caboose (all ages)

4016 Frederick Boulevard, St. Joseph 64506; (816) 232–1839 or, if closed, call (800) 785–0360; www.stjomo.com. Open Monday through Saturday 8:30 A.M. to 4:30 P.M. March through December.

This is the best place to get information about the Pony Express sites as well as the many other attractions around the city. If it's closed, try the Convention and Visitors Bureau office at 109 South Fourth Street.

First Street Trolley (all ages)

Catch it at one of several local hotels or at the center of town; (816) 271–5380 or (800) 785–0360. Trolley operates Tuesday through Saturday 10:00 A.M. to 6:00 P.M. June through September. An all-day pass is $3.50 for adults, $1.75 for seniors and children ages 6 through 17; ages 5 and under free. Single-trip fares are 50 cents.

Ride all day, getting off at any of the ten museums downtown, or just stay on the trolley and ride the one-hour circuit for a great tour of the city. The trolleys are authentic reproductions of streetcars used at the turn of the twentieth century.

Robidoux Row Museum (all ages)

Third and Poulin Streets, St. Joseph 64501; (816) 232–5861; www.stjomo.com. Open Tuesday through Friday 10:00 A.M. to 4:00 P.M., Saturday and Sunday 1:00 to 4:00 P.M. May through September; shorter hours other months. $; children ages 12 and under free.

This series of connected houses built by Joseph Robidoux in the 1840s has been restored and often hosts historic reenactments and demonstrations of pioneer crafts. The site includes the restoration of Robidoux's personal quarters and even includes some of his belongings.

Amazing
Missouri Facts

How long did the Pony Express operate?

April 1860 to October 1861
18 months

Pony Express Museum (all ages)

914 Penn Street, St. Joseph 64503; (816) 279–5059; www.ponyexpress.org. Open Monday through Saturday 9:00 A.M. to 5:00 P.M., Sunday 1:00 to 5:00 P.M., year-round. $; children ages 6 and under **free.**

You can relive the moment on April 3, 1860, when a rider named Johnny Fry waited anxiously atop his horse, Sylph, for a cannon to sound the signal to begin the first run of the Pony Express. The museum is housed in the original Pike's Peak Stables, and you can pump water from the same well that was used to water the horses. It's a great museum for children, who can sit on a wooden sawhorse equipped with a saddle and handle an authentic reproduction of the *mochilas* (saddlebags) that carried the mail or walk inside a typical relay station situated along the route. A diorama with special effects re-creates the desert air, mountain cold, and some of the smells encountered along the riders' trips between Missouri and California. Twenty-one interactive exhibits allow visitors to experience every aspect of this glorious experiment, from choosing horses suitable for the trip to tapping out messages on a telegraph, the invention that put the Pony Express operation out of business.

The headquarters of the company that operated the Pony Express, the Central Overland California and Pike's Peak Express Company, is located just a few blocks away from the stables in the Patee House Museum.

Patee House Museum (all ages)

Twelfth and Penn Streets, St. Joseph 64503; (816) 232–8206; www.stjoseph.net/ponyexpress. Open Monday through Saturday 10:00 A.M. to 5:00 P.M., Sunday 1:00 to 5:00 P.M. April through October. Open weekends only November and January through March. Closed in December. $; children ages 5 and under **free.**

Once an elegant 140-room hotel, the building now is a wonderful and strange conglomeration of nooks and crannies filled with artifacts and antiques from the town's past. It seems that the people in this city don't throw anything away—they just donate it to the Patee House. If you or your children can't find anything interesting here, you're not trying. In addition to the restored Pony Express headquarters office, there's a row of simulated storefronts from the late 1800s called the "Streets of St. Joe," featuring a general store, a photographer's studio, a daguerreotype shop, a Victorian home, a dentist's office, a jail chronicling a century of crime, an optical shop, and several horse-drawn vehicles. The museum also houses a full-size steam engine you can climb into, old radios and telephones, tools, quilts, furniture, clothes, a room full of mechanized toys, and thousands of artifacts too numerous to mention. Children will also want to ride "Wild Things," a hand-carved wooden carousel with full-size endangered-species animals. Don't leave without visiting the old-fashioned Buffalo Saloon in the train depot. If a volunteer's on duty, you can get soft drinks and popcorn. Plan on spending at least an hour in the museum—there's plenty to see.

Jesse James Home Museum (all ages)

Twelfth and Penn Streets, behind the Patee House Museum, St. Joseph 64503; (816) 232–8206; www.stjoseph.net/ponyexpress. Open Monday through Saturday 10:00 A.M. to 4:00 P.M., Sunday 1:00 to 4:00 P.M. From June through August the home is open until 5:00 P.M. $; children ages 5 and under free.

This is the tiny four-room house where, on April 3, 1882, fellow gang member Bob Ford shot the famous outlaw from behind to collect a $10,000 reward. It's a small but intriguing place. You can see the legendary bullet hole in the wall, the gouges in the floor where souvenir seekers took pieces of blood-stained wood to sell, and photographs and informa-

Pass Some Time on the **Parkway**

St. Joseph residents are justifiably proud of the Parkway, a beautiful scenic system of boulevards that winds for 26 miles and connects several city parks. The system was developed in 1918 by George Burnap, an internationally known landscape artist who understood the long-term benefit of a "green belt" within an urban area. The Parkway is a favorite among bikers and hikers.

- **Krug Park,** St. Joseph Avenue and Krug Park Place, is great for hiking, picnicking, or simply hanging out on the playground. This 163-acre park has a castle and the North American Animal Exhibit with buffalo, deer, and longhorn cattle. During the month of December the park is lighted to create a dazzling drive-through display.

- **King Hill Overlook,** King Hill Drive, has a breathtaking view of the south side of the city and eastern Kansas. This area was once a Native American ceremonial ground.

- **Huston Wyeth Park**, Poulin and Elwood Streets, is located on the river bluffs and provides a great view of the point where wagon trains crossed the Missouri River to begin the journey west. The picnic areas in the park are good vantage points for watching the river.

tion about the James family and Jesse's lawless career. There also are artifacts removed from James's grave when he was exhumed in 1995 for DNA tests, the results of which showed a 99.7 percent probability that the man in the grave was Jesse James.

Glore Psychiatric Museum (ages 10 and up)

3406 Frederick, St. Joseph 64506; (816) 387–2310 or (877) 387–2310; stjosephmuseum.org. Open Monday through Saturday 9:00 A.M. to 5:00 P.M. Free admission; donations accepted.

This unusual and sometimes unsettling museum's artifacts and exhibits are designed to show the public how the treatment of mental illness has changed over time. The museum explains the 125-year history of what was first called "State Lunatic Asylum No. 2." Many once-accepted instruments of treatment (torture?) are explained in exhibits or on display, including the Bath of Surprise, O'Halloran's Swing, the Tranquilizer Chair, and the Hollow Wheel. Also on display are "Yellow Rose," a 1966 Chevrolet Monte Carlo, and "Juke Box Hero," a 1990 Toyota pickup, vehicles that were customized by vocational education students at Woodson Academy, a self-contained school for patients at the former Woodson Children's Psychiatric Hospital. The macabre yet true story told by the exhibits makes the museum interesting to adults and popular with adolescents and teenagers. This museum is operated by the organization St. Joseph Museum Inc.

Cool Crest Garden Golf (all ages)

1400 North Belt, St. Joseph 64506; (816) 232–2663. Open Monday through Saturday 10:00 A.M. to 11:00 P.M., Sunday noon to 10:00 P.M.; call for winter hours. Admission is $4.00 per round.

This miniature golf course's unique setting of beautiful flower gardens, bronze statuary, cool waterfalls, electrical "hazards," and nostalgic music has been pleasing families for more than fifty years.

Wyeth-Tootle Mansion (all ages)

1100 Charles Street, St. Joseph 64501; (816) 232–8472; www.stjosephmuseum.org. Open 10:00 A.M. to 5:00 P.M. Tuesday through Saturday year-round, 1:00 to 5:00 P.M. Sunday January through March. $

The second and third floors of this Gothic mansion dating from 1879 have an array of exhibits and artifacts illustrating the cultural and natural history of St. Joseph, while the first floor has been returned to its original setting as an elegant late-nineteenth-century home. The mansion is operated by St. Joseph Museum, Inc.

Black Archives of St. Joseph (all ages)

509 South Tenth Street, St. Joseph 64501; (816) 232–8471; www.stjosephmuseum.org. Open 10:00 A.M. to 1:00 P.M. Tuesday and Thursday, 1:00 to 4:00 P.M. Wednesday and Friday. $

The story of the black experience in St. Joseph—including information about African-American musicians, school desegregation, and a local Hall of Fame—is presented in this museum. Located in the former convent of the Twin Spires Complex, it is a member of the complex of museums owned and operated by St. Joseph Museum, Inc.

St. Joseph Saints (all ages)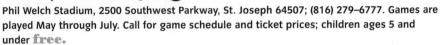

Phil Welch Stadium, 2500 Southwest Parkway, St. Joseph 64507; (816) 279–6777. Games are played May through July. Call for game schedule and ticket prices; children ages 5 and under **free.**

This team in the Mink League of the National Baseball Congress started play in 1996 in Phil Welch Stadium, a ballpark dating from 1939 and once used by a Western Association team. You'll have a chance to get real close to the college athletes who play on the team, as well as the players on other regional teams from Iowa, Nebraska, and Missouri.

A Cosby Family **Adventure**

There are times when a family outing starts out in high gear and is nerve-wracking from the time you start out until you get back to the hotel or on the road home. Other times the pace just seems to be perfect, almost leisurely, and provides the maximum enjoyment possible. That's the way we found our trip to St. Joseph: leisurely, entertaining, and downright enjoyable.

We started at the Pony Express Museum. The kids loved sitting in the same kind of saddle the riders used, pumping water from the very well used to water the riders' horses, and exploring a replica relay station. Next we went to the nearby Patee House Museum, a former 140-room hotel where the Pony Express headquarters was located.

Patee House is one of the most interesting and eclectic museums in Missouri. We explored the "Streets of St. Joe," a row of simulated storefronts from the late 1800s. The kids were very interested in a room full of mechanical toys, and we all climbed aboard a full-size steam engine. We even lucked out in the Buffalo Saloon in the train station; a volunteer was on duty and sold us sodas and popcorn.

After a little more exploration, we walked around the building to the Jesse James Home, the tiny house where James lived when Bob Ford, a gang member, shot him down. The photographs were interesting, and the legendary bullet hole in the wall was a little macabre. We also agreed later that it felt a little eerie standing in the small living room as the guide explained the incident as it is believed to have happened.

We decided to have an early dinner and stopped in at Jerre Anne Cafeteria and Bakery, 2640 Mitchell. Nothing fancy here, just fantastic meals and incredible desserts. We took extras for the road.

Society of Memories Doll Museum (all ages)

Twelfth and Penn Streets, St. Joseph 64503; (816) 233–1420 or (816) 364–6165; www.stjomo.com. Open Tuesday through Saturday 11:30 A.M. to 4:30 P.M., Sunday 1:00 to 4:00 P.M. May through September and then by appointment. Children ages 12 and under must be accompanied by an adult. $; children ages 4 and under **free.**

This impressive collection includes more than 800 dolls, including modern Barbies and Cabbage Patch Kids, bisque and china dolls, and even covered wagon dolls dating from the 1840s. There is wonderful old, child-play-size furniture, and several dollhouse and individual "rooms" decorated around specific dolls.

National Military Heritage Museum (all ages)

701 Messanie, St. Joseph 64501; (816) 233–4321; www.nationalmilitaryheritagemuseum.org. Open Monday through Friday 9:00 A.M. to 5:00 P.M., Saturday 9:00 A.M. to 1:00 P.M. $; children ages 5 and under **free.**

This museum in progress is located in what was the city's first police station, a brick building designed by Harvey Ellis. Displays are being added as restoration frees up additional space in the 20,000-square-foot structure. Exhibits honor all branches of the military from the early 1800s to present. Artifacts on display include three Vietnam-era helicopters with replica weapons, a World War I trench mock-up, a small-arms display, and other military items.

Albrecht-Kemper Museum of Art (all ages)

2818 Frederick Boulevard, St. Joseph 64506; (816) 233–7003 or (888) 254–2787; www.albrecht-kemper.org. Open Tuesday through Friday 10:00 A.M. to 4:00 P.M., Saturday and Sunday 1:00 to 4:00 P.M.; closed Monday. $; children ages 11 and under **free.**

The museum hosts traveling exhibits and has a permanent collection of more than 1,300 works, including a fine collection of eighteenth-, nineteenth-, and twentieth-century American art. Artists on display include Missouri artists George Caleb Bingham and Thomas Hart Benton, as well as N. C. Wyeth, Mary Cassatt, John Taylor Arms, Rembrandt Peale, Wayne Thiebaud, Wolf Kahn, and Edward Curtis.

Amazing Missouri Facts

Where is the highest point in the state?

At 1,772 feet, Taum Sauk Mountain near Piedmont.

Missouri Department of Conservation (all ages)
On campus of Missouri Western State College, 701 NE College Drive, St. Joseph 64507;
(816) 271–3100. Open Monday through Friday 8:00 A.M. to 5:00 P.M. Free admission.

This pocket museum outside the office of the Department of Conservation has several exhibits with a conservation theme, including several mounted specimens and a small aquarium, along with a short, marked nature trail. This is also the best place to pick up the brochures you need if you plan on visiting one or more of the department's excellent conservation areas.

Belt Bowl (all ages)
210 North Belt, St. Joseph 64596; (816) 233–1054. Open daily 8:00 A.M. to 10:00 P.M. Fees are $2.75 per game; shoe rental is $1.75.

If you have a little time to kill and need to get out of the Missouri summer heat for a while, the proprietor here will put bumpers in the gutters for the little ones if lanes are available.

Western **Shopper's** Heaven

Western shoppers can find plenty of places to browse in town.

Silver Fox Indian Trading Post. 5104 King Hill Avenue, St. Joseph 64504; (816) 238–7560. Open Monday through Saturday 9:00 A.M. to 4:30 P.M. This interesting shop sells hundreds of Native American items and artifacts including pottery, bolos, collar tips, pipes, and hat bands.

St. Joe Boot. Belt Highway and Highway 36, St. Joseph 64507; (816) 232–8128. Open Monday through Friday 9:00 A.M. to 6:00 P.M., Saturday 9:00 A.M. to 8:00 P.M., Sunday noon to 5:00 P.M. Here you'll find Western fashions and accessories, in addition to more than 4,000 boots for men, women, and children.

Bill's Saddlery. 20496 County Road 306, St. Joseph 64505; (816) 279–7392. Open Monday through Friday 8:00 A.M. to 5:00 P.M. Step back in time and see custom saddles being made the way they were at the turn of the twentieth century. The business also sells hand-crafted leather goods, bags, belts, and purses.

Stetson Hat Factory Outlet. 3601 South Leonard Road, St. Joseph 64503; (816) 233–3286. Open Monday through Friday 8:30 A.M. to 4:30 P.M., Saturday 8:00 A.M. to 4:00 P.M. Here you can buy Western felt and straw hats, dress hats, and caps of all types.

For More Information

St. Joseph Convention and Visitors Bureau. 109 South Fourth Street, St. Joseph 64501; (816) 233–6688 or (800) 785–0360; www.stjomo.com.

Mound City

As you travel north along the Missouri River, you'll notice the rural character of the countryside that makes the northwestern corner of the state excellent for wildlife viewing and outdoor recreation.

Squaw Creek National Wildlife Refuge (all ages)

Highway 79 to Highway 159 and then 3 miles west, (660) 442–3187; midwest.fws.gov/squawcreek/. Refuge is open daily from sunrise to sunset. Visitor center is open 7:30 A.M. to 4:00 P.M. Monday through Friday, 10:00 A.M. to 4:00 P.M. Saturday and Sunday mid-March through May and mid-October through early December. Free admission.

This is an opportunity that shouldn't be missed. It is one of the best locations in the state for year-round wildlife viewing. Snow geese, Canada geese, mallards, white pelicans, eagles, and other types of birds stop off here during their fall and spring migrations, providing you with a chance to observe the noisy confusion and the awesome sight. At these times there are hundreds of thousands of waterfowl feeding and resting on the marshes. This area attracts more wintering bald eagles than any other area in the state, possibly in the lower forty-eight states.

Start at the visitor center at refuge headquarters to get information, and be sure to bring binoculars so you can spot birds and wildlife from afar. There is an auto road that circles the marsh and pools, providing excellent viewing from the comfort of your car. Hiking trails, wayside exhibits, and a viewing tower are also on-site. Fall and spring are the best times to observe migrating populations of waterfowl, which you will see flying in lines strung out across the sky for miles around the refuge. Sunrise and sunset are the most active times of day for the wildlife.

Rock Port

Missouri Tourist Information Center

I–29 rest area, exits 110 and 111, Rock Port 64482; (660) 744–6300; www.visitmo.com. Open 8:00 A.M. to 5:00 P.M. daily.

This is the place to stock up on printed materials for attractions throughout the state.

Craig

Big Lake State Park (all ages)

11 miles southwest of Mound City off Highway 111, 204 Lake Shore Drive, Craig 64437; (660) 442–3770 or (800) 334–6946; www.mostateparks.com. Campsites are $8.00 per day for tents, $14.00 per day for RV electrical hookups. Call (877) 422–6766 at least forty-eight hours in advance for camping reservations. There is an $8.50 registration fee. For information about motel rooms, call (660) 442–5432.

Camping and picnicking are not allowed in the Squaw Creek National Wildlife Refuge, but you can find facilities in this 625-acre park, which includes a natural oxbow lake formed when the Missouri River shifted course. The lake is popular for boating and waterskiing, and there are eighty campsites, housekeeping cottages, a swimming pool, and a twenty-two-unit motel and dining lodge.

Savannah

Ol' MacDonald's Farm (all ages)

15603 County Road 344, 3 miles north of I–29 and Business 71, Savannah 64485; (816) 324–6447. Open April through December. Tent camping is $15 per day, RV campsites range from $18 to $24 per day.

This ninety-acre, full-service recreation park has facilities able to accommodate trailers, tents, and recreational vehicles. The complex has a laundry room, seven small lakes for fishing, a sand volleyball court, and a dining room open Monday through Saturday from 6:00 A.M. to 2:00 P.M. You can fish, hike, ride paddleboats, or take a trail ride on horseback. Camping guests get many activities **free**; more than two persons per campsite pay $2.00 per day each.

Cameron

Wallace State Park (all ages)

Highway 35, 6 miles south of Cameron, 10621 North East Highway 121, Cameron 64429; (816) 632–3745 or (800) 334–6946; www.mostateparks.com. Open year-round. Campsites are $8.00 for tents, $14.00 for RV electrical hookups. Call (877) 422–6766 at least forty-eight hours in advance for camping reservations. There is an $8.50 registration fee.

The rugged wooded terrain here contrasts with the rolling farmland of this part of the state. This 501-acre park has four of the prettiest and most varied hiking trails in the region, offering dense woods, open meadows, and streams. There are eighty-eight campsites, and small Lake Allaman offers swimming, fishing, and boating for electric motorboats only. Go by the office for a map.

Jamesport

As you approach this town, which is the largest Amish community in the state, you'll pass carriages and farmers tilling the land with horse-drawn equipment. The Old Order Amish who live in this area maintain a nineteenth-century lifestyle and shun modern conveniences and technology. You and your kids can enjoy the charm of stepping back in time among people who aren't just pretending. The town has twenty-six specialty craft stores, including a carriage store and rug and broom store, where you can watch craftspeople at work, and sixteen antiques shops. There are several excellent restaurants and bakeries where you can buy home-baked meals and goodies. Many of the farms in the area sell quilts, homemade candy and bread, crafts, furniture, and clothing. Get a map in one of the stores in town and go exploring. Amish stores are closed on Thursday and Sunday. For more information, call (660) 684–6146; www.jamesportmo.com.

Laclede

There are two extensive wetland areas close to town that provide outdoor recreation and prime opportunities to watch waterfowl, shorebirds, bald eagles, and aquatic mammals such as river otters and muskrats. If your family is on a quest for wide-open spaces, head north on Missouri Highway 5. You'll see some of the least-populated areas and least-traveled roads in the state. Fewer than 150 cars a day use the northern end of this highway as it heads into Iowa.

Gen. John J. Pershing Boyhood Home State Historic Site (all ages)

Highway 5, 1 mile north of Laclede, P.O. Box 141, Laclede 64651; (660) 963–2525 or (800) 334–6946; www.mostateparks.com. Open Monday through Saturday 10:00 A.M. to 4:00 P.M., Sunday noon to 5:00 P.M. $; children ages 5 and under **free.**

This is the house where Pershing lived from ages six through twenty-one, when he left for West Point, earned the nickname of "Black Jack" in a storied career, and worked his way up to become the highest-ranking military officer in U.S. history. In 1919 Congress bestowed

Amazing
Missouri Facts

Who was the highest-ranking officer ever in the military?

Gen. John J. "Black Jack" Pershing, born near Laclede, Missouri.

Theater in **Trenton**

North Central Missouri College and the Grundy County Friends of the Arts cooperate to bring live family productions to this small town. The Arts and You series offers music concerts, children's theater, and individual performing artists from August through April at various community locations. For a schedule of events and ticket prices call the Trenton Chamber of Commerce at (660) 359–4324; www.trentonmochamber.com.

on Pershing the rank of General of the Armies, an honor only given posthumously since then to Gen. George Washington during the bicentennial in 1976. The one-room country school where Pershing taught from ages nineteen through twenty-one also has been moved to the site from its original location about 8 miles away. Both buildings are furnished as they would have been when Pershing was there from the 1860s until 1881; the school has the desk he used.

Pershing State Park (all ages)

29277 Highway 130, Laclede 64651; (660) 963–2299 or (800) 334–6946; www.mostateparks.com. Open year-round. Campsites are $8.00 for tents, $14.00 for RV electrical hookups. Call (877) 422–6766 at least forty-eight hours in advance for camping reservations. There is an $8.50 registration fee.

The park has thirty-nine campsites, two hiking trails, and two small lakes stocked with bass, bluegill, and channel catfish. One of the trails is a 1½-mile hike that takes you through woods and over an interpretive boardwalk through a wetlands along Locust Creek. The other trail is 3 miles long. Special events include **Halloween Storytelling** on the weekend before Halloween and the nearby **Pershing Balloon Derby,** a flight of hot-air balloons just outside the park, generally held on Labor Day weekend.

Locust Creek Covered Bridge State Historic Site (all ages)

Highway 36, 3 miles west of Laclede; send mail to P.O. Box 141, Laclede 64651; (660) 963–2525 or (800) 334–6946; www.mostateparks.com. Open daily sunrise to sunset. Free admission.

This is the longest remaining covered bridge in Missouri. When after World War II the creek channel changed, the bridge was left high and dry. A footbridge makes it accessible to hikers.

Fountain Grove Conservation Area (all ages)

County Road W south from Highway 36; drive 5 miles to the entrance; send mail to Route 1, Box 122B, Chillicothe 64601; (660) 938–4124; www.mdc.state.mo.us/areas.

This wetlands has a variety of wildlife living on more than 7,000 acres and is open to small boats. There are primitive camping sites, hiking trails, and even an auto tour route. The levees, service roads, and trails often offer the best viewing, although they are restricted during waterfowl hunting season from October until mid-February, so call ahead during that time for availability.

Sumner

Swan Lake National Wildlife Refuge (all ages)

From Highway 36, take Highway 139 south 12 miles, then take County Road RA south to the refuge entrance, Route 1, Box 29A, Sumner 64681; (660) 856–3323; http://midwest.fws.gov/SwanLake/. Refuge hours are dawn to dusk March 1 through October 15; closed remainder of year for hunting. Visitor center is open year-round Monday through Friday 7:30 A.M. to 4:00 P.M. Observation tower is open year-round from dawn to dusk.

Covering more than 10,000 acres, this wetland environment has two lakes, an observation tower where you can get a great view, and a visitor center where you can get information about the refuge and animals in the area. A video about Swan Lake explores wildlife in the area and tells how the Civilian Conservation Corps started a refuge here in 1937. The refuge now encompasses the 1,200-acre Swan Lake and 3,000-acre Silver Lake. Boats with up to ten horsepower are allowed on Silver Lake, which is stocked with buffalo, channel catfish, carp, and crappie. Follow the levees, service roads, and trails for the best viewing.

Macon

Outdoor recreation such as boating, skiing, camping, fishing, and hunting is popular in these parts, thanks to Long Branch Lake, a 2,400-acre lake formed about 1980 when the Army Corps of Engineers dammed the east fork of the Little Chariton River. The history of the project as well as cultural information about the Native Americans who once inhabited this region is contained in a visitor center with exhibits on U.S. Highway 36, 2 miles west of U.S. Highway 63. Call (660) 385–2108.

Long Branch State Park (all ages)
Highway 36, 3 miles west of Macon, 28615 Visitor Center Road, Macon 63552; (660) 773–5229. Open year-round. Campsites are $8.00 for tents, $14.00 for RV electrical hookups. Call (877) 422–6766 at least forty-eight hours in advance for camping reservations. There is an $8.50 registration fee.

This 1,734-acre park has eighty-two campsites, a sand beach for swimming, picnicking areas with two shelters, three boat-launching facilities, and on three sides fronts Long Branch Lake, which is filled with bass, walleye, crappie, and several kinds of catfish.

For More Information

Macon Area Chamber of Commerce.
218 North Rollins Street, Suite 102A, Macon 63552; (660) 385–2811; www.maconmo chamber.com.

Amazing
Missouri Facts

What famous World War II American general was born in Clark?

Omar Bradley

Kirksville

Kirksville, the home of Truman State University, hosts several events that attract visitors from all over the region.

- **Shrine Pro Rodeo.** *Rodeo Arena, NEMO Fairgrounds, Highway 11, P.O. Box 934, Kirksville 63501; (660) 627–1704. Third weekend in June.* The largest rodeo in this part of the state has competition in several events, including barrel racing, saddle-bronc riding, calf roping, steer wrestling, team roping, and bull riding. The net proceeds from the event each year are donated to the Shrine hospitals.
- **NEMO District Fair.** *NEMO Fairgrounds, Highway 11, P.O. Box 287, Kirksville 63501; (660) 665–8800. Last full weekend in July.* The fair has big-name country music entertainment, a demolition derby, 4-H and FFA exhibits, and carnival rides.

Thousand Hills State Park (all ages)

Highway 157, off Highway 6; Route 3, Kirksville 63501; (660) 665–6995 or (800) 334–6946; www.mostateparks.com. Open year-round. Campsites are $8.00 for tents, $14.00 for RV electrical hookups. Call (877) 422–6766 at least forty-eight hours in advance for camping reservations. There is an $8.50 registration fee. In season, which is Memorial Day through Labor Day, cabins range from $55.00 to $65.00 for four people; lower off-season rates. Dining lodge is open daily from 11:00 A.M. to 9:00 P.M. in season, with shorter winter hours. Swimming is **free** to cabin guests; for day visitors it's $2.00 for adults, $1.50 for children ages 3 through 11; children ages 2 and under **free.**

This 3,200-acre wooded state park surrounds 600-acre Forest Lake and offers camping, hiking, boating, and picnic facilities. It has a fee swimming area with showers and lockers, a full-service marina, seven duplex cabins, and a dining lodge featuring full meals and sandwiches. The park has a petroglyph site believed to be part of ceremonial grounds used by Native Americans from A.D.1000 to 1600, complete with original rock carvings. Summer activities include evening programs, nature hikes, and pontoon-boat rides. The lake is outside Kirksville but owned by the city, which places a small city sticker on boats using the lake and limits motor size to ninety horsepower.

Festivals

DECEMBER–JANUARY

Eagle Days. Squaw Creek National Wildlife Refuge, near Mound City; (660) 442–3187. December or January. During this time you can view hundreds of bald eagles and learn about the comeback of our national symbol. The event includes guided eagle tours, a movie about eagles, captive eagles on display, and various exhibits.

MAY

Apple Blossom Festival. Citywide in St. Joseph; (800) 785–0360; www.stjomo.com. First weekend in May. For starters there's the Apple Blossom Parade, then concerts, dances, and a softball tournament.

AUGUST

Trails West. Civic Center Park, Eleventh and Frederick Avenues, St. Joseph; (816) 233–0231 or (800) 216–7080. Third weekend in August. This festival has an arts-and-crafts show, musical entertainment, lectures, melo-dramas, rousing historical reenactments, food booths, and children's activities, including an art tent with hands-on art projects and performances by jugglers and magicians. It's a great weekend of inexpensive entertainment for the whole family.

SEPTEMBER

Spirit Festival. Kansas City; (816) 221–4444 or (800) 366–3378. Labor Day weekend. One of the nation's largest Labor Day weekend events, this festival features more than thirty national jazz, blues, rock, reggae, country, gospel, and swing acts along with local and regional artists, exhibits, arts, crafts, children's pavilion, and carnival midway.

SantaCaliGon Days. Independence Square in Independence; (816) 252–4745; www.santacaligon.com. Labor Day weekend. Celebrating the pioneer heritage of Independence, the festival includes entertainment, an interpretive area with demonstrations, and food and crafts booths. **Free** admission.

Southside Fall Festival Roundup. Hyde Park and Alabama, St. Joseph; (816) 238–3515; www.southsidefallfestival.org. Third weekend in September. This three-day-long festival and rodeo features food, crafts, entertainment, a petting zoo, a grand parade, and professional rodeo cowboys plying their trade at the Stockyards Arena. The festival is **free**; admission to the rodeo $–$$.

SEPTEMBER–OCTOBER

Renaissance Festival. Adjacent to Sandstone Amphitheater in Bonner Springs, Kansas; mail to P.O. Box 32667, Kansas City 32667; (816) 561–8005; www.kcrenfest.com. Several Saturdays and Sundays during September and October. More than 150 costumed characters perform music, demonstrate arts and crafts, and simply carry on as folks did during the Renaissance. Jousts, sword fights, and other appropriate activities are constantly under way and more than 150 crafts booths sell items. $$–$$$; children ages four and under **free.**

OCTOBER

Applefest Celebration. Weston; (816) 640–2909. First full weekend of October. You can press your own apple cider and sample delicious apple treats, the most popular being the apple dumplings. Vendors provide a variety of other food, and your family can watch dancers, listen to musicians, and participate in **free** hands-on children's activities. Several nearby farms sell apples and host other family activities.

Pumpkinfest. Pony Express Museum, 914 Penn Street, St. Joseph; (816) 279–5059 or (800) 530–5930; www.ponyexpress.org. Second weekend in October. The spirit of the fall harvest is celebrated here with a **free** family arts festival featuring live entertainment, a children's costume parade, festival rides, pumpkin games, food, and the lighting of the "Great Pumpkin."

Where to Eat

KANSAS CITY

Arthur Bryant's Barbecue. 1727 Brooklyn Avenue, Kansas City 64124; (816) 231–1123; and 8201 NE Birmingham Road at Station Casino, Kansas City 64160; (816) 414–7474. Brooklyn location is open Monday through Thursday 10:00 A.M. to 9:30 P.M., Friday and Saturday 10:00 A.M. to 10:00 P.M., Sunday 11:00 A.M. to 8:00 P.M. Birmingham location is open Sunday through Thursday 11:00 A.M. to 10:00 P.M., Friday and Saturday 7:00 A.M. to 1:00 A.M. For decades, Arthur Bryant's famous barbecue sauces, its original mild and its sweet and tangy spicy, have been making Kansas City's ribs, beef, pork, turkey, and sausage something to write home about. The kids can get french fries, and you can add beans, but everyone will love the barbecue. $$

Gates and Sons Bar-B-Q. 3205 Main Street, Kansas City 64111; (816) 753–0828, and 1221 Brooklyn, Kansas City 64127; (816) 483–3880; www.gatesbbq.com. Both stores open Sunday through Thursday 10:00 A.M. to midnight, Friday and Saturday 10:00 A.M. to 1:00 A.M. This original Kansas City restaurant chain has been serving customers since 1945 and is considered one of the best barbecue purveyors in the country. You can get a hot and spicy version of their sauce, and the menu includes sandwiches, ribs, sausage, chicken, and mutton. $$

Kansas City Masterpiece. 4747 Wyandotte Street (on the Plaza), Kansas City 64112; (816) 531–3332. Open daily at 11:00 A.M., closes Monday through Thursday 10:00 P.M., Friday and Saturday 11:00 P.M., Sunday 9:30 P.M. The famous barbecue sauce splattered on fantastic baby back ribs, hamburgers, buffalo (yes, real buffalo) burgers, and more. $$$

Stephenson's Old Apple Farm. Highway 40 and Lee's Summit Road, 16401 East 40 Highway, Kansas City 64136; (816) 373–5400. Open Monday through Saturday 10:00 A.M. to 10:00 P.M., Sunday 10:30 A.M. to 9:00 P.M., with special Sunday brunch upstairs from 10:30 A.M. to 2:00 P.M. Apple fritters to die for; after all, there is a working apple farm out back. But you won't want to miss the hickory-smoked turkey or ham steak, the brisket, or the baked turkey, and kids can actually get a vegetable with their meals. $$

Stroud's. North, 5410 Oakridge Drive, Kansas City 64119; (816) 454–9600, and south, 1015 East Eighty-fifth Street, Kansas City 64131; (816) 333–2132. North, which is closer to downtown, is open Monday through Thursday 5:00 to 9:30 P.M., Friday and Saturday 11:00 A.M. to 10:30 P.M., Sunday 11:00 A.M. to 9:30 P.M. South location stays open thirty minutes longer and opens an hour earlier. Full meals include incredible pan-fried chicken, shrimp, chicken-fried steak, pork chops, and much more, and you get a potato, vegetable, and choice of soup or salad. $$

Winstead's. 101 Brush Creek Boulevard, Kansas City 64112; (816) 753–2244. Open Monday through Thursday 6:00 A.M. to midnight, Friday and Saturday 6:00 A.M. to 1:00 A.M. Hamburgers, fries, shakes, all the things kids love are available at this Winstead's on the Plaza and several others around town. $

INDEPENDENCE

Gates and Sons Bar-B-Q. 10440 East Highway 40, Independence 64055; (816) 353–5880; www.gatesbbq.com. Open Monday through Thursday 11:00 A.M. to 11:00 P.M., Friday and Saturday 11:00 A.M. to midnight, Sunday 11:00 A.M. to 10:00 P.M. This restaurant is part of the Kansas City restaurant chain. $$

NORTH KANSAS CITY

Chappell's Restaurant and Sports Museum. 323 Armour Road, North Kansas City 64116; (816) 421–0002. Open 11:00 A.M. to midnight Monday through Saturday. The initial attraction is walls that are completely covered with what the restaurant claims is the largest sports memorabilia collection in the country. But it's the prime rib to die for, great sandwiches, kids' menu with chicken fingers, and well-stocked bar that will keep you coming back. $$

ST. JOSEPH

Barbosa's Castillo. 906 Sylvanie Street, St. Joseph 64501; (816) 233–4970. **Barbosa's East,** 4804 Frederick Avenue, St. Joseph 64506; (816) 232–0221. Both locations are open 11:00 A.M. to 9:00 P.M. Monday through Saturday; East only is open Sunday 11:00 A.M. to 8:30 P.M. The homemade food is fantastic at both locations, although Barbosa's Castillo has better atmosphere because it is located in an old Victorian home. Don't pass up the nachos and enchiladas, and you can't miss with the burritos and tacos. $$

Jerre Anne Cafeteria and Bakery. 2640 Mitchell Avenue, St. Joseph 64507; (816) 232–6585. Open Tuesday through Saturday 11:00 A.M. to 7:00 P.M. Family diners won't want to miss the home cooking and baking available here for more than seventy years.

The restaurant has provided an ever-changing selection of entrees, vegetable dishes, salads, and desserts to die for. $

JAMESPORT

Country Cupboard. Old Highway 6, Jamesport 64648; about 9 blocks west of the four-way stop downtown; (660) 684–6597. Open Tuesday through Thursday 6:30 A.M. to 8:00 P.M., Friday and Saturday 6:30 A.M. to 9:00 P.M., Sunday 8:00 A.M. to 8:00 P.M. Scrumptious pork tenderloin sandwich and barbecue ribs top a menu that includes chicken-fried steak and onion rings. $$

Gingerich Dutch Pantry and Bakery. Four-way stop downtown, Jamesport 64648; (660) 684–6212. Open 10:30 A.M. Monday to Friday, close 9:00 P.M. Monday and Friday, 5:00 P.M. Tuesday and Wednesday, 3:00 P.M. Thursday; Saturday hours 7:00 A.M. to 7:00 P.M. This fabulous Mennonite restaurant serves Amish-style meals, including pies and bread baked daily, sandwiches, and full meals. $$

Where to Stay

KANSAS CITY

Best Western Country Inn (Worlds of Fun). 7100 NE Parvin Road, Kansas City 64117; (816) 453–3355 or (800) 528–1234. Checkout time is 11:00 A.M.; check-in time is 3:00 P.M. Eighty-six rooms, outdoor heated pool, continental breakfast. Children ages 12 and under **free.** $$$

Citi Centre Plaza. 1215 Wyandotte Street, Kansas City 64105; (816) 471–1333 or (800) 354–0986. Checkout time is noon; check-in time is 3:00 P.M.; 190 rooms, exercise room, sauna, continental breakfast. Children ages 18 and under stay **free**; children ages 12 and under eat **free** in restaurant. $$$$

Embassy Suites Country Club Plaza. 220 West Forty-third Street, Kansas City 64111; (816) 756–1720. Checkout time is noon; check-in time is 3:00 P.M.; 266 rooms, indoor pool, sauna, exercise room, cooked-to-order breakfast. $$$$

Holiday Inn Sports Complex. 4011 Blue Ridge Cutoff, Kansas City 64133; (816) 353–5300 or (800) 465–4239. Checkout time is noon; check-in time is 3:00 P.M.; 163 rooms, indoor pool, sauna, exercise equipment. Children ages 19 and under **free.** $$$

Hyatt Regency Crown Center. 2345 McGee Street, Kansas City 64108; (816) 421–1234 or (800) 233–1234. Checkout time is noon; check-in time is 3:00 P.M.; 731 rooms, outdoor heated pool, health club, sauna. Children ages 18 and under **free.** $$$$

Marriott Country Club Plaza Hotel. 4445 Main Street, Kansas City 64111; (816) 531–3000 or (800) 227–6963. Checkout time is noon; check-in time is 4:00 P.M.; 296 rooms, indoor pool, health club. $$$$

Marriott Downtown. 200 West Twelfth Street, Kansas City 64105; (816) 421–6800 or (800) 228–9290. Checkout time is noon; check-in time is 3:00 P.M. 983 rooms, indoor lap pool, exercise room, continental breakfast. Children ages 5 and under **free.** $$$$

North Kansas City Days Inn. 2232 Taney Street, Kansas City 64116; (816) 421–6000 or (800) 329–7466. Checkout time is noon; check-in time is 2:00 P.M. Ninety rooms, continental breakfast. Children ages 17 and under **free.** $$$

Super 8 (Worlds of Fun). 4321 North Corrington Avenue, (across the highway from Worlds of Fun), Kansas City 64117; (816) 454–8788 or (800) 800–8000. Checkout time is 11:00 P.M.; check-in time is 2:00 P.M. Sixty-eight rooms, outdoor pool May through September, continental breakfast. Children ages 12 and under **free.** $$$

ST. JOSEPH

A.O.K. Business 71, 3¼ miles north of St. Joseph, 12310 County Road 360, St. Joseph 64505; (816) 324–4263. Open year-round. The ten-acre campground has fifty-three RV electrical hookups, hot showers, rest rooms, picnic tables, shelters, a playground, fishing, a self-service laundry, and a store with food and camping supplies. Tent camping is $10 per day, RV electrical hookups are $20 per day. $

Best Western Classic Inn. I–29 and Highway 169, St. Joseph 64507; (816) 232–2345. Checkout time is 11:00 A.M.; check-in time after noon. Fifty-two rooms, continental breakfast, outdoor pool, exercise room, sauna. Children ages 12 and under **free.** $$

Drury Inn. 4213 Frederick Avenue, St. Joseph 64506; (816) 364–4700 or (800) 325–8300. Checkout time is noon; check-in time is 3:00 P.M.; 133 rooms, Quick-start breakfast, outdoor pool, exercise equipment. Children ages 18 and under **free.** $$$

Motel 6. 4021 Frederick Avenue, St. Joseph 64506; (816) 232–2311. Checkout time is noon; check-in time is anytime; 117 rooms, outdoor pool. Children ages 17 and under **free.** $

Museum Hill Bread & Breakfast. 1102 Felix Street, St. Joseph 64501; (816) 387–9663; www.museumhill.com. This 1880s Italianate mansion in the Museum Hill District boasts one of the best views in St. Joseph. Its beautiful original woodwork and many architectural gems make it an exceptional place to stay. Best of all, the owners are kid-friendly. $$

St. Joseph Riverfront Historic District Hotel. 102 South Third Street, St. Joseph 64501; (816) 279–8000 or (800) 824–7402; checkout time is noon; check-in time is 2:00 P.M.; 170 rooms, whirlpool, sauna, fitness center, indoor heated pool, lounge, and restaurant. $$$

Stoney Creek Inn. 1201 Woodbine Road, St. Joseph 64507; (800) 659–2220 or (816) 901–9600. Check-out time is 11:00 A.M., check-in time is 3:00 P.M. This North Woods–themed hotel has 129 rooms, with themed suites with whirlpool and fireplaces, an indoor-outdoor pool, and continental breakfast. $$$–$$$$

Walnut Grove Campground. Business 71, 3 miles north of St. Joseph, 12501 County Road 443, St. Joseph 64505; (816) 233–1974. Open April 1 through November 1. Clean rest rooms, private hot showers, RV electric hookups, nineteen shaded sites, and a dumping station. Tent camping is $10.00 a day for two people, $15.00 per day for pull-through trailers with RV electrical hookups. There is a $2.00 per person fee for more than two guests in tent or RV. $

JAMESPORT

Marigolds Inn and Gift Shop. Highway F, 3 blocks west of four-way stop downtown, Jamesport 64648; (660) 684–6122 or (800) 884–5946. Checkout time is 11:00 A.M.; check-in time is 3:00 P.M. This twelve-unit hotel, built by Amish craftsmen in 1998, won't be hard to find: It's painted bright orange with rust and green trim. The rooms are painted and stenciled in five themes—Western, birdhouse, garden, cabin, and Americana—and have clouds painted on the ceilings and furnishings to match the themes. There's also an outside deck with tables that is surrounded by gardens and a meeting room for reunions. $$

General Index

M

N

Y

Activities Index

Historic Sites and Homes

Museums and Art Galleries